The Divine Spark Within

Excavating the Mysteries of Sophia and the Deep Christ

Dan Morse

SOPHONIA PRESS

Published 2022
Printed in the United States of America
ISBN (paperback): 979-8-9868000-4-2

Quotes from *The Mysterious Story of X7* © 2010, rights residing with Findhorn Press, now Kaminn Media, used by permission.

Cover design: Daniel Holeman, www.awakenvisions.com.

Wooden Thomas Cross. Photo by Mathen Payyappilly Palakkappilly. Creative Commons Attribution-ShareAlike 3.0 Unported (CC BY-SA 3.0)

Belyaev, Vasili. *Sophia the Holy Wisdom of God*, Church of Spilt Blood, St. Petersburg, Russia, c. 1890. Public domain.

Jesus with Beard, 4th century, Catacomb of Commodilla. Public domain.

Thomas Cole: *The Departure*, 1837 and *The Picnic*, 1866. Public domain.

Portrait photo by Dan Morse.

Sophonia Press

sophiaproject8@gmail.com

www.sophiaproject.net

DEDICATION

To Carl Jung,

Gershom Scholem,

and

Henry Corbin:

Spiritual Archeologists and Pioneers.

And to the burgeoning seedling of an exuberant Self within.

Contents

List of Illustrations

The research, analysis, and insights presented in this volume have come together through the conduit of the author's subjective experience. He honors how this material might be meaningful according to the reader's unique subjective experience.

Introduction

The human condition is a mystery so vast that it is impossible to take in its full scope and meaning. Innumerable scientific discoveries into the nature of both physical and metaphysical reality have helped bring some clarity to our perplexing existence; yet, they seem woefully inadequate to answer the big questions of life. Who are we, in this body vessel, entering into this world anew through the miracle of birth? And what is our mission here, our role to play, in this theater of the living?

Though organized religions have contributed much to these existential questions, below the foundation stones of churches, synagogues, and mosques lie the aquifers of deep wisdom. Not easily grasped by common, everyday thinking, these "living waters" occasionally seep into religious doctrine, but more often, they flow and churn beneath the worshipper's awareness.

One source of this extensive wisdom stream led to the development of a religious tradition, generally called "Gnosticism." As the black sheep of Christianity, Gnosticism has had a troubled life. This enigmatic religious and philosophical movement flourished for a few hundred years, roughly from 100–400 CE, until it was suppressed and essentially overtaken by the dominant Roman version of early Christianity.

Yet, after nearly 2000 years of banishment, the Gnostic teachings are now slowly coming back into prominence. Since the late 1970s, with the publication of the majority of their recovered scriptures, this ancient religious system has become readily available for all to study with virtually no threat of persecution. As the significance of this tradition becomes more widely appreciated, it offers immense value in this modern era when the dominant religions seem to be having difficulty keeping up with the increasingly complex challenges of these modern times.

In one of his most popular Gnostic sayings found in the *Gospel of Thomas*, Jesus said, "If you bring forth what is within you, what you bring forth will save you. If you do not bring forth what is within you, what you do not bring forth will kill you" (Logion 70 in GT for *Gospel of Thomas*. See List of Abbreviations and Gnostic text web links on page 259 and also at www.sophiaproject.net/post/list-of-abbreviations-and-text-web-addresses.)

This saying is both endearing and highly disturbing. It can even be distilled down to "Bring it forth or die." If this is an actual saying preserved from Jesus's own lips, just what is he trying to tell us? What is it that we are so urgently being asked to bring forth?

Among the many treasures found within the Gnostic gospels, this saying might be considered low-hanging fruit, catchy, with a curious, ironic twist. Like the symbol of Eve's apple and other biblical metaphors, it can be understood in innumerable ways. However, from what I have come to understand and what will be explored below, this dictate points to one of the most central and crucial enigmas of our times: this mystery of a dormant divinity within that can save us, individually and collectively, from the seemingly unresolvable issues of our day.

An Overview

This book will conduct a theological and spiritual excavation of three mysteries: 1) an ancient creation story that features a lead character known as Sophia, 2) the man commonly known as Jesus Christ, whose ministry as portrayed in the New Testament is a shadow of his original teachings which were largely suppressed, and 3) Christ's message of something that must be brought forth, which equates with a phenomenon known in the Gnostic tradition as the Divine Spark Within. Through these three mysteries, we will be breaking out of the dominant historical and theological narrative of the origins of Christianity as codified in the Bible. From the rubble of this Gnostic tradition and its fragmentary literature is found an unusual story about Jesus Christ and his consort, barely known even to this day, named Sophia. Even more astounding, the clues to this mystery will point to how we as members of the human species can step out from behind the bars of an invisible system of control and disempowerment to reclaim our birthright as uniquely powerful beings of higher consciousness.

As this book weaves through these three mysteries, evidence will suggest that, in the 1st century CE in the area known at the time as Palestine, there was the sudden emergence of high wisdom teachings introduced by a man known as Jesus Christ. These novel revelations included elaborate descriptions of a distinct myth of origins, as well as a complex cosmology that was far more detailed than the stories in the Book of Genesis and in the books of the New Testament. This New Wisdom Revelation became the primary source for the 2nd century philosophical and religious movement known as Gnosticism. However, eventually, in just a few centuries, both this creation story and the history of its origins were almost completely lost. Instead, they were replaced by or assimilated into what is known as the Roman version of Christianity, which by the 5th century, was quickly becoming the dominant religion throughout the Roman Empire. This became the standard "orthodoxy" of authorized doctrine, which pushed out the "heterodoxy" of diverse religious ideas. (Keep in mind that the codified Roman Church orthodox tradition is different from the Eastern Orthodox Church, which split from Rome in 1054.[1]) This analysis is in stark contrast to the dominant historical viewpoint that Christianity came first, which was then bastardized by what are considered to be the Gnostic heresies.

Recovering both the story of this sudden appearance of high wisdom and the creation story found within it will help us locate where we, humanity, are found within the vast span of creation. As with many indigenous tribes, the telling and, at times, enactment of creation stories can facilitate a process of return, and hence a collective renewal as a culture comes back into alignment with its origins and purpose. This particular creation story, with its unique meta-view, can orient us back to our origins, to who we were originally designed to be, and guide us through the current and most precarious crux of humanity's process of maturation.

This creation story suggests that there was a plan to seed the lower world, here on this earthly planet, with physical bodies for higher light beings to inhabit, but the plan went awry. A lead player in this cosmic drama was known as Sophia. Her desire to meet with the Divine Source ultimately led her to fall into an epic drama of struggle and torment at the hands of some less than godly oppressors. Her process of soul searching and pleas for help led to one of the great, though largely lost, epic dramas in religious literature: Christ's rescue of Sophia.

The story of Sophia's descent and restoration offers humanity a model of our evolutionary challenges, including how we are grappling with the reality of an invisible but insidious higher dimensional system of control. Indeed, who we are, where we came from, who we were designed to be, and who we are destined to become are all suggested within this epic tale of Christ and his beloved, Sophia.

Specifically, I will be delving into this material using these three distinct mysteries: 1) The Creation Story of Sophia – A Mystery Play, 2) The Deep Christ – A Mystery Thriller, and 3) The Divine Spark Within – A Holy Mystery.

The Creation Story of Sophia: A Mystery Play

There is a complex story of creation buried in the pages of the ancient Gnostic texts. A lead character in this story is named Sophia, hence the title, the Creation Story of Sophia. Where this myth of origins came from is the subject of much inconclusive debate. Though the most prominent explanation is that it gradually emerged out of Jewish mystical trends, my thesis points to it as having a specific identifiable source in the 1st century CE. This then spawned some of the earliest trends of Gnosticism that developed in the following few hundred years.

Similar to how I have presented this Myth of Sophia in "bardic" musical presentations since 1998,[2] I will be offering it here as a sort of Mystery Play. Mystery Plays date back over a thousand years, where Bible stories were staged in simple theatrical fashion during European church services, much like contemporary Christmas nativity pageants are enacted around the world, typically by children. I am playing with the word "mystery" here, where elements of intrigue and suspense, as well as the oftentimes undefinable qualities of the sacred, are entertained. In four distinct acts, this Sophianic mystery play will be put on stage with scripts taken from the Gnostic texts, intermixed with narration and some analysis. With this, my wish is for the creation story to come alive in the reader's imagination.

This ancient creation drama is highly unique and advanced, possibly unsurpassed in scope, an archetypal story of archetypal stories. In the words of Joseph Campbell, it is a monomyth,[3] which, like the Hero's Journey, is a primary myth from which many variations have come.

This myth is also a metaphor for the human initiatory journey through incarnation. Like the stages of initiation,[4] Sophia goes through her separation from Source followed by a chaotic fall where she has to find her way through a life-changing ordeal. In this way, Sophia is a model for our own process of spiritual development and what could be called the Soul's Journey, as will be explored in Chapter 7.

This creation story is also about the interplay of relationships between the masculine and feminine archetypes, with Christ being the great masculine counterpart to the feminine Sophia. How western civilization has endured an extensive suppression of the divine feminine principle for thousands of years is indicated by this myth. It also points to one of the key themes of alchemy and depth psychological theory; the sacred marriage between the opposites, reuniting the sacred masculine and feminine, and who we humans are in relationship to the divine.

The Deep Christ: A Mystery Thriller

This book will investigate how this figure known as Jesus shows up both in the creation story of Sophia and historically in the 1st century in a very different way from how he is depicted in the New Testament. Instead of just being limited to his three-year ministry where lessons were given mainly as parables, in various early Gnostic texts, Jesus is the one who presents this complex story of origins and performed rituals of liberation with his disciples.

Significantly, Jesus appears as a lead character in the creation story of Sophia within an epic tale of cosmic courtship. These are two beloveds who became separated due to Sophia's descent into the lower world of earthly matter. Going far beyond how he is prominently featured in the New Testament, here, Jesus Christ straddles between the highest levels of divine source and what he calls the Regions of the Left, the realms of chaos controlled by selfish gods. His mission to rescue Sophia, he explains, was one of the central purposes behind his incarnation into this world. This is a mystery thriller that sleuths the historical and theological footprints of this man, raising key questions about the very foundations of not only Christianity and Gnosticism but the very personhood of Jesus.

We will delve into numerous lost and forgotten scriptures where these stories are told with so-called "soft eyes," holding off on making any definitive conclusions. There are too many questions about what happened historically and too many layers of misinformation to explain it all simply according to the New Testament's version of this man. Because of his broader and more esoteric role, as uncovered in this investigation, I will be referring to him more generally as the Deep Christ as opposed to, for example, the Esoteric Jesus, or other names of this sort.

The Divine Spark Within: A Holy Mystery

One of the most obscure enigmas of the Gnostic tradition is something that is referred to as the Divine Spark hidden within us. It is referenced in the ancient texts as something invaluably precious and rare and suggests powerful abilities within our human form. Yet, this spark has remained largely unrecognized, untapped, and out of reach for much of human history.

Whether a metaphor or a real phenomenon, the Divine Spark has been cryptically referred to by many names in the Gnostic tradition, where it is called a seed, a pearl, and a droplet of "hidden Light" that is the very substance of the original Source Creation. Behind Jesus's Bring Forth saying found in the Thomas Gospel, there is a holy mystery. More than a spark, it is this latent internal fire that seems to be a key to helping us break out of the limitations of our current spectrum of spiritual experience.

The spark motif involves the complex Gnostic story of the creation of man, presented in Chapter 18, which is quite different from the one found in the Book of Genesis. Here, lower gods called "archons" had a primary hand in the creation of the Adamic species. However, Sophia tricked the demiurge, the lead archon, into blowing the Divine Spark into Adam. She also sent Eve, the luminous essence of Sophia, to Adam to help him wake up to his true nature. Adam and Eve then became the prototype for the human struggle, where we are tasked with working to activate our more Light-filled being that has been shrouded from us.

To step into our higher potential, these ancient texts suggest that it is our task to bring forward our pure selves, where negativity and angst have fallen away. This is not to negate the essential process of what can be called "soul work." Instead of ignoring the dark corners of our emotional pain and trauma, we need to enter into these areas with love and compassion, where both healing and recovery can be gained. However, as the Deep Christ taught, the goal is to ultimately enter a vibrational frequency that comes into sympathetic resonance with an original Source Light energy, called the Great Power. When our internal condition is attuned to a precise frequency, according to his teachings, this results in an emergence of profound new human attributes. In Chapter 21, I will present an overview of this process known in the ancient texts as the Bridal Chamber.

Interweaving the Three Mysteries

All three of these mysteries are necessary to land the broad thesis of this book, which points specifically to human beings' unique role in this creation story. Downplaying or neglecting one of these would be as ineffective as trying to sit on a two-legged stool. So, I invite the reader to move between their interconnectedness as the bigger picture gradually unfolds.

Part I of this book presents some necessary background to understanding these three mysteries. I will go into the historical context of the 1st century in the land of Israel, where a unique Wisdom Revelation, I believe, first emerged. I will also give background information on three key themes that can help navigate these mysteries: Gnosticism, Sophia, and the Deep Christ. Part II will present the complex creation story of Sophia. Part III will investigate clues to the unusual appearance of the Deep Christ in this creation story and in the 1st century that is quite different from the familiar Jesus of the New Testament. Part IV will explore this theme of the Divine Spark Within. Part V will bring a culmination of all these explorations with a focus on what humanity is grappling with during these current transitional times, offering clues to how we can overcome the seemingly insurmountable challenges of our day. This is a model by which we can pursue both personal and collective spiritual transformation with the help of a specific wisdom teaching called the Bridal Chamber.

Though this investigation will be primarily rooted in the Christian and Gnostic traditions, the underground Wisdom stream is by no means limited to just these two. The Kabbalah, especially that of Isaac Luria (1534–1572), has many overlaps with the Gnostic system and offers key insights that help fill in some of the details of this creation cosmology. Besides the Kabbalah, this original Wisdom Revelation of Christ likely seeded numerous esoteric traditions which arose in the subsequent centuries, including Islamic (Sufi) Gnosticism,[5] Manichaeism,[6] Persian traditions as presented by Henry Corbin, The Chinese Luminous Religion from Daqin,[7] alchemy, the medieval grail legends, Jungian depth psychology, and more. Due to the need to narrow the scope of this book to get a more thorough understanding of the key sources of this Wisdom stream, the inclusion of material from these other systems will be limited.

Many of the characters found within this historical New Wisdom Revelation are primarily men. My hope is that, by helping to reclaim the divine feminine traditions of Sophia, the long arc of male dominance in the cultural religious milieu can be increasingly humbled.

I have sought to be responsible as a researcher to secure the findings in these investigations using first- and second-generation texts instead of relying solely on the inferences of other scholars. Though some claims made in this book may seem far-reaching, I believe they rest on the solid ground of ancient textual insight. That this thesis is, to some degree, novel in the field of Gnostic research may be explained by how we are still barely coming out of the muddle of disinformation that surrounds Gnosticism and early Christianity. We are still in the early stages of a thorough analysis of the very recent publication of the vast majority of Gnostic codices that were lost for much of the last 2000 years.

It is recommended that, when stepping into these pages, the reader does not get too caught up in any of the epic figures in this drama. In this mystery theatrical thriller, *you* are the most important character. It is your life that is central in all of this and is one which I urge you to not lose sight of as we step into this complex tale. Nothing in this book needs to override your inner sense and beliefs. Indeed, how the great mystery might be working in your life is connected deeply to your personhood and your unique history. Only you know what particular nutrients of insight or wisdom might help feed your own development as a spiritual being. In the same way, this book is an expression of my deep self that carries a throughline of inquiry rooted in my personal spiritual and psychological journey. When coming across material that doesn't resonate with you, I invite you to not toss this all aside but rather tap into your own deeper sensibility to find the movement, the language, image, or archetypal motif that does speak to you.

That said, I now invite your inner imaginal process to be engaged with what is on show here. It is not easy to translate this information into real-world applications, though it points to something profoundly significant. Like a beacon, it leads us forward, or like an inner spark, it flashes a clue to something almost unfathomable.

PART I

BACKGROUND

1

Introduction to the

First Century Novel Revelation of Wisdom

The whole premise of this volume has been inspired by my fascination with the archetypal motif of Sophia. As I will describe in Chapter 19, since my late adolescence, the name Sophia had a personal significance to me, which drew me into an extensive investigation into how she appeared in the proto (meaning formative) Gnostic and classic (Sethian) Gnostic traditions. From this research, I have come to understand that there was a unique esoteric theological system that first appeared in a comprehensive fashion in the 1st century CE. This system, however, eventually became lost, persecuted, or assimilated into the tradition known as Christian orthodoxy. A helpful way to understand the sudden appearance of this body of high information is in the concept of a new revelation of wisdom.

A Novel Wisdom Revelation

In the land we know as Israel, there were collisions of highly tumultuous political and religious forces that resulted in the devastation of Jerusalem and a diaspora of Jews from this homeland in the aftermath of the Jewish Wars of 66–70 CE. Amidst this tumult, there appears to have emerged a body of original and highly advanced wisdom teachings.

Based on my research, I postulate that, though influenced by various religious or spiritual traditions available at that time, this novel revelation emerged rather suddenly in a whole and comprehensive fashion. Over time, however, this unique body of teaching was interpreted and reworked to where the original revelation became almost unrecognizable. It is largely the task of this book to excavate from recovered ancient manuscripts the substance of this unique revelation.

Wisdom is a keyword that dovetails with a vast "wisdom tradition" that spans many religious and philosophical systems. Though there is no one dominant theory of where this system came from, consensus scholarship suggests that one of the most prominent of the wisdom traditions, known as Gnosticism, took shape in the first few centuries CE — not as the result of a sudden revelation, but rather having gradually developed out of various religious and esoteric influences, including Persian, Egyptian, Jewish, and Greek (Platonic). However, so few documents survived the tumult of these origins that it has been virtually impossible to get a clear picture of these formative stages.

The Greek word *Sophia,* meaning "wisdom," denotes a religious and spiritual motif that, though appearing to a limited degree in the Old Testament, suddenly exploded with prominence in the first few centuries CE as a key figure, characterized as feminine, in a complex story of creation. This Sophia creation story, as some Gnostic texts suggest, was delivered by a man who presented himself as having first-hand access and witness to the origins of creation. This person has been identified as Jesus Christ in some of the Gnostic texts, though it requires a broader lens to take in the complexity of who this person was beyond his more familiar depictions in the New Testament scriptures. To step outside of the confines of how he is commonly known in Christianity and to acknowledge the greater depth of his mystical teachings, I have come to refer to him as the Deep Christ.

Found in fleeting, sometimes cryptic references within the earliest phases of this Gnostic tradition, there is a key theme that emerges of a powerful but latent human potential, referred to as the Divine Spark Within. Though this has been shrouded from us through the ages, we can begin to restore it from a distant, lost memory with the help of what can be called the Mysteries of Sophia.

A Synopsis of the Novel Wisdom Revelation

The following is more of an overview of this thesis of a New Wisdom Revelation that will be investigated throughout the course of this book.

A man commonly known as Jesus became connected to a profoundly cosmic higher self whom he identified as Christ. In the ancient texts, he described at length how this expanded consciousness aspect of himself descended from the highest levels of creation. Having access to this cosmic viewpoint, he was able to see a meta-view of the origins of creation and how it unfolded down to his own time in 1st century Palestine.

In his original teachings and lost writings, he presented a complex cosmology and myth of creation that was far more detailed than the story found in the Book of Genesis. Written accounts of this suggest that there was a plan from the highest regions of original creation to create physical bodies in our world that could be used as "dwellings" for high beings called "Children of Light" to inhabit. A figure known as Sophia pioneered this project, but she was captured by selfish and powerful gods known as "archons," who stripped her of her divine Light and tormented her within the prison of this material world. In response, the high Christ, who is identified as Sophia's consort, disguised himself to descend undetected past the regions of archonic control and into this world to rescue Sophia from her enslavement.

The Gnostic rendition of the creation of Adam and Eve, which may have also emerged from this extensive New Revelation, can, at times, be quite different from the Judeo-Christian tale found in the Book of Genesis. As portrayed in these long-lost Gnostic texts, humanity was born into a world ruled by unseen overlords, where connections with our higher and original divine creation were eclipsed. A key theme is that humans have a spark of divine Light within us, planted there at the behest of Sophia during the inception of our species. What is more, Jesus Christ himself engaged in eucharistic and baptist rituals that were specifically designed to awaken this spark and free his followers and humanity as well from what he described as an overarching condition of enslavement.

This vast creation tale is so extraordinary and radical that it was persecuted and buried to the point of being nearly completely erased from historical memory. Even though this cosmology and Deep Christ teachings flourished in the first few centuries CE, by the end of the 4th century they were framed as a bastardization or heresy of true Christianity and became either lost or subsumed into a dominant form of this new religion whose seat of authority was in Rome. The "orthodox" or definitive Christian rendition of the story of Jesus and his teachings is a distant echo of this original revelation. Lost were teachings about a complex higher cosmology, Sophia, and our inner spark. Fortunately, there are surviving texts that make it possible for some version of this more original New Revelation to be pieced together. These materials include 1) recovered Gnostic texts, 2) writings from those who sought to discredit these teachings, called heresiologists, and 3) clues that we can decipher from the orthodox biblical writings such as from St. Paul. It is toward this process of reconstructing the lost treasure of this highly significant original teaching, even reverse engineering it back toward its 1st century origins, that is the primary task of this book.

2

Historical Context of the New Wisdom Revelation

Identifying a New Revelation that appeared at the beginning of the Christian era may be stating the obvious, as Jesus's impact on the world spawned a whole new religion. However, this story includes more than what is told in the pages of the New Testament.

To begin to find our bearings in this thesis of a New Revelation, I'd like to first look into the context of the place and times in which this event happened, specifically the 1st century CE in the Middle East. This is necessary to not only find our footing in the earliest beginnings of this unique creation story of Sophia but also to set the stage for an extraordinary investigation into the enigma of the Deep Christ. If we resort to just seeing the Bible as unbiased history, then the trail of clues to the Deep Christ, as has happened through the course of the last 2000 years, will once again be obscured or lost.

A Historical Look at 1st century CE Palestine

Through the course of multiple invasions by the Babylonians, Persians, Greeks, and Romans, in this harsh land at the crossroads known at the time as Judaea or Syria Palestine, the Jewish population survived. For more than eight hundred years in the first millennium BCE, their desire to gain self-governance and openly practice their religion and customs without restriction was regularly stripped by the invaders.

Finally, around 140 BCE, the Jewish Hasmonean Dynasty came to power by overthrowing the Greek Seleucid rule. These victorious and brutal Maccabees (meaning "hammer") finally brought religious freedom to their people, lasting on and off for some eighty years until, in 63 BCE, Judaea came under Roman rule, and Herod "the Great" eventually became the Roman proxy ruler. He was tolerant of Jewish religious practices, claiming he was part Jewish. His remodeling of Solomon's Temple on Mount Moriah was a sign of this endorsement. However, he had no patience for Jewish resistance to Roman rule. So intent was he to stamp out any Jewish threats from the former Hasmonean clan that he made the surprising and odd move of marrying the Hasmonean princess Mariamme, perhaps to assimilate this family line into his own lineage. When Herod allegedly murdered their two sons, likely fueled by his fear of a Maccabean resurgence, this caused Augustus Caesar to famously quip of the kosher ruler, "It is better to be Herod's pig than his son." These were clearly unusual times and most important for understanding the context of this Novel Revelation of Wisdom.

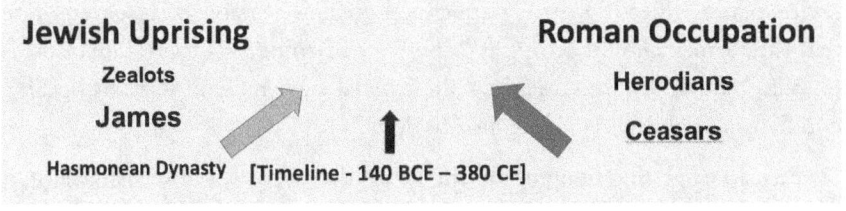

Historical Context of the New Wisdom Revelation: Illustration 1

Illustration 1 (of 3 shown below) shows the tension of the Jewish uprising amidst a tolerant but, at times, brutal Roman occupation, especially in the 1st century CE. James, called "the Righteous," was a central Jewish religious leader who featured in a tragic turn of events that ultimately led to the Jewish Wars and the sack of Jerusalem by the Romans in 70 CE.[1] Robert Eisenman (1997) has written extensively about these tumultuous events in the Middle East in the 1st century, and I draw heavily from his research.

The Sadducees and Pharisees, whom Eisenman calls the "establishment priests," conducted Jewish religious practices approved by their Roman overseers. The orthodox Jewish resistance, on the other hand, was carried out by a group of Jews who zealously demanded stricter adherence to the Laws of Moses. These "zealots" (a general and not historically precise term) were greatly offended by the Herodian authority that would only tolerate Jewish religious practices as long as they remained subservient to Roman laws. Strict Jewish practices automatically violated these laws by not bowing to Caesar over their own God. Its most radical wing, called the Sicarii, were the guerrilla jihadists who hid curved swords under their cloaks as they conducted strategic assassinations of their Roman overlords and approved priests.

Though Jesus likely interfaced with James and the anti-Roman Jewish groups, I do not subscribe to Reza Aslan's thesis in his book *Zealot* (2013) that Jesus himself was a radical extremist preaching for the cause of Jewish sovereignty. Though Aslan falls short of grasping the broader picture of these pivotal historical events, to his credit, he helps pull back some layers of the New Testament Jesus as being a repackaged version of an earlier and more original one — a thesis that I will explore more at length in this book.

Aslan writes that there was a long process through later edited texts of "transforming Jesus" from a radical Jewish nationalist into a peaceful loving savior figure with little earthly attachments. This version of Jesus was one that the Romans could accept and the Roman emperor Flavius Theodosius (d. 395) made the Jesus teachings the official state religion in what became codified as established Christian orthodoxy.[2]

Instead of getting hung up on the thesis that Jesus was a Jewish zealot, it is better to understand the figure of James, whose life intermingled with Jesus, as being arguably the most important Jewish anti-Roman religious figure of 1st century Jerusalem. James was a man of great religious integrity who was revered for his "righteousness." The prominent disciple, St. Peter, was directly connected to James's leadership, as was St. Paul. Yet, James's role in all of this, as portrayed in the New Testament's version of this history, was simply as one of Jesus's disciples, and his role as religious patriarch in the Jewish zealot movement was completely erased.

What happened to this figure James is a classic example of how the New Testament also contorts some distinct historical figures such as St. Thomas into characters more in alignment with a less Jewish, less political, less mystical, Roman-sponsored agenda. For example, two figures named James are found in the New Testament in close proximity to each other: James the

Less (Mark 15:40, son of Mary) and James the Greater (disciple of Jesus, son of Zebedee), both having nothing to do with his prominent role as anti-Roman Jewish religious leader. What is more, the historical drama of the stoning death of James, as indicated by the 1st century Roman Jewish historian Josephus, appears to have been completely replaced in the New Testament with what Eisenman describes as a wholly fictitious character known as St. Stephen.[3]

To add to this confusion around these key players, it turns out that, according to the Bible, James was actually Jesus's brother. There are two references in the Gospels that James was one of Jesus's brothers (Matthew 13:55 and Mark 6:3). According to Eisenman, the orthodox Christian designers reluctantly acknowledged James as the brother of the Lord only because there is a zealot-flavored book that was included in the New Testament called the Epistle of James.

Indeed, just how persistent this biblical version of history has been entrenched through the centuries, such as how James and the Jewish zealot movement were essentially written out of the narrative, is an example of what we are up against in uncovering the context of the 1st century where Jesus lived.

At this point, it is important to bring clarity to the difference between two phenomenal text discoveries from that period because there is often confusion between the two.

The Jewish Dead Sea Scrolls and the Gnostic Nag Hammadi Library

I will be drawing heavily from a key Gnostic collection called the Nag Hammadi Library, which is distinct from a collection also discovered in the dry Arab desert in the 1940s known as the Dead Sea Scrolls. People often confuse these two though, in fact, they are very different, and this is important in finding our way to this 1st century Novel Revelation.

According to Eisenman, the Dead Sea Scrolls are largely 1st and 2nd centuries CE documents associated with this Jewish zealot movement. The Jewish uprising (66–70 CE) was fiercely persecuted, and these temple scrolls were hidden away, with more being added during the last Bar Kokhba flare-up of this movement in the 2nd century.

Eisenman, a scholar of 1st century Christian history and preeminent Dead

Sea Scroll researcher, played a pivotal role in releasing the microfiche copies of these scrolls from a suspiciously closed group of Catholic scholars who sought to frame these scrolls as having originated in the 1st century BCE. Eisenman's analysis of these texts places them more in the 1st and 2nd centuries CE (Baigent and Leigh, 1993), raising questions about the accuracy of the New Testament version of history.

Christian historical accounts seem to either have confused or deliberately obscured the relationships between the zealots and the early Jesus movement. The common history of a Christian "Jerusalem Church" and its first bishop James in the "Apostolic Age" does not make sense when understanding the complexity of this reactionary and profoundly Jewish group. The task of untangling the mess of this history, therefore, poses an enormous challenge in uncovering what I recognize as an original Wisdom Revelation.

My approach in this investigation is, in part, inspired by Eisenman (1997, 2014), who has written two extensive volumes that seek to dissect the way in which this 1st century history was distorted. He deciphers some specific strategies used by the early Christian scriptural architects, who were, to some degree, motivated by the agenda of the emerging orthodox tradition. This was to whitewash anything that was a threat to Roman rule, which, I believe, included any movement toward individual spiritual empowerment not tied in with a regulated religious authority.

The Dead Sea Scrolls sprang from a fierce messianic Jewish nationalism that saw the Hellenizing trends associated with St. Paul as being highly heretical. On the other hand, as I will explore extensively, the Nag Hammadi Library is a textual record of a tradition called "Gnostic" that not only broke from its Jewish theological roots but also constituted an egregious Jewish heresy.

The Essenes played an important role in this history and likely had a strong influence on the spiritual and esoteric development of John the Baptist and Jesus. But this is complicated by the Essenes' participation in the Jewish messianic nationalist movements, as Eisenman has discussed (1997). The Essenes were not distinctly Gnostic but were aligned with a more Jamesian and Jewish apocalyptic tradition which, at times, was in direct contradiction to the emerging Gnostic movements.

The Novel Revelation of Wisdom

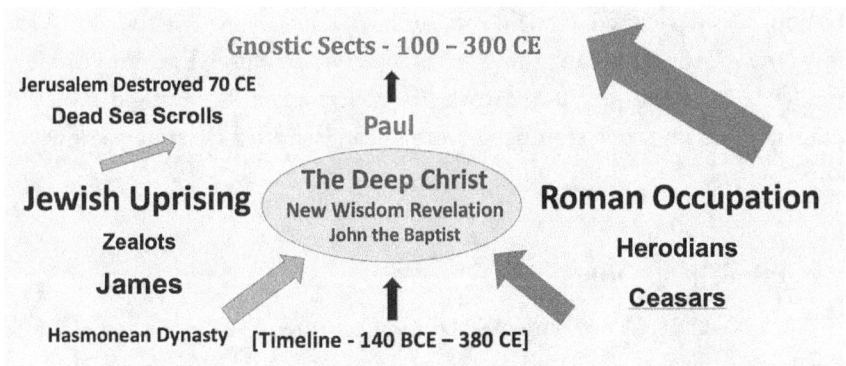

Illustration 2

Dropped into the middle of this Jews vs. Rome conflict (Illustration 2) is a Novel Revelation of high wisdom teachings. Beginning with John the Baptist with his own proto-Gnostic teachings (Mead, 1924), this revelation emerged in its most comprehensive form from this person known as Jesus, whose message stretched far beyond those found in the Bible. Due to the enigmatic teachings that describe his own journey in a complex story of creation that sprang from what the prominent Gnostic Valentinian called the Deep, I will be referring to him more generally as the Deep Christ. There were also some key players who contributed to this spiritual innovation, including St. Thomas, Mary Magdalene, and Philip, who appear to have been a part of Christ's inner circle. This constellation of characters forms an epicenter of 1st century wisdom teachings that will be the primary focus of both our Sophianic Mystery Play and Deep Christ Mystery Thriller.

St. Paul and the Gnostic Tradition

St. Paul's role in the advent of the Gnostic tradition during his lifetime is complex, controversial, and largely overlooked. Evidence suggests that he was an important player in the dissemination of this New Revelation. As the primary architect of a Hellenized version of Christianity, Paul worked to weave esoteric teachings into his religious system (Pagels, 1975) that were designed to stay below the radar of the less informed public and be non-threatening to the Roman authorities. However, Paul's version of Christianity was eventually adapted to become the "universal" (i.e., the only) acceptable version of Catholic Christianity, and the "apostolic" tradition of popes and bishops was developed to anchor the authority of the new religion to its base in Rome. Beyond St. Paul, there are many clues to this 1st century mystery thriller to be found in the theatrical fog that surrounds key figures of this drama, especially when stumbling on the strangest of all characters known as Simon.

From Gnostic to Orthodoxy

This New Revelation emerged amidst this intense religious upheaval of the 1st century centered in Jerusalem. By the end of that century and the beginning of the 2nd century, there began to form various schools and sects that we now know as Gnostic.

One of the earliest sects in the schools of Gnosticism, generally known as "Sethian" (Turner, 2001), are, I believe, some of the closest second-generation offspring of the novel 1st century Deep Christ teachings. According to some scholars, including the editor of the 1978 English translation of the Nag Hammadi Library, the roots of this Sethian Gnostic tradition are distinctly non-Christian.[4] Over time and with later editions, however, these Sethian writings became increasingly "Christianized," and the more original teachings were largely lost or assimilated into Christian orthodoxy. It is this particular Sethian Gnostic tradition that I believe holds many clues to this 1st century Wisdom Revelation.

It would be hard to over-stress the influence that the Roman occupation of Palestine factored into all of this. Rome was battling an unrelenting uprising that mobilized more than twenty thousand soldiers in a brutal siege to reclaim Jerusalem from a religious movement that refused to surrender. The toll that the Jewish Wars took was so great that Rome sought never to let another religious movement create such turmoil.

In the earliest days of Christianity and its mystical sister, Gnosticism, like Judaism, the two were seen as a threat to Roman rule. The Gnostic system in particular was quite radical, and its esoteric teachings and high initiatory practices brought a sense of spiritual empowerment to its adherents. This was certainly not acceptable as it fostered too much personal independence from Roman state power.

The French Catholic bishop Irenaeus (c. 130–202 CE) was a good example of an early Christian theologian who worked with the Roman leadership to begin to shape this emerging new religion that was distinctly non-Jewish into something acceptable to Rome (Pagels, 2003). He also worked hard to demonize this Gnostic system as a Christian heresy rather than what is arguably something quite the opposite. In his *Against Heresies*, Irenaeus argued at length how this Gnostic version of the Christ story was corrupt and how its endless speculation and strange depictions of divine cosmologies and fallen angels had no place in what was becoming Christian orthodoxy.

The apostle Peter became the central figure around which the "Petrine" Roman religion was organized. Gradually in the 2nd, 3rd, and 4th centuries, the contemporary version of Christianity began to take hold amidst a maelstrom of competing versions.

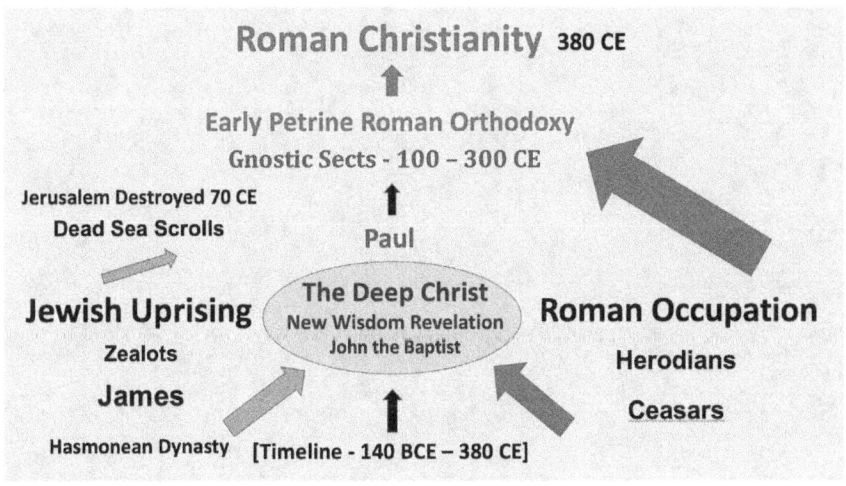

Illustration 3

The Triumph of Roman Orthodox Christianity

Eventually, a Roman-sponsored Christian Church secured the lead role over Celtic, Alexandrian, Jerusalem, Syrian, and other church variations. At the Council of Nicaea in 325 and finally, in 380 with the Edict of Thessalonica, a concise declaration of belief called the Nicaean Creed became the foundation for the anti-Gnostic, Roman orthodox version of Christianity (Illustration 3). Not only were the Gnostics virtually wiped clean from the face of history, but the source and inspiration behind their movement, this New Revelation of Wisdom, was also buried beneath the unyielding bedrock of St. Peter's religion.

Roman Christianity became the victor which wrote the history, and, as Eisenman attests, trying to dig our way out of the many layers and piled-up centuries of their version of history is a nearly impossible job. This historical excavation, however, is an effort to get closer to the bottom of it.

3

Introduction to Gnosticism

To trace back to the origins of this 1st century Wisdom Revelation, it is important to be familiar with the strange tradition known as Gnosticism. In this investigation, I will be, in essence, reverse engineering the lost traditions of Sophia and the Deep Christ, from Christianity to Gnosticism to their largely lost and obscured 1st century innovations. In this way, a clear understanding of Gnosticism is pivotal.

To be clear, I do not consider Gnosticism to be the sole carrier of truth, and I am not a practicing Gnostic. Rather, I honor how this incredibly rich religious system feeds into the underground streams of so many depth and wisdom traditions, from the Kabbalah to the Cathars, from medieval alchemy to the theories of Carl Jung. This multifaceted esoteric tradition, related to the Perennial Philosophy, is vast, and I believe its many rivulets are attempting to grasp phenomena that are beyond any one group's capacity to fully systematize.

The word Gnostic is sometimes confused with the term "agnostic," meaning "I don't know and I don't pretend to know" (about God, etc.). Some would argue that this is the best bottom line for everybody to stay humble with a "beginner's mind." As helpful as this may be, however, agnosticism is different from what is being presented here.

Gnosticism is a religious and spiritual movement that generally emerged after 100 CE (2nd century) and flourished for roughly 300 years before it was largely extinguished or assimilated into orthodox Christianity, Neo-Platonism, and alchemy. It spanned a wide area, from Rome to Babylon, though it appears to have had two central locations during its early formation: Alexandria, Egypt, and in the regions of northern Syria, specifically in an ancient city called Edessa, in modern-day Sanliurfa in southern Turkey. Judaea/Palestine was an important epicenter of this movement as well, though finding the footprints of Gnostic development through the later part of the 1st century in this area is virtually impossible, given how thorough these tracks have been erased.

The word Gnostic comes from the Greek *gnosis*, a word used in the early texts meaning knowing or, according to its own tradition, a sort of non-intellectual direct, perhaps mystical, comprehension of something beyond the hard facts of this material world.

Bentley Layton (1987) writes that this term "gnosis" was in common use in the 2nd century and referred to a certain kind of "knowing," which can best be described as having an "acquaintance with." This involves having a personal familiarity with something as opposed to just knowing the bare facts of it. For example, rather than knowing where San Francisco is, to have gnosis is to *know* San Francisco, having grown up there. This term "gnosis," however, over time, began to be used to refer to a person's intimate familiarity with a deep knowing that often came from spiritual or divine inspiration.

Problems with the Word "Gnostic"

To even call this unique and fleeting tradition by this name Gnostic is to invoke, at times unconsciously, a sort of disdain, even disgust, so thorough has been the campaign to demonize it by orthodox Christianity. Though Gnosticism has enjoyed a revival of interest in the last fifty years, still so battered has the word Gnostic been over the centuries that even today, scholars such as those within the famed Jesus Seminar of the Westar Institute toy with throwing the term out altogether.[1]

From the 4th century to today, Gnosticism has not been welcomed in Christian or Catholic churches — something I discovered firsthand. I brought my interest in Gnostic philosophy to an Episcopal priest in Northern California some years ago, where we had what I thought was an open and respectful dialogue. However, the following Sunday, this priest, who clearly had little academic familiarity with the Gnostic tradition, made it quite clear in his sermon that this sex-obsessed, conspiracy-riddled, heresy cult, popularized by Dan Brown's *The Da Vinci Code,* was not welcomed in the church. Although feeling a little betrayed, I realized that this cleric genuinely believed that Gnosticism was a disgrace and he was only doing his job by upholding his priestly vows designed to guard against such heresies. Just as it had for the past 1600 years, this largely misunderstood and often misrepresented form of mystical Christianity was being told to just get lost.

Given all of this, it is tempting to avoid the term Gnostic completely because the very word invokes such controversy, leading many, including myself at times, to consider other alternative labels. "Proto-Christian," "early Christian mysticism," "Coptic Christianity," or "the Way of Gnosis" have been proposed, and, to some extent, these are helpful descriptors. However, these are more general and do not accurately identify the spiritual and religious movement defined by its distinct language and cosmology. To use these terms, I believe, could fall into the trap of continuing to turn a blind eye to this unique tradition and further obscuring its already highly elusive history.

In 1966 at the International Congress on "the Origin of Gnosticism" held in Messina, Italy, there was a consensus decision to use the term "gnosis" to mean "knowledge of the divine mysteries reserved for an elite" and the term "Gnostics" was agreed upon to identify this religious group that emerged largely in the 2nd century CE.[2]

This idea that Gnosticism is "reserved for the elite" carries an all-too-common view that this seemingly rogue Christian sect saw itself as "special" and privy to secret teachings only available to a select group. In this light, Roman Catholicism (meaning universal), which sought to make itself available to all, appears well-intended. However, I think that "reserved for the elite" is better understood in light of the need for these teachings to remain private and guarded to not only manage the dissemination of advanced and often misunderstood teachings but also to avoid persecution. This was especially true after the mid-4th century when religious books that ran counter to the orthodox standard were banned and the campaign to eliminate this "heresy" kicked into high gear. It is interesting to note that Gnostics in general were open to the developing Christian religion and worked to translate their system into being more compatible with the emerging orthodoxy, where some of their texts became more "Christianized". Unfortunately, Christianity eventually did all it could do to discredit the Gnostic tradition.

I have concluded, therefore, at least for now, that no other term better identifies this novel psycho-spiritual movement of the first few centuries CE than Gnostic. In fact, reclaiming this very word can help unearth the long-buried and suppressed spiritual treasures within this tradition.

The Gnostic Texts

According to Bentley Layton's *The Gnostic Scriptures* (1997), the various Gnostic sects had specific features that were uniquely Gnostic and not Christian. They utilized certain linguistic terms unique to them, and there was a strong sense of group identity built around not only this language but also religious rituals, specifically various baptisms. Most importantly, there is a "complex and distinctive myth of origins"[3] that is the prime source material for my rendition of the creation story of Sophia.

So thorough was the elimination of the Gnostic texts that for much of the last 1600 years, we have only known of this religious movement from Christian writings that sought to discredit them. Known as "heresiologists," these early Christian writers took upon themselves the task of picking apart what they saw as Christianity-gone-rogue. Gnosticism consequently became identified as "the first heresy" and was what put the derogatory use of the very word *heresy* on the map.[4] Ironically, it was the extensive writings of 2nd– 5th century Christians like Irenaeus (130–202 CE), Hippolytus of Rome (c. 170–235 CE), and Epiphanius of Salamis (c. 310–403 CE), where writings on these heresies became the only available record of this obscure tradition for most of Christian history. Research of Gnosticism prior to the late 1970s relied largely on these writings.

The campaign to erase this tradition was so thorough that a total of only four of the innumerable codices (bound books, not scrolls, made from papyrus paper) that existed from that time have been dug up from either layers of dirt or found in musty basements of monasteries and university libraries.

In the late 18th century, the first of the long-lost Gnostic texts were recovered called The Bruce Codex.[5] These were an incredibly rare collection that had miraculously survived the purges of the 4th and 5th centuries.

The Bruce Codex was purchased in Egypt by an antiquities dealer named Bruce in 1769 and contains extremely rare Gnostic inner teachings, specifically the *Book of the Great Logos According to the Mystery*, also called the *Book of IEOU* (IE), or the *Book of Jeu*. This is a 3rd-century text that, I believe, falls quite close to the epicenter of the highly advanced Novel Revelation of proto-Gnostic teachings.

The second cache of recovered Gnostic texts is called the Askew Codex. This was purchased by Anthony Askew in 1785 from a London bookseller and contained a remarkable 356 pages, including the largest of the Gnostic texts called the *Pistis Sophia* (PS). I will be drawing heavily from this *Pistis Sophia* text to present the creation story of Sophia. This codex also contains a fragment of what has become known as *The Gospel of Mary* (GM). The Bruce and Askew collections were initially translated in the 1890s with a high degree of scholastic rigor by German Coptologist Carl Schmidt, although the value of his work was not fully appreciated until they became more widely available in English translations in the late 1970s.

Another 5th-century collection called the Berlin Codex, discovered in Egypt in 1896, was found wrapped in white feathers in a Christian burial site and included the *Gospel of Mary*, *Sophia of Jesus Christ* (SJC), the *Apocryphon of John* (AJ), and the *Act of Peter* (AP).

The Nag Hammadi Library

In 1945, a fourth massive buried stash of Gnostic codices from the 4th century was discovered. Translated from the Coptic, these were eventually published in English in 1978 as the Nag Hammadi Library (NHL). Having escaped the orthodox heresy hunters of the early Christian era, this collection added forty new books to the far fewer recovered Gnostic texts to date, bringing profound new insights into this lost tradition as well as giving more details about the specifics of their creation story. The *Gospel of Thomas* (GT), with its famous Bring Forth quote, is currently the most well-known book in this collection. Though it does not include specifics of the complex creation story, this text is a good introduction to the Gnostic teachings of Christ.

I want to again emphasize that it has only been since the late 1970s that nearly all of these recovered texts became readily available to the public. Elaine Pagels (1979), one of the translators in the 1978 English edition of the Nag Hammadi Library, wrote her seminal book *The Gnostic Gospels,* which first introduced many people to this curious religious trend. Prior to the 1978 publication of the Nag Hammadi Library, G. R. S. Mead, Jung, and others helped further our understanding of this extremely spare body of work. But the publication of this enormous collection opened the floodgates of discovery and insight into this obscure movement. Hence, it has been a mere forty-five years that we have been able to more clearly consider the significance and magnitude of these texts.

We are now in a fertile time period where this treasure can be more thoroughly mined. Less than a half century is a mere moment in religious historical time and is why I believe scholarship is still trying to digs its way out of the vast campaign to obscure and discredit Gnosticism. From my own twenty-five years of research, especially into the Sophianic component of these texts, I offer my insights, which at times may include bold claims. Such is the excitement and risks of delving deeply into a tradition that has been taboo for so long.

Like Christianity, Judaism, and Islam, there are endless variations of the Gnostic tradition, with many sects and branches. The Nag Hammadi Library itself is an assorted collection that includes Gnostic, Hermetic, and Platonic writings that were popular amongst this group in the mid-4th century. In 367 CE, the famous St. Athanasius (who the Episcopalian Priest I mentioned earlier told me he had learned about in seminary) banned all "non-canonical" Christian books. Though there are conflicting reports of the collection's discovery, this may have been the impetus behind an anonymous and heroic monk's effort to hide an invaluable stash of Gnostic books just outside the St. Pachomius Monastery near modern-day Nag Hammadi, Egypt.

The Earliest Gnostics Called Sethian

It is within this collection that scholars have identified some of the earliest writings of this extensive Gnostic tradition. John D. Turner (2001) has presented the most comprehensive overview of what gradually came out of the haze of Gnostic formation in a system generally called "Sethian." We learn that the 4th-century Roman bishop and heresiologist Epiphanius identified this tradition based on its frequent reference to the lesser-known offspring of Adam and Eve named Seth. This Gnostic philosophical stream is believed to have originated in both Egypt and Syria (modern-day southern Turkey). A distinct feature of these Sethian texts is their myth of origins, which I will be presenting as the creation story of Sophia. That Seth was the Son of Adam or Son of Man adds intrigue to this being a title associated with Jesus.

The Sethian *Apocryphal (Secret) Book of John* (AJ) was likely the most popular book of the Gnostics as two copies of it were found in the Nag Hammadi Library, adding to the one that had already been recovered fifty years prior in the Berlin Codex. The famed Valentinian tradition, perhaps the most well-known of the Gnostic schools, was greatly influenced by the earlier Sethian materials.

Three main ideas are unique to this Sethian Gnostic system: 1) a detailed creation cosmology (cosmogony), 2) a unique interpretation of the Genesis story of Adam and Eve, and 3) a specific ritual of baptism, which involved an esoteric process of being immersed not in water but by a divine Light known as the "living waters."

Other Gnostic books that are not specifically identified in this grouping also contain the specific creation mythology of Sophia, and hence, we might consider a broader category of texts as being "Sophianic." Later, more Christianized texts such as the *Tripartite Tractate* (TT) and the *Gospel of Truth* (GTr) show how Sophia is deleted from the story or overlaid with the concept of Logos and the Church replacing her as the bride of Christ.

Books within the Sophianic category include *Pistis Sophia* (PS), *Books of IEOU* (IE), *Apocryphon of John* (AJ), *Eugnostos the Blessed* (Eug), *Sophia of Jesus Christ* (SJC), *Second Treatise of the Great Seth* (ST), *Trimorphic Protennoia* (TP), *Apocalypse of Peter* (APe), *Acts of Thomas* (AT), *Gospel of Philip* (GP), *Hypostasis of the Archons* (HA), *On the Origin of the World* (OW), and the *Exegesis on the Soul* (ES).

In this entire collection, no complete rendering of the creation story survived. For the story presented here, I draw mainly from the prominent 2nd century *Apocryphon of John* and the *Pistis Sophia*, though other texts contribute as well.

Not only is this figure Jesus Christ himself featured as a main character in the creation story, he himself is, at times, the one who is the storyteller. This is extraordinary and fuels the need to broaden the scope of our understanding of who this man was. How do we reconcile how Jesus is featured prominently in these texts in a manner so different from how he is portrayed in the New Testament? It is this question that points us to the jewels of the 1st century New Revelation and to the more original teachings from which the Sophianic tradition emerged.

4

Introduction to the Creation Story of Sophia

Excavated from scraps of 1600-year-old Gnostic writings, there is a curious fragment: "Wisdom sendeth forth her children."[1] Who is this Wisdom, and who are her children?

What and Who is Wisdom — Sophia?

The word Sophia, Greek for wisdom (*chokmah* in Hebrew), has been around for a very long time. The further back we go in the western and Judeo-Christian traditions, the less she had specific anthropomorphic features. To the Greeks, wisdom was mainly an attribute, a feature of one's broader skills of understanding. This was not just about accumulating information, but it involved abilities of discernment, heartfelt understanding, and being pragmatically effective in the world. Pythagoras coined the love of wisdom into the now common word, philosophy.

This word "wisdom" features prominently in the Old Testament,[2] such as in the Book of Wisdom, where the human attribute is associated with something more than mere knowledge of facts. Michael Meade refers to wisdom as being a cross-fertilization between vision and maturity, a virtue clearly worth cultivating.

The seven sapiential or Wisdom books (*Sapientia* is Latin for wisdom) of the Old Testament include the Song of Songs, Job, Psalms, Proverbs, Ecclesiastes, Sirach, and the Book of Wisdom. This wisdom tradition of the

Old Testament primarily emerged from exiled Jewish priests who were being held in Babylonian captivity in the 6th century BCE.

In these books, the quality of wisdom is referred to largely as a moral principle.

"Is not wisdom found among the aged? Does not long life bring understanding?" (Job 12:12).

"My mouth will speak words of wisdom; the meditation of my heart will give you understanding" (Psalms 49:3).

However, in these Old Testament books, there are sparse and vague references to wisdom being, more than just a personal attribute, an actual identity.

"I, wisdom, was with the Lord when he began his work, long before he made anything else. I was created in the very beginning, even before the world began" (Proverbs 8: 22-23).

"God by wisdom founded the earth; by understanding he established the heavens" (Proverbs 3:19).

Here, a feminine wisdom figure is part of the original creation. However, descriptions of who this character was, where she came from, and what her role in creation might have been are scant. At least this was the case until the 1st century CE when, fairly suddenly, there began to emerge a whole new body of literature that focused specifically on this feminine creator goddess.

Scholars have tended to view the origins of Gnosticism as having gradually evolved from Egyptian and Greek philosophy and a revival of Platonic writings at the time. They have also recognized that this creation story that is uniquely Gnostic was also highly unusual in that it was "not the spontaneous product of a tribe or culture,"[3] in contrast to the thousands of creation stories from innumerable indigenous tribes around the world.

In contrast to this, evidence points to how this creation story came onto the scene of the 1st century CE in what I am calling a New Revelation. There emerged quite suddenly a complex creation story that pointed to our place in a tragic yet hopeful drama. In the centuries that followed, the primary teachings of this revelation were obscured almost to the point of nonrecognition. However, with the writings of heresiologists like Irenaeus and also Gnostic codices that survived from that time, there are enough textual references to piece together this unique myth of origins.

The Gnostic Sophia: A Synopsis

Sophia is sometimes an elusive character in this vast Gnostic creation story who, over time, was written out of the script entirely. However, as she is presented in these rare pre- (or "proto," meaning formative) orthodox texts, she is clearly one of the great heroines of humanity. Though she is often depicted as having been overcome with pretension, which led to her "fall," I have come to believe that her venture into this lower world of "chaos" was part of an attempt, along with her consort, Christ, to create "bodily dwellings" into which divine beings could inhabit. This plan was thwarted, however, by self-serving "gods" called archons, who were able to trap Sophia and steal the seed stock of this new being, her divine Light. Mournful "Songs of Sophia," presented by Christ in the *Pistis Sophia*, were pleas for her beloved "Light of lights" whereupon she was rescued her from her plight. The plan for creating beings of Light eventually continued, however, whereby the spark of Sophia was planted into Adam at the inception of humanity. This inner divine Light still lies largely latent within us, longing to be remembered and reconnected with its mother source flame, Sophia.

The creation story of Sophia is an epic tale of courtship that weaves between two lovers and reaches across the span of cosmic history toward the earliest beginnings. It is also a love song that can be heard in the smallest and most personal spaces of our inner world.

The Creation Story of Sophia: A Mystery Play

To separate this creation material out from the rest of what is presented in this book, I invite the reader to imagine this story being presented in the form of a Mystery Play. Mystery Plays were a popular medieval European tradition that flourished between the 9th and 16th centuries. Instead of just sitting in church listening to the preacher interpret Bible stories, often in Latin, which nobody could understand, people started to add simple stage productions to the church service. At times, it would be actors posing in picture form, called a tableau. These plays sometimes included whole villages, where hundreds of people gathered in the town square for theatrical presentations of stories like the Good Samaritan or the Last Supper. Modern-day Christmas nativity pageants played out in churches around the world are relics of this tradition.

The word "mystery" in this context was used to refer to the miracles associated with biblical events in both the Old and New Testaments. But this word also pointed to how the various craft guilds would take on the responsibility of presenting certain Bible stories for the town's play, year after year, making it their own. For example, the textile guild might appropriate the Annunciation of Mary and the mason guild the crucifixion. It was the secrets or mysteries of their trade that brought a special flavor to their stage production. More importantly, however, I am playing with the word *mystery* here in pointing to these treasured though elusive esoteric wisdom teachings.

The sections of this story presented below that constitute the various acts of the Mystery Play include loosely portrayed scenes composed of text quotes, prose narration, and some analysis. Instead of the familiar biblical scenes, in this Sophianic Mystery Play, I will be portraying vast sweeps of cosmic beginnings to this sometimes-otherworldly stage. Prominently featured is a goddess known as Sophia, who appears both as an original expression of what is known as the Holy Spirit and as an adventurous youth. This is a love story of despair and great hope. And, if I am getting the story right, this drama continues even into our present time, where each one of us is a key player on the stage.

5

Introduction to the Deep Christ

*The son revealed the everlasting, and all the unknown was known. He revealed
what is hard to interpret and what is secret, and he preached to those who live in
silence with First Thought, and he revealed himself to those who are in darkness,
and he clarified himself to those in the abyss. To those in the hidden treasuries he
told ineffable mysteries, and he taught unspeakable doctrines to all those who
became children of the light.*

-    *Trimorphic Protennoia,* (TP) Nag Hammadi Library.

In the first few centuries CE, many sects and religious trends ultimately
became subjugated by a centralized authority of orthodox Christianity.
Anything that didn't fit into a Roman-approved version was either merged
with this religious organization or was deemed a heresy and banned. As a
result, earlier and perhaps more accurate histories of this man Jesus were
marginalized and lost.

Where did Jesus's ministry take place, what were his teachings, where had
he come from, who was in his family, and how long did he live? Answers to
these questions can be found, to some extent, in the New Testament — by
far the most prevalent source for the historical accounts of the life of Jesus.
However, recent scholarship offers a more disciplined exploration of this
man's life outside of the near-total dominance of the New Testament
"history."

The stories of Jesus were written many decades after the events depicted, and, despite the overwhelming acceptance of these stories as "gospel," there are many questions about how historically accurate they may be. It is interesting to note, for example, that the letters of St. Paul were written prior to the Gospels,[1] but they provide virtually no details about Jesus's life.

The Gnostic texts, however, present a very different description of this man and hold invaluable clues to a Christ story that is more complex and esoteric in his teachings. Here, Jesus teaches less in parables and more in elaborate descriptions of the structure of the cosmos, from its origins down to the quantum regions of our human form. This is in great contrast to how he is presented in the New Testament, with elaborate stories of his birth and death, all of which are largely absent in the Gnostic texts. How can we make sense of this?

As a point of reference to this question, let us look at another primary character in this mystery drama who also straddled Gnosticism and Christianity and was a key player in both of these monumental religious systems.

St. Paul was Both Gnostic and Christian

In Gnostic scholar Elaine Pagels's (1975) lesser-known book, *The Gnostic Paul*, she presents a compelling analysis of how this prominent 1st century figure, St. Paul, interspersed into his authentic writings references to the more esoteric teachings of this Gnostic tradition. In his letters, Paul included clues and symbolic code words that point to these mystery teachings. However, these clues were couched in language that was easier to understand for those unaware of the deeper meanings. In this way, Paul sought to bridge the teachings of gnosis with a religious system that was simpler and more available to the less studied general population. According to Clement of Alexandria (150–215 CE), the famed Valentinus himself and one of the great 2nd century philosophers and teachers of this Gnostic tradition claimed that his Gnostic system came from St. Paul.[1]

As Pagels explores this, she posits a most important question: How can Paul be known as the originator of both Christianity and Gnosticism?[2] It is hard to imagine that Paul had Gnostic leanings when his reputation says almost the opposite. Paul was the main architect of the Hellenist version of

Christianity that became the template upon which the new, anti-heretical orthodoxy of the early Roman Church was drawn.

Some years ago, I attended Pagels's address on her book *Revelations: Visions, Prophecy, and Politics in the Book of Revelations* (2013) at the Westar Institute.[3] In the Q and A, I had the good fortune to ask her a question, which gets to a key theme of this Christ investigation. My question went something like this:

"Similar to how Paul appears to be both Gnostic and Christian as you describe in your *Gnostic Paul* book, Jesus also shows up quite differently in both the New Testament and the Gnostic texts. How are you reconciling the way that both the Christians and the Gnostics attribute their inspiration and the origins to this man, who is depicted so differently in these two traditions?" Unfortunately, I was unable to gain any notable insights from her answer, though she did say that she could have written much more about the Gnostic Paul.

Despite Pagels's significant contributions to this broad study of Gnosticism, she, like so many other scholars, seem to have a general tendency to gloss over the differences between the two Christs, as if they were in some way not that much different. Yet, as I will explore in this book, there is a vast gulf between them, a chasm that lies at the heart of our Deep Christ Mystery Thriller.

My recommendation, as we embark on this inquiry, is to basically set aside the many stories and associations one has of him. This is not to say that you need to forgo your own beliefs or personal relationship you have with him, whatever that might be. Indeed, the subjectivity of each person's religious and spiritual beliefs is essential and a bottom line, which no person should diminish in another. However, because the findings presented here can be so contrary to what is commonly known about Jesus, it is best to just start with a clean slate and see what unfolds from there. Holding hard-set preconceptions of who Jesus was, such as the stories of his birth and death, can make this discovery process more challenging.

The Gnostic Jesus

To be honest, I have not stepped into this inquiry into the Gnostic Jesus very enthusiastically. The lead character, Jesus, in the more common

Christian mystery plays of old, has gotten plenty of attention over the last 2000 years. Surely, Jesus has, for better or worse, been fertile ground for endless projections by countless people over the centuries. Sometimes I wonder what more can possibly be said about him? And yet, following the thread of Sophia led me to an unavoidable inquiry into Jesus as he appears in the Gnostic tradition.

From this investigation, I have come to suspect that a clear understanding of this strange Gnostic portrayal of Jesus has evaded a more differentiated analysis drawn from the now numerous Gnostic scriptures. There seems to be an automatic tendency to fill in the image of Jesus based on the established template of how he appears in the New Testament. People just want to complete the picture that the Gnostic Jesus is simply another way of looking at the biblical Jesus and just leave it at that. Forget that these texts claim that he continued his teachings for years after the crucifixion. Ignore how this Gnostic Jesus spoke at length with tremendous detail about the nature of the trinity, the primary three-fold creation — something which is nearly completely absent in the New Testament.[4]

My sense is that Jesus is so established as a beloved and largely unquestioned historical figure who holds such a deeply rooted place within the collective psyche that there is an almost automatic blurring of any differences in how he is portrayed in these two traditions. Furthermore, the Gnostic portrayal of Jesus carries a mythological flavor which makes it easier for this generalized Gnostic savior to be intermingled with his biblical version.

From my research, however, the Gnostic Jesus appears to carry a more original depiction of this savior figure than the Jesus of the four Gospels, who is defined more within a later Petrine-based Roman system.[5] Though some scholars, like the esteemed John Turner, suggest that Christ enters into the Gnostic texts as part of a "Christianizing" trend, this does not explain how the early Sethian tradition is riddled with references to a specific savior figure who has distinct features such as his direct relationship to Sophia. These unique features essentially disappear in the progressively Christianized texts, suggesting that this is a later development.

Though I present what is basically an introduction to the thesis of a pre-Christian, Gnostic Christ, and one which is virtually impossible to prove, it nevertheless raises the question of whether the very personhood of Jesus may have had a historical identity whose real-life footprint was more in line with the character of the Gnostic Jesus than of the later, less cosmological Jesus of the four Gospels. Though this question will have to remain definitively unanswered in this book, I will be tracking clues to how the Jesus of the New Testament may have been preceded by a man who presented a novel Revelation of teachings that carried greater mystical depth than is largely assumed, a Deep Christ where "they say he came for all, but in truth, [he] came for her [Sophia], who came for all."[6]

On Myth and History

The word *myth* holds rich but varied meanings. A culture, for example, has living myths, where the deep churnings of the underlying beliefs, rituals, and milieus work outside the realm of conscious thought. Here, archetypal stories provide a mythological template upon which a culture continually evolves. This is a positive meaning of the word *myth* as is espoused within the field of Jungian psychology.

In contrast to this, I will be using the term *myth* here to refer to a process of mythologizing where, over the course of time, there is a blurring or even romanticizing of historical details. A good example of this is in the best-selling book of all time, the Bible.

In the New Testament, there are many examples of how Jesus is linked with characters and events in the Old Testament that some, like Robert Eisenman, believe were edited into the Gospel stories in order to underline that Jesus was a fulfillment of the Jewish anticipation of a coming messiah. For example, did the story that appears in the Gospel of Matthew (2:16-18) about the early 1st century mass murder of all male children in the area of Bethlehem really happen? As is now largely recognized, there is no historical evidence that such a horrific event ever occurred around the year zero in this region of Palestine.[7] This legend was likely superimposed into this Jesus story from the Old Testament tale of the Egyptian Pharaoh's killing of all children born in that year who might fulfill the prophecy of a newborn who would eventually threaten his power. Jesus is hence depicted as the new Moses, who would lead his people into the promised land, complete with the Killing of the Innocents myth being folded into the New Testament as historical fact. This is a classic example of how the New Testament stories were embellished by Old Testament references to help provide a historical precedent for this

Jesus, as Eisenman has discussed.

The historical portrayal of not only Jesus and James but also the disciple Thomas of the Gospels has also been distorted. Furthermore, one wonders if details of the circumstances of Jesus's life were avoided in the New Testament in a way that helped distance him from the raging religious, political, and theological controversies that were perhaps just too messy to include. Or, as we will explore, the spiritual system of the Deep Christ might have been just too outrageous to be adopted wholly by the later orthodoxy. And so, in the end, modern-day readers are getting a toned-down, cleaned-up, and mythologized version of this man.

At the same time, the creation story of Sophia has been largely dismissed as some old fanciful myth with strange gods and a heroic rescue by a descending Jesus. But given, I believe, how this 'myth" is central to a 1st century novel Revelation, there may be more here than a mere stylized fairy tale. Perhaps this Sophianic creation story is a complex description of cosmic origins that lies outside our three-dimensional frames of understanding and is rendering history rather than mere myth.

The challenge is that people can get attached to the overly-familiar histories and stories and so cling to them even when presented with evidence that there might be some mythologizing going on. On the other hand, stories found within the texts involving the Gnostic Christ are dismissed by scholars as myths that sprang out of the imaginations of creative theologians who made their way into the lore of religious sects, conveniently overlooking that there may be some historical basis to these creation stories.

Attempts to question these Gospel "histories" are generally not welcomed by the carriers of the traditionally accepted narrative. Robert Eisenman has expressed frustration at just how deeply entrenched the biblical version of Jesus is that it acts as a massive bulwark against any serious scholastic inquiry into what historically, i.e., factually, might have been going on at that place in that time.[8]

The Gnostic creation story, as with much of the Gnostic theology, is typically seen as a myth that developed over a couple of hundred years, perhaps from a group of Jewish mystical philosophers who developed maps of the divine realms and rituals of purification[9], until it gradually took a clearer shape in the 2nd century.[10] My findings into the Deep Christ, however, diverge from this thesis of Gnostic origins.

Especially when looking at Sophia, or worse, the archons, this intersection of myth and history can be quite problematic. The authors and scribes of these Gnostic stories sought to distinguish these unusual cosmic characters from being merely mythological. An author of one of the Gnostic scriptures found in the Nag Hammadi Library was so convinced of the factual existence of the otherworldly characters that he or she composed a text called *The Hypostasis* (fundamental reality) *of the Archons* (HA). Carl Jung, himself the master of archetypal myth, stepped out of his norm to consider that there was something more to Sophia and the archons beyond mere myth.

To tease apart what is myth and what is history is to help reclaim something that has been lost. We are looking for greater clarity and precision with regard to our origins as humans that can point us toward becoming more of who we were originally intended to be. We are living in a time when it seems that we have lost our evolutionary compass. Forces of humanity's own creative capacities have been recklessly pursued to where our very survival is increasingly brought into question. It is most fortunate that, with the excavations of these lost Sophianic Revelations, we now have a novel and enormously valuable map of where we came from, where we are going, and what might be required for us to find our way out of this existential plight.

6

The Hymn of the Pearl
Prelude to the Three Mysteries

Stepping into the three complex mysteries of Sophia, Christ, and the Divine Spark will necessarily be challenging, given how ancient and obscure they are. However, a short story offers a very simple version of all three of these, combined into one tale, that is not told but rather sung by a favorite character in the Gnostic tradition, St. Thomas.

This disciple, as referenced in the New Testament, is known as Doubting Thomas, who is featured in a somewhat gruesome post-crucifixion scene. Thomas didn't believe that Jesus had resurrected until he touched the holes of his crucified and resurrected body (John 20:24-29). What is less known, however, is that St. Thomas was one of the great disseminators of this novel Gnostic and proto-Christian teaching into areas as far away as India. It is believed that the *Gospel of Thomas* of "bring forth what is within you" fame was written in the ancient city called Edessa in Northern Syria. An even lesser-known codex that also likely emerged in the 2nd century out of Edessa was called the *Acts of Thomas* (AT).

The *Acts of Thomas* features a long story of how Jesus managed to get his "brother" Thomas to India. Included are two hymns, both allegedly sung by St. Thomas himself. One is called the "Wedding Song of Sophia," and the other is called the "Hymn of the Robe of Glory" or, more generally, "The Hymn of the Pearl." The lyrics of this latter song tell the tale of a prince who comes from "the East" from the kingdom of his parents, the king and queen of the land. He is given the task of going down to Egypt to find the "one Pearl."

The Hymn can be read as a mythological template, where each of the elements of the complex stories of Sophia, the Deep Christ, and the Divine Spark are interwoven. It is equally significant that this is a rich archetypal tale of the soul's journey, involving trials of that deep part of ourselves on our passage through life.

This story contains not only the themes of these mysteries, it also has a similar fourfold structure as found in the creation story of Sophia. In the next chapter, I will outline this format as it appears in the Hymn. This will be the template that I will use to investigate the three mysteries throughout the course of this book.

Here is my rendition of the story that draws from Mead's translation of the Hymn from the *Acts of Thomas* (AT).

The Hymn of the Pearl

A long, long time ago, there was a prince, or a princess, if you prefer, who lived in an amazing kingdom under a king and queen who tended to the land in a manner that elicited great admiration from the people.

The prince grew with love and care: "In the wealth and the glories of my upbringers, I was delighting, from the East our home" (AT).

One day, his parents came to him and said, "It is time for you to go on a journey, down to the lands where you have never been. Your task is to find the one most precious Pearl guarded by a terrible dragon." The prince closed his eyes and realized that the path of his life mission was now before him.

His parents removed the coat of many colors that he had worn for all of his days. He packed his bag, left the East, and went down into the foreign land.

He wandered through villages and forests he had never seen before. Soon, he began to see people wearing different clothes and speaking in a foreign tongue. He was intrigued by them and took delight in their unusual customs. All the while, he asked, "Where is the Pearl?" "Ah, way over yonder," they told him as he continued to travel deeper into this unfamiliar country.

In time, he became very comfortable with this intriguing culture, getting to know the people better, hanging out with them, hearing their music, and eating their food. Gradually, as the prince reports, "I forgot that I was a king's son and became a slave to their king. I forgot all concerning the Pearl for which my parents had sent me. And from the weight of their food, I sank down into a deep sleep" (AT).

Not hearing from him for a time, his parents became very concerned. They did not understand what had happened to him. They sent a letter carried by an eagle who flew it over the land until, finally, it found the prince.

Seeing the eagle land on his bedside window sill, the prince grabbed the letter, opened it, and began to read.

"Oh, you prince, have you forgotten? There's a Pearl to be found where treasures do abound. Won't you wake up?"

He read this letter, shaking off his hangover. "What is this letter? What is going on here?" Waking from his slumber, he began to remember where he came from. He remembered his mission: the Pearl!

And at that point, he set out with singleness of purpose, whereupon he found the Pearl, guarded by a ferocious monster.

"I began to charm him, the terrible loud breathing serpent. I lulled him to sleep and slumber. And I snatched up the Pearl and turned to the house of my mother and father" (AT). Upon his return, his parents welcomed him with open arms and with gratitude for the success of his mission. They brought him his robe of glory, which was once again placed over him. And all was well in the kingdom.

7

The Four Stages of the Soul's Journey

Via Positiva, Negativa, Creativa, and *Transformativa*

A Structure for Exploring the Three Mysteries

As will be explored more in the pages below, this ancient tale of the Pearl offers a simple nutshell version of the story of Sophia. This prince (Christ) goes down and successfully reclaims the lost pearl (the spark of Sophia) whereupon he can return to his place of origin.

This myth is also an archetypal map of the soul's journey. The word *soul* here refers to our deep self, that aspect of our being that overarches the everyday ups and downs of life. With time and the accumulation of experience, there is a deepening and a gaining of wisdom, where we are fully in the world and not just at the mercy of it. This concept of the soul's journey is modeled by Sophia, known as the *anima mundi*, the soul of the world.

In his seminal book, *Original Blessing*, Matthew Fox (1983) promoted a model of The Four Paths of Creation Spirituality.[1] This four-fold template, I believe, offers a valuable means of understanding the broad process of growth and transformation. This is a map of the path of initiation for the hero and heroine on his or her journey, as well as the path of the child who passes through the key stages and challenges of life. This is a profound map of the archetype of initiation and change, which will be the structure used to investigate the three mysteries of Sophia, Christ, and the Spark.

Here is a description of each of these four stages as outlined in the Hymn of the Pearl.

Via Positiva

Via Positiva represents the bounty of our beginnings, our origins, where there is a source of unconditional support and nurturance for a life to come. The young prince is found in his well-endowed home. "In the wealth and the glories of my Up-bringers, I was delighting, from the east our home..." (AT). This is the place every child deserves to enter at birth, a place where they are loved, valued, and given emotional nourishment and physical protection from the harshness of the bigger world. This home also includes the king and queen archetypes at their best, where "source" manifests as a wellspring of divine order and love. In this fourfold model, the Via Positiva is the Way of an original, inherent state of grace and innocence.

Via Negativa

From this place of origin, there is inevitably a descent, the Via Negativa. The prince matures to the point where he is ready to step outside the nest, so to speak, where it is natural and important for him to explore beyond the safety and comfort of his home. "I left the East and went down." In the three-fold stages of a classic indigenous rite of passage process (that, unfortunately, does not include an initial Positiva stage), this is known as the "separation." In Jung's model of psycho-spiritual alchemy, this is the falling apart, called nigredo — the dropping into the depths of one's soul. It is here that the prince gets lost. "I forgot that I was a king's son and became a slave to their king. I forgot all concerning the Pearl for which my parents had sent me, and from the weight of their [food], I sank down into a deep sleep" (AT).

Via Creativa

The prince then undertakes the process of remembering. Here, the hard knocks of incarnation, of being in a body in this world, point to a higher purpose and newfound sense of direction. This is the way of Creativa, of inner sourcing, where no one can rescue a person but one's self. This is where the vision comes to the vision quester and where creative exertion moves through the blues-song of hardship and into the power of resiliency. There is a danger here, however, where one might fail to move through this Creativa phase and instead retreat into a place of victimhood, passing blame on all that isn't right in the world. This can result in the failure to progress out of the soul-deepening Negativa and cutting short this initiatory rite of passage. Indeed, many a prince and princess have been caught in the Negativa, where the need to push through the Creativa was too difficult to undertake.

The Creativa is where we find ways of expressing the deepest part of ourselves, where others can then be moved by our expressions. What is our calling? What skill do I need to develop that can be as an instrument to my unique heart song, my gift to this world? "I began to charm him, the terrible loud-breathing serpent. I lulled him to sleep and to slumber, chanting o'er him..." This is the big initiatory challenge of the soul's journey, to bring forth what is within.

Via Transformativa

The final stage of this cycle of change is called Via Transformativa. This is where we reap the ultimate rewards for our efforts. "And I snatched up the Pearl and turned to the house of my mother and father." This is the breakthrough stage, where the caterpillar emerges from its cocoon in its transformed state, the Prince now being adorned by his Robe of Glory.

A key to this final stage is that, as opposed to what is required of us in the Creativa phase, we can't *will* this to happen. Any attempt to force it to come to us further distances us from this ultimate achievement. Rather, it is through our being present in a refined consciousness, where the rambunctious mind is calmed, that the doors to this great treasure might open. As I will investigate more fully, these stories may point us to unfathomable transformational possibilities.

At the same time, this fourth stage brings us to a place of action, where we are faced with a new task: to bring the gift of our transformation into the world, to help others, and to be an agent of change in society at large. This is the boon retrieved from the hero's journey that helps reinvigorate the culture. Gandhi and Martin Luther King were wonderful role models for this. As our soul-song neutralizes the control and tyranny of the fierce dragon, whatever that might be, we are also helping to inspire the possibilities for more collective human transformation.

The Four Paths Structure to Exploring the Three Mysteries

This fourfold process will be used as a template in which to explore each of the three main themes of this volume.

As presented in Part II, the creation story of Sophia follows a plotline that starts from a point of origin (positiva), through her fall into matter (negativa), into creative songs of redemption that leads to a turning (creativa), where Sophia's transformation lifts her out of exile and into her current place of majesty in the higher angelic realms. (These four stages correspond precisely to the Four Acts model of this creation story in Bentley Layton's *The Gnostic Scriptures*.[2])

In sleuthing the mystery thriller of the Deep Christ, in Part III, this will be an archeological dig into who this man was, what he was teaching, and what his relationship to Sophia was. How he shows up so differently in the Gnostic tradition in comparison to the Jesus of the New Testament will be a descent through the stages of the Negativa that constitutes novel research with profound implications. This will lead to an obscure historical figure who offers, I believe, a central clue to the mystery of this Deep Christ, known as Simon Magus.

In Part IV, we will explore the multiplicity of the theme of the Divine Spark Within using this fourfold model. The Positiva section will work to extract this quintessential treasure from the dense and obscure Gnostic texts as well as in other sacred traditions. The Negativa exploration will continue in the creation story of Sophia to tell the story of Adam and Eve. This involves the planting of the Divine Spark by Sophia as part of Plan B after her effort to seed this corner of the universe with higher Light beings was thwarted. In the Creativa section, I will be sharing my story as it relates to this theme of the Divine Spark and how this writing project dovetails with the movement of the Sophianic Spark within me, thus encouraging the reader to find their own unique footsteps on this journey as well.

In Part V, I will bring all these themes to a culmination in the last section, Via Transformativa, by looking specifically at our limitations of spiritual consciousness and what we can do to step into a higher level of being. In a more poetic verse, I will look at how this has significance for us personally and for humanity as a whole.

This book can be used as a resource guide for navigating the maze of ancient scripture. However, I am hoping that it can also be a spark in itself that urges you the reader to stay in touch with your personal story, where you might find the glint of the most precious pearl of the divine within you.

PART II

THE CREATION STORY OF SOPHIA

8

Source Creation and the Great Emanation

Act I of the Creation Story of Sophia – *Via Positiva*

Welcome to the first Act of our Mystery Play on the creation story of Sophia.

I have gathered the raw elements of this story from the early Gnostic texts, as well as from the Jewish mystical tradition known as Kabbalah. The Kabbalah has a long and varied history. An acclaimed scholar and student of the Jewish mystical traditions, Gershom Scholem (1978) identified the earliest of the Kabbalist texts, from the 1st century CE, called the Bahir, which likely spawned a vast array of texts that flourished in the 12th and 13th centuries in France and Spain. The Kabbalah could be considered a close Jewish relative of Gnosticism, and there are numerous overlaps in their creation cosmologies. From my research, it appears that the Kabbalah was inspired by the earlier Gnostic tradition, which then developed into its own unique system through influences of medieval Jewish mysticism. The Kabbalah offers a valuable point of reference in helping to chart this creation story that I have drawn mainly from the Gnostic texts.

Keep in mind that this creation drama can be traced back, as I will explore, to the 1st century and is written with far more elaborate detail than the arguably later Gospel of John, with its one-paragraph description of origins, "In the beginning was the Word, and the Word was with God, and the Word was God" (John 1:1).

There are many variations to the themes and players who appear in this Sophianic creation story. However, there is a fairly consistent and coherent narrative that I have found described in these texts, and I will be painting this story with broad brush strokes to help avoid having to get caught up in the textual variations.

Regarding the problem of gender, the cultural context of the times when these scriptures were written was largely patriarchal, and I believe this factored into identifying the Godhead here described below as Ineffable-Ein Soph as "he" and "father." However, there are also references to "him" being androgynous, and so, to help pull back from the long-standing bias toward a Father God, I will be adjusting the pronouns accordingly.

A Synopsis of Act I of the Creation Story

There was once a lone being who knew of nothing beyond itself. Finally, it withdrew its mind deep into itself. There followed a massive emanation of unimaginable Holy Light. This was a threefold emanation: A Holy Spirit Mother (Higher Sophia), a steadfast masculine face of God, and a third, the offspring, a Divine Form. From there, male-female paired emanations called aeons exploded to fill a new heavenly realm called the Pleroma. The female of the last of these emanations is the main heroine of this story, the younger Sophia.

Now, onto our Mystery Play.

The curtain opens!

The Creation Story of Sophia

Act I: *via Positiva*

The Ineffable-Ein Soph

Imagine, if you can, that in the very beginning, the whole Universe was totally contained in one lone Being. In the beginning, or specifically, before the beginning, there was a singularity who was completely alone. The origins of this sole Being are entirely unknown. Nothing in the Universe knows where it came from.

This being is often referred to as the Ineffable. "S/he is unbegotten" (TP). "Having no birth." "S/he-Who-Is is ineffable" (Eug), a complete mystery.

In the Kabbalah, this singularity is called Ein Soph (without limit), "outside of which there is nothing."[1]

"S/he is the Father-Mother of everything…above corruption, which is pure light into which no eye can look" (AJ-D).

Imagine that this single "monad" (AJ) was the only thing in the Universe, only there was no universe! Nothing was separate from this one, totally inclusive Being. This one Being was all that existed, and it had a unique consciousness, a personality with thoughts and feelings.

"Nothing is above it. Nothing rules it. Since everything exists within it. It does not exist within anything. Since it is not dependent on anything. It is eternal" (AJ).

This is our origin, this is us, this is "The All." When I pray, I invoke this Being. It still exists, though it is no longer completely alone.

Inside the Ineffable-Ein Soph

Some extremely rare scriptures attempt to describe what existed inside of the Ineffable Being prior to the Great Emanation. From the Kabbalah, made available by Scholem. "…Above all the emanated powers, there exist in 'the root of all roots', three hidden lights which have no beginning, 'for they are the name and essence of the root of all roots and are beyond the grasp of thought,"[2] "its immanence in the depths of its own being."[3] These were the seeds that were to become the threefold nature of the Great Emanation, equating with the Christian concept of the Trinity. Ein Soph is a passive, inner mystery that then manifests into creative expression.

Below is what I believe to be an illustration of what the Kabbalah is referring to as the three hidden lights within Ein Soph prior to the emanation. This is from a book called *The Book of the Great Logos According to the Mystery*, or the *Book of IEOU* (IE), one of the most obscure of the early Gnostic texts, likely not meant for the uninitiated. It includes multiple schematic illustrations and descriptions of the esoteric teachings and rituals of the "living Jesus," including this one.

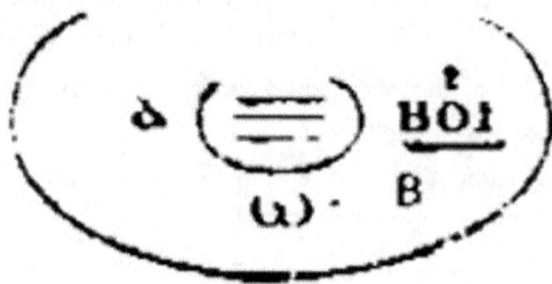

The three lines in the center are "the voices" that will "sing praises" upon being emanated (IE).

This Being, with its threefold interior "voices" that will "sing praises", is like a massive furnace of energy and Light called the Ein Soph Or, the Unlimited Light.

Tzimtzum (Contraction)

There is a highly unusual detail in the original creation cosmology of the Kabbalah and the Gnostic system. At the very beginning, the mind of this lone Being, its self-awareness, actually pulled back deeper into itself. This is called, from the Kabbalah, the *Tzimtzum*, meaning contraction. There was some inner process by which the consciousness of Ein Soph went deep into itself, which then allowed it to emanate. This corresponds with the two opposing movements in childbirth: contraction and pushing outward. The blue dot in the center of the source Light featured on this book's front cover is an illustration of this contracted aspect of the Ineffable. In the *Book of the Great Logos* (IE), it is written, "God who withdrew Himself into Himself."[4]

Isaac Luria was a prominent 16th-century Kabbalah mystic teacher who brought to prominence this idea of God's original contraction into himself. According to Luria, God sought to make room for the world by abandoning a region within "Himself". Deep within was a kind of mystical primordial space into which He withdrew. From there, the subsequent explosion of creation was initiated. The first act of Ein Soph is therefore not a step outside but a step inside, recoiling, falling, or withdrawing into itself. At the earliest beginnings, "instead of emanation we have the opposite, contraction."[5]

In the Islamic tradition, there is a saying (*hadith*): "I was a treasure that longed to be known, and so I created the world."[6] This suggests that some emotional longing accompanied this contraction from within this Singularity, which then led to an explosion of Great Light.

The Great Emanation with a Three-Fold Nature: Female Thought, Masculine Face, Anthropos (the Son)

Found within these Gnostic texts are elaborate descriptions of what were called the "three powers." "Three powers came forth from him; they are the Father, the Mother, (and) the Son, from the living silence, what came forth from the incorruptible Father. These came forth from the silence of the unknown Father" (GE).

The Gnostic Christ referred to this as "The Great Power" (CGP) and also the "First Mystery" (PS).

The following is a closer look at each of these three powers.

1. Divine Mother Thought (Pronnoia), Higher Sophia, Holy Spirit

As this Great Emanation took place, there burst forth a Holy Light that filled the Universe. Or, more precisely, it was the Universe. Though there are three aspects of this original emanation, this feminine aspect is spoken about at length in the Gnostic texts, where hymns of praise are sung to her. If the Ineffable was "Mind," then this feminine expression was known as "Thought," called in Greek, *Pronnoia*.

The female Thought equates to the higher aspect of a twofold Sophia and also to the concept of the Holy Spirit. She spreads her beauty throughout the vast regions as a Great Emanation. In the Kabbalah, this equates with the outpouring of Ein Soph, called Sephirot.[7]

The Ineffable's "thought" performed "a deed and she came forth" (AJ).

"And Its thinking became a thing. She appeared. She stood in Its presence in the brilliance of the light; she is the power which is before the All" (AJ).

"The invisible Spirit (Ineffable-Ein Soph) rejoiced over the light which had come into being, the one who was the first to appear from the primal power, which is Its Pronnoia" (AJ).

"She is the spring of the living water" (AJ).

"I am first thought, the thought that is in light. I am the movement that is in all, she in whom the realm of all takes its stand, the firstborn among those who came into being, she who exists before all" (TP).

"She is called by three names, although she exists alone since she is perfect. I am invisible within the thought of the invisible one. I am revealed in the immeasurable, ineffable things. I am intangible, dwelling in the intangible. I move in every creature" (TP).

She moves within us. May She be remembered.

2.   The Masculine Face of this Ineffable. Called Father, Ancient of Days

This Ineffable-Ein Soph emerged as both the feminine Light of this Holy Spirit and a masculine face or "forehead." This is a highly ambiguous part of the story but correlates to the Kabbalah's idea of the Ancient of Days, who came from what was referred to as the "Ancient of Ancients" (i.e., Ein Soph, the Ineffable).

This masculine aspect of the original creation exhibits a quality of distance, of being solely in the location of the original creation, as opposed to the feminine "Thought," who emanates throughout the All. There is a reference to an interaction between these original masculine and feminine beings that is extraordinary. "Nor was He called Father before [Mother-Thought] called Him Father" (GR). This gives us a clue as to what was unfolding as the Female Divine Light Mother looked at this masculine aspect that emerged and saw him, giving him a name: Father. This profound first creation might just be the Universe's first experience of love. It is at this point that the Ineffable-Ein Soph comes out of its loneliness and is finally met with the eyes of care and tenderness.

Christ calls this masculine being "Father," although, in certain texts, he seems to be calling the Ineffable "Father" as well (or "Fore-Father as in Eug). He is also referred to as "Mind" (*nous* in Greek). We are dealing with such vast unfathomable sweeps of creation, and this reference to "Father" can have different identifications in the various versions and interpretations found in the Gnostic texts.

The name Barbelo appears often in the Sethian texts such as the *Apocryphon of John* and, I believe, is referring to both the primary female and male aspects of this Great Emanation.

3. Anthropos, Adam Kadmon, Christ: The Archetypal Divine Template

From this Holy Light Mother and Steadfast Father came a third, their offspring. This is referred to as a son (though there is also a female/daughter aspect called Pistis Sophia, as we will explore below).

Jesus says in the *First Book of IEOU*, "I radiated forth in this small idea as one originating from my Father. I bubbled up and I flowed forth from it. I radiated forth from it. It emanated me forth and I was the first emanation from within it. And I was its whole likeness and its image. As it emanated me forth I stood in its presence" (IE).

This third is also called Word (Gnostic, orthodox), Logos (Philo, Gnostic, orthodox), Son of Man (Gnostic, orthodox), Christ (Gnostic, orthodox), Christos (Greek), Christus (Latin), Anthropos (Gnostic), Adam Kadmon or the Primal Androgynous Man (Kabbalah), Light of Lights (PS), Nous (Greek, Gnostic), Man of Light (PS), Allogenes/Autogenes (Gnostic), and the Standing One (Simonian).

"In the beginning, he decided to have his likeness become a great power. Immediately, the principle (or beginning) of that Light appeared as Immortal Androgynous Man. His male name is 'Begotten, Perfect Mind'" (Eug). It is this concept of the Great Power that is a key clue to tracking the mystery of the Deep Christ.

"And [the Ineffable] gazed into Barbelo (male-female aspects of the Great Emanation) in the pure light which surrounds the invisible Spirit and Its luminescence, and she conceived from It. It begot a spark of light in a light resembling blessedness…" (AJ). "It is a hidden Light, bearing a fruit of life, pouring forth a living water from the invisible, unpolluted, immeasurable spring, that is, the unreproducible Voice of the glory of the Mother, the glory of the offspring of God…" (TP). These are rare and precious references to the motif of the creation of a spark of light, the quintessential energetic that Christ helps to bring to humanity. It is this spark that is the offspring of the union of the first great experience of Love, the Light that radiated a reflection of the Ineffable back to itself.

The Pleroma

Male-Female pairs of angelic beings called "aeons" emanated out into this heavenly realm like ripples from a stone dropped in water. The divine universe of original creation is called the Pleroma, translated as "Fullness," which equates with the Christian concept of heaven. The presence of these sacred aeons holds geometric anchors to the structure of this divine universe. These aeonic deities serve to uphold their position within the great temple of this heavenly realm, and it was Sophia's abandonment of her location that resulted in a great disruption within this balance, as we will explore in the next chapter.

The Younger Sophia

Just before the closing curtain of this first Act of the Mystery Play, entering from stage right comes the heroine of our story. She is the youngest feminine goddess of the 32 pairs of aeons of the heavenly realm and is filled with Light. She is known as Sophia. She could be considered the daughter of the higher Sophia, the feminine emanation of the Ineffable, the Pronnoia/Thought. In these Gnostic texts, little is written about her prior to her fall. However, there was one very striking reference about her.

"The perfect Savior said: 'Son of Man consented with Sophia, his consort, and revealed a great androgynous light. His male name is designated 'Savior, Begetter of All Things.' His female name is designated 'All-Begettress Sophia.' Some call her 'Pistis'"" (SJC).

Sophia and Christ are a pair who reside in the highest and lowest regions of the great emanation, known in the Valentinian system as Bythos (the Deep) and Ennoia, the Light of "Thought." This pair is also identified as holding a certain dimension in the geometric pattern of this heavenly realm, the Pleroma.

It is at this point in the mystery play that Sophia is about to embark on a most remarkable journey.

9

The "Fall" of Sophia

Act II of the Creation Story of Sophia

Via Negativa

Welcome to the second act of the Sophia Mystery Play. Featured are plot twists and turns that truly qualify it as via Negativa. Here, Sophia embarks on a harrowing descent. She first attempts to fly up toward the incredible Source Light (Ein Soph Or), but, unable to reach it, she turns and falls from her heavenly home to a torturous hell below. Here, we meet the very strange beings called "archons," or lower angelic beings, who steal her Light and trap her in the material world.

The classic interpretation of this Gnostic story places heavy blame on Sophia for creating a cosmic catastrophe. As I delve deeper into this mystery play, as well as the Deep Christ mystery thriller, we will see how the following version might have been a later distortion of a more original one, in which Sophia is seen not as a tragically flawed goddess due to her folly but as heroic and "innocent" of the circumstances that led to her "fall." First, let us present the classic version of the Fall of Sophia.

The curtain opens.

Sophia Goes Toward the Light

Sophia is the youngest of the "aeons," or energetic expressions of the divine source emanation. Sophia and Christ are a pair who are not only matched in the highest regions of the Great Emanation but are also identified as holding the outermost space in the geometric pattern of the heavenly Pleroma, called the 13th aeon — a dimensional arena that lies far outside the 24th aeon, the source emanation.[1]

Sophia, as a being of Light, sees a Light in the distance that is far more glorious than her own. Jesus continues his narration.

"I (Jesus) will tell you the mystery, how this befell her" (PS:29, i.e., *Pistis Sophia* chapter 29).

"It came to pass when Pistis Sophia was in the thirteenth aeon... that Pistis Sophia gazed into the height. She saw the light [of the Ineffable] and she longed to reach to that region, and she could not reach to that region. But she ceased to perform the mystery of the thirteenth æon"[2] (PS:30).

Here, Sophia, the daughter of the Holy Spirit, sees this First Mystery of the emanation and becomes overwhelmed with the desire to join with it. Sophia, being young, doesn't like to play by the rules and instead follows her passion. She becomes ecstatic when she catches a most incredible glint of Light at the center of the heavenly realm. Without thinking, without planning, without making arrangements, she leaves her post and flies toward the Light, like a moth to the flame.

As she is ascending the aeonic realms, the other divine pairs, though they are below her, outside the Pleroma, are dismayed at how she abandoned her position in the great architecture of this original divine universe. "...All the rulers in the twelve aeons, who are below, hated her, because she had ceased from their mysteries, and because she had desired to go into the height and be above them all. For this cause then they were enraged against her and hated her...." (PS:30).[3]

Sailing upwards, however, Sophia was stopped from reaching that inner sanctum of Source Creation, prevented by some unseen limit or boundary.

Sophia's "Fall"

Having been prevented from reaching her ultimate glory, the Great Palace of the First Mystery, she turned her sights to see another Light. What she did not know was that this was the false light of the "demiurge." The demiurge is a Platonic word used in the Gnostic tradition to refer to the king of the archons. Thinking that it was the Light of the central source, she was drawn to it, thereby tumbling down out of the Pleroma into the realms of chaos.

Sophia recalls, "I gazed ... into the lower parts and saw there a light, thinking: I will go to that region, in order that I may take that light. And I went and found myself in the darkness which is in the chaos below..." (PS:32).

Yaldabaoth and the Archons

"And when she saw (the consequences of) her desire, it changed into a form of a lion-faced serpent. And its eyes were like lightning fires which flash. She cast it away from her, outside that place, that no one of the immortal ones might see it, for she had created it in ignorance ... And she called his name Yaldabaoth" (AJ).

There are different versions of this part of the story, and it is unclear if Sophia "created" the archons or if they were already there during her fall and then turned to persecute her.

In the *Pistis Sophia*, Jesus continues, "...She went forth from her own region, the thirteenth aeon, and went down to the twelve aeons [outside of the Pleroma]. The rulers of the aeons pursued her and were enraged against her because she was drawn towards grandeur. And she went forth also from the twelve aeons, and came into the regions of the chaos and drew nigh to that lion-faced light-power to devour it. But all the material emanations of Self-willed [Yaldabaoth] surrounded her, and the great lion-faced light-power devoured all the light-powers in Sophia and cleaned out her light and devoured it, and her matter was thrust into the chaos; it became a lion-faced ruler in the chaos, of which one half is fire and the other darkness, that is Yaldabaoth, of whom I have spoken unto you many times" (PS:31).

This is an extraordinary paragraph. Jesus is not only explaining how Sophia became essentially kidnapped by these strange beings called archons, but he also indicates that he has spoken extensively with the disciples about this lead archon he calls Yaldabaoth. One wonders if there are yet to be recovered lost texts of these teachings. Here, Christ describes how he traversed the highest regions of creation, where he was able to see outside the lower realms of chaos.

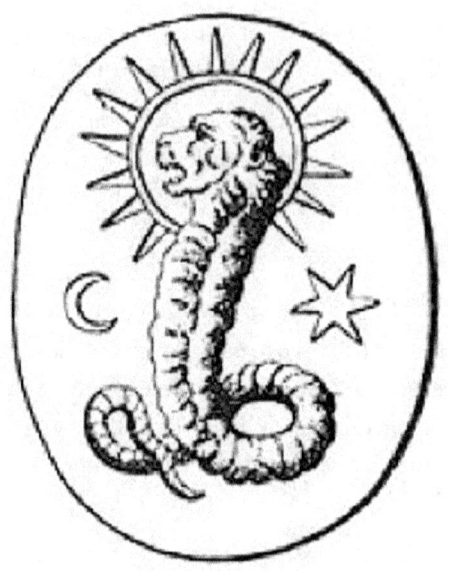

17th-century image of the demiurge, Yaldabaoth.

"Yaldabaoth is the chief ruler. He took great Power from [Sophia], left her, and moved away from his birthplace. He assumed command, created realms for himself, with a brilliant flame that continues to exist even now" (AJ-D).

Stealing her Light

"When then this befell, Sophia became very greatly exhausted, and that lion-faced light-power set to work to take away from Sophia all her light-powers" (PS:31).

"She fell down into a body and came to this life, then she fell into the hands of many robbers" (ES).[4]

Sophia was tortured, tormented, ridiculed, and forced to barely survive on parched soil and bare rocks, lost in the desert of hardened light called matter. The archons showed no mercy. And Sophia wept.

"And when I looked unto the height, I saw all the rulers of the æons, how in their numbers they looked down on me and rejoiced over me, though I had done them no ill; but they hated me without a cause. And when the emanations of Self-willed [Yaldabaoth the demiurge] saw the rulers of the æons rejoicing over me, they knew that the rulers of the æons would not come to my aid; and those emanations which sore pressed me with violence took courage, and the light which I had not taken from them, they have taken from me" (PS:32).

Becoming lost in the far depths of chaos, Sophia mourns over having lost her home and her family. "And because of the delusion of my light, I have become a stranger to my brothers (fellow aeons), the invisible ones, and also to the great emanations of the Barbelo" (PS:32).

Meanwhile, Yaldabaoth increased his power and, with no connection to the divine source, undergoes the process of being a creator God within the material world, presenting himself as the One God.

The Gnostic Christ reports: "And having created [...] everything, he [Yaldabaoth] organized according to the model of the first aeons which had come into being, so that he might create them like the indestructible ones. Not because he had seen the indestructible ones, but the power in him, which he had taken from his mother, produced in him the likeness of the cosmos. And when he saw the creation which surrounds him and the multitude of the angels around him which had come forth from him, he said to them, 'I am a jealous God, and there is no other God beside me,'" (AJ).

We are now deep into the Mystery Play as this tragic Act of the creation story of Sophia comes to a close.

10

Reflections on Sophia and the Archons

Part II of the Creation Story of Sophia (continued)

Stepping back from the plotline of this Mystery Play, it is helpful to look more closely at this strange tale. Carl Jung once wrote a most intriguing reflection on Sophia and the archons: "I have much more sympathy with Sophia than with the demiurge but faced with the reality of both my sympathy counts for nothing."[1] This is a striking quote from a man who was profoundly aware of the treasures that had remained untapped in the largely lost Gnostic tradition. Here, Jung is acknowledging that the phenomenon of Sophia and the king archon, the demiurge, constitute not a fairy tale but an objective reality.

John Lamb Lash (2006), who wrote one of the few contemporary books that delve into this whole Sophia story, prefers to use the word "mythos" to describe something that is not just seen as mere fiction.[2] He clarifies that this is a story that attempts to describe actual events that are unfolding even in the present time and are not just storybook myths.

Like Jung, St. Paul seems to say quite explicitly that both Sophia and the archons are a reality. "But we speak the wisdom of God in a mystery, the hidden wisdom which God ordained before the ages for our glory which none of the princes of this world knew...." (1 Corinthians 2:7-8). This writing, likely from Paul's own hand and not a later redaction, offers a rare window into a cosmology that he seems to have been quite familiar with.

If this Sophianic myth is in fact history with real otherworldly characters, then it should elicit far more attention from our culture than it has thus far received. With that in mind and to further investigate these mysteries, let's first look more into the key player in this drama, Sophia.

The Descent of Sophia

From her position in the heavens, Sophia fell into lower dimensionality, and trapped by these lower gods, lost her Light. She tumbled into the spiritually rough density of matter. This idea of Light or spirit being bound within matter, as exemplified by Sophia, is an archetypal motif found in many spiritual traditions.

According to this Gnostic rendition, one wonders, is Sophia merely an archetypal figure, a troubled superwoman of mythical status? Or is she a real deity, a true-to-life conscious being? I prefer to think of her as being both. Much like Christ, she is both archetypal and real.

Sophia is a mythological motif that represents our true inner nature buried deep within us. She is the quintessential expression of the soul's dive into the hardship of life and is referred to as the soul of the world, Jung's *anima mundi*. She is also, according to Jung, a "reality."

As in many fairy tales, Sophia is the girl who has dreams but is instead cast out or kept in the basement, a Cinderella of the stars. Sophia is quintessential youth, joy, the desire for truth, and unrestrained passion. But as the archetype of initiation will have it, naïve youthhood must be tempered in the trials of the soul's journey. Filled with charm and charisma, Sophia sails toward the sun, but if left to continue her flight, at some point, her creative spark could gradually turn into pompous grandiosity — something that happens to many who have ignored the humbling lessons of the soul's passage. And yet, as Christ describes, more than mere archetype, she is an actual deity, who descended from the higher regions into our earthly realm.

Within the Gnostic creation story, Sophia is depicted as a double figure. She is a high and original divine feminine figure of creation called *Pronnoia*, the Thought emanation from Divine Mind. And she is also, like a daughter, a complex figure who runs away from her position in the heavens to become trapped in the lower dimensions of the material world. Lash posits quite literally that Gaia, the earth, is Sophia bound in matter. Though I have not come to this conclusion, this thesis is intriguing to consider.

There are so many cross-references within the texts that give credence to this theme of the Descent of Sophia. They constitute a core of the earliest traditions of Gnosticism and, I believe, likely sprang from a 1st century New Revelation prior to the rise of Gnosticism. Though some scholars argue that it gradually emerged over the course of a couple of centuries, and indeed there are many influences from prior to the 1st century that factor into this mythos, still, I have not found specific antecedents to this uniquely complex Sophianic myth prior to this time. In the following centuries, many variations were then written, extending from the 1st century origins until her story gradually disappeared behind the brighter lights of the definitive orthodox Christian version.

Some of the Gnostic texts specifically blame Sophia for a profound cosmic mishap that resulted in her fall. The *Apocryphon of John* describes Sophia as specifically being responsible for the creation of the archons. This is hard to swallow in this modern era, when it is typically the woman who is blamed — a trend that goes as far back as the Bible's first woman, Eve. To denounce this goddess Sophia as the source of humanity's failings is not easy to hear. However, if we take a closer look, we may not want to be so quick to blame Sophia.

Sophia Came to "Build Bodily Dwellings"

Some Sethian Gnostic texts equate Jesus with this man known as Seth (the Son of Adam), the lesser-known offspring of Adam and Eve. In a most remarkable Gnostic text, the *Second Treatise of the Great Seth* (ST), Jesus Christ is credited with being the narrator. This text, I believe, is possibly one of the closest to the original expressions of this 1st century Deep Christ and his Revelation of Wisdom, as I will explore further in the next chapter.

Christ speaks: "For those who were in the world had been prepared by the will of our sister Sophia...because of the innocence which has not been uttered. And she did not ask anything from the All, nor from the greatness of the Assembly, nor from the Pleroma. Since she was first, she came forth to prepare monads and places for the Son of Light and the fellow workers which she took from the elements below to build bodily dwellings from them. But, having come into being in an empty glory, they ended in destruction in the dwellings in which they were, since they were prepared by Sophia" (ST).

This represents a far different context to the idea of Sophia's fall than what is more commonly known. The Gnostic Jesus is saying that she went ahead to "prepare monads and places for the Son of Light" as a sort of logistics event scout for a project that involved far more than some misguided adventures. This does not sound like an accident nor a result of folly. "She took materials from the elements below to build bodily dwellings from them." This indicates that Sophia came to this world intentionally to work with the denser elements of matter as part of a broader plan to seed the divine-human template, the Anthropos/Primal Man, here on Earth — a plan that "ended in destruction." This is extraordinary and offers a revision of what is most commonly found in the Gnostic texts that effectively blame Sophia for her grandiosity, where she acted without her consort and, as a result, created the whole mess of the archons.

Perhaps it is an example of how a story can change over time, much like the game of "telephone." Instead of Sophia coming with a distinct and noble purpose, the story devolved, even within the span of the short-lived Gnostic tradition, into her being the one who left home without her husband and then got into a heap of trouble. Putting blame on her is understandable in light of the deeply entrenched patriarchal culture that was so prominent in that era.

Regardless of whether her problems were the result of hubris or a failed mission, what is most consistent in the texts is that, upon her descent, she became trapped by these lower "gods." Setting aside the issue of blame, it is at least apparent that the plight of Sophia's enslavement is a central plotline of the whole Sophia and Christ drama described in these Gnostic texts.

As will hopefully become clearer, this is a story of profound importance to an ultimate understanding of who we are and what our place might be in the whole mystery of creation.

The Problem of the Archons

"For we are not contending against flesh and blood, but against the principalities, against the powers, against the world rulers of this present darkness, against the spiritual hosts of wickedness in the heavenly places," (Ephesians 6:12).

St. Paul is an odd player in the mystery thriller of the Deep Christ. Was he really a Gnostic-leaning purveyor of Christ's esoteric teachings as claimed by Valentinus and, as I will explore later, Marcion? Did St. Paul actually believe in the reality of the archons, the "spiritual hosts of wickedness in heavenly places"? Here in his letter to the Ephesians, Paul seems to be making a rare but distinct reference that these sinister, otherworldly rulers are real.

The word archon, from the Greek word "arche," meaning beginning or original, was used in ancient Greece in reference to a person's position as a ruler or political leader. In the first few centuries CE, however, the term archon took on a whole different meaning within the Gnostic system. Here, the word referred to leaders or heads of the lower heavens (aeons), sometimes seen in relation to the seven inner planets of our solar system. A key feature of their rule could be described as having exploitative abuses of power and, as I will explore in Chapter 20, we humans are mere pawns in their game.

So, what are the Archons?

All indications from these ancient sources suggest, as Jung affirmed, that they are, in fact, real. One text in the Nag Hammadi Library, *The Hypostasis* [or fundamental reality] *of the Archons* (HA) states this quite explicitly.

In the *Pistis Sophia* and the early Gnostic Sethian *Secret Book (Apochryphon) of John*, Jesus (allegedly) talks specifically about the archons, including the lead archon, "Yaldabaoth, of whom I have spoken unto you many times" (PS:31). He is not talking in general about some ancient mythological god who displayed fantastical attributes. Rather, he is talking about a real creature with specific features, as seen apparently from his own first-hand encounters with him. This is a "lion-faced Light-power" ... "one half is fire and the other darkness" (PS:31), whose "eyes were like lightning fires which flash" (AJ).

Also, it is extraordinary that the lead archon, Yaldabaoth, is quoted as saying, "I am a jealous God, and there is no other God beside me." This has a strong resemblance to the Hebrew God Yahweh, who dictates a Second Commandment, "Thou shalt have no other gods before me" (Exodus 20:3), and, "I, the Lord your God, am a jealous God…" (Exodus 20:5). Linking this Hebrew God with the demiurge as found within this Gnostic tradition is one of the most scandalous and controversial twists in this mystery.

How can we even begin to understand the strange phenomena of Yaldabaoth and the archons?

Making Sense of the Archons

One of the primary reasons, I believe, most people have never heard of the Gnostic Sophia is because of how hard it is to grasp the enigma of the archons. Within the whole Sophianic cosmology of the Gnostic system, it is almost impossible to separate Sophia from the archons. Hence, in the Christianizing of this earlier material, rather than deal with the thorny idea of the archons, with its implication that "Our Father" might be the demiurge, I suspect that the Church fathers found it easier to simply dispense with the entire cosmology of Sophia and the archons.

As we shall see, the core themes of this creation story, including Sophia, Jesus's descent, the Divine Spark, Eve as a Sophianic intervention, and Seth as offspring of Adam and Eve, all revolve around what could be called the "problem of the archons." Some people believe that the meta-view of humanity's ancient history of struggles, as suggested by Jesus in the Gnostic scriptures, is the result of the archon's indomitable rule over humanity, which might best be described as an illusional "matrix." If this is true, then this would not only be a big deal, but it would be *the* big deal in the overall picture of humanity's evolutionary development.

Alien Archons?

John Lamb Lash (2006) suggests, as do others, that the archons, as described in the texts, are reptilian-like alien creatures. This, of course, opens a Pandora's box of controversy.

If archons exist, whatever they are, then they clearly reside outside the normal spectrum of human observation and awareness. Are they physical, non-terrestrial, or etheric? Are they mythological creatures of old, or are they in existence today? Who or what are they, and where do they reside? Given the "reality" of the archons, we might find some footing in an investigation into these beings by looking at a difficult and highly controversial topic; namely, extraterrestrials.

There is a general reluctance within society at large to view the study of alien life as a legitimate field beyond just science fiction. To consider otherwise risks destabilizing some long-standing belief systems in our culture. Hence, the whole question of non-terrestrial life forms is therefore relegated to the fringes and discredited as "conspiracy theory." For those who choose to step into this untamed jungle of the enigma of extraterrestrial life, it is easy to become overwhelmed. Furthermore, in order to responsibly navigate this subject, one has to avoid being pulled into speculation fueled by paranoia or grandiosity, which takes well-developed critical thinking skills, psychological maturity, and an open mind.[3]

The whole subject of extraterrestrial aliens has been pushed to the fringes of modern culture ever since the "weather balloons" crashed in Roswell in 1947. Fortunately, there have been recent developments that allow for a more open national conversation about this.[4] Some say that the decision was for the US government to have a policy of denial against acknowledging the possibility of extraterrestrial life and that this policy has been adhered to into the present. When Carl Jung (1979) wrote *Flying Saucers: A Modern Myth of Things Seen in the Sky*, he fathomed them as an archetypal image, such as one might encounter in a dream. He didn't necessarily write them off as fiction, however, noting that eyewitness accounts from highly trained Air Force pilots were hard to ignore.

For anyone brave or foolish enough to step into the enigma of the archons, there are plenty of recent discussions to be found, indicating that this topic is gaining traction in the culture. This might be for better or worse, as the whole phenomenon of fringe investigations can be a problem in itself. Ranging from reasonable inquiries to outlandish speculation, the risk of looking into the archons is that myopic views, untethered from clear discernment, can be accompanied by, in Jungian terms, unprocessed shadow projections.

In the last decade, social media and what I call "alt-media" or a sort of break-away journalism arena, spurred on by the limits of a corporate-influenced "mainstream" media, is causing a significant impact on the balance of norms in both news and human relations, in what is being termed a "post-truth world" (Patten, 2018). Indeed, the issue of archons opens the door to a shadowy world that is so offensive and outrageous that it is more often discussed (and, I believe, misunderstood) in the jungle of conspiracy speculation. At the same time, it is unfortunately completely ignored by the vast majority of people who are unwilling to even consider this "fundamental reality."

Because the predominant consensus culture is unwilling or unable to consider the idea that humanity is being subjected to some extra-physical overlords, the whole topic gets tossed out into the untamed fringes of our social consensus, where basic critical thinking skills can be greatly limited. The solution to this is not to overlook this phenomenon of the archons or simply dismiss it altogether. Rather, this whole topic requires well-developed psychological maturity to be delved into responsibly.

It might be that this rampant alt-media subculture is a byproduct of some growing pains of our collective consciousness, where we are taking early rickety steps away from a more limited worldview that has held the scope of our awareness in too constricted a manner. Though I believe, for example, that the alt-media phenomenon is part of an effort to escape the grip of the carefully managed corporate or "legacy" press (Higdon and Huff, 2022), still, this breakaway subculture is fertile ground for all sorts of regressive and prejudiced social movements to grow. So, how do we navigate this archon phenomenon without losing our sane human bearings?

There is, however, a way to engage in this most difficult topic without getting caught up in the endless speculations around who, what, and where these strange beings are. The following is a recommended approach to finding some stable and reasonable ground in dealing with this subject, somewhere between the dystopian "reality" of the archons and the instinct to just ignore them altogether.

The Pre-Verbal Trauma Model of Grappling with the Problem of the Archons

In the first two years of a child's development, few memories are retained. When a young child has an intense experience, such as some form of emotional or physical trauma, it is rare for that event to be retained in their conscious memory as they get older.[5] There may be somatic symptoms or subconscious hints that point to that trauma. Overall, however, the memories of the overwhelming experiences are not available to their conscious mind, partly due to the lack of language at that stage of development. The only clue that there was even some grave injury is how the trauma might impact the older person in the present, such as when there are irrational fear responses, phobias, or psychosomatic symptoms. Here, the pre-verbal trauma can be identified according to the present-time effects of that initial trauma.[6]

In the same way, we might see archons as lying outside the normal range of conscious human awareness. If they are real, then we have little historical memory, context, or conscious framework for understanding them. Much like the impact of early childhood trauma, all we can do is see the effects they are having on us and respond to these accordingly.

There is much we can do by bringing more focus to the *effects* of the archons, whether or not we are willing to consider that they are real. To understand the full impact of the lower gods, we need to look into the last phase of the Sophia Mystery Play, the creation of Adam and Eve, presented in Chapter 18. Chapter 20 will also review insights from the Deep Christ about how we humans are affected by the archons.

Archons in This World?

Does there exist a meta-level of manipulation and control of humanity by some otherworldly overlords who acted to thwart our earliest inception with the capture of the Light of Sophia? Are there intersections between key players in positions of world power where, in this 21st century, manipulation and blackmail are steering the actions of power elites that exploit humanity for the archon's own selfish needs? Have we been subjected to subtle manipulations that keep us more in an "enslavement" paradigm that blocks innate abilities to connect with higher dimensional support? If all of this is the case, then might the very process of claiming both higher consciousness and new levels of love and wisdom constitute radical acts of rebellion and liberation? These are all highly significant questions to consider and are central to these mysteries.

The Gnostic Jesus gave some good advice to his followers, as recorded in the *Letter of Peter to Philip*.

"'Lord, tell us: In what way shall we fight against the archons since the archons are above us?' Then a voice called out to them from the (Savior) saying, 'Now you will fight against them in this way, for the archons are fighting against the inner man. And you are to fight against them in this way: Come together and teach in the world the salvation with a promise. And you, gird yourselves with the power of my Father and let your prayer be known. And he, the Father, will help you as he has helped you by sending me'" (LPP).[7]

It is significant that Christ is saying that the archons are fighting against "the inner man" or, perhaps, that part of us associated with our Divine Spark. Christ is saying something which only recently is beginning to become more understood: that these nefarious overlords are specifically targeting our latent potential and that this inner spark is their great enemy. It is extraordinary that, even 2000 years later, this idea is now only beginning to get traction. This is understandable, however, given the high level of sophistication in how the archons affect us which is almost completely invisible to the vast majority of humanity.

His reference to "Teach in the world the salvation," I believe, refers to processes of support and intervention from the highest levels of creation that are available to us as we tune our consciousness to those subtle realms. The idea of a "promise" seems to indicate that the Gnostic Christ was saying, "Hang in there, there will eventually be an end to this."

One of the central theological concepts of the Pauline Christian system was that of "faith" (pistis in Greek). Carl Jung clarifies that St. Paul was not advocating a mere blind faith in some belief. Rather, whatever inclinations, intuitions, or direct numinous experiences we might have, for example, it is our trust or faith in the legitimacy of these experiences that lead us through uncertainty.[8] The challenge is for us to keep our faith in the knowing of our inner gnosis through times of doubt. Given how ominous this problem of the archons might be, perhaps we can trust that there is a means by which we can overcome them.

Now, onto the next highly dramatic Act of the Mystery Play.

11

The Rescue of Sophia

Act III of the Creation Story of Sophia

Via Creativa

Any challenge we face confronts us with a choice. Do we step toward the unknown, no matter how daunting it may seem, or do we decide to retreat from it? The via Creativa, the path of the creative, is what is necessary when faced with an initiatory ordeal. To fall back or collapse in the face of it is to regress where growth is not achieved. The creative process, in general, is the expressive and energetic movement, the mustering of one's inner strength and inner truth that pushes against the undertow of suffering. In my earlier years, I did not take full responsibility for my life's direction until I realized that holding onto the idea of myself as a "victim" was keeping me small and disempowered.

Blues music is a wonderful example of the power of creative expression, where, in the face of suffering, the emotional movement that accompanies soulful songs and rhythms helps us move through the pain. The mere acknowledgment and expression of that pain can often in itself become the creative solution out of that pain.

In the last section of this story in Chapter 10, via Negativa, Sophia had fallen into this material world where her Light was stripped from her by her tormentor, Yaldabaoth. In this next Act of our Mystery Play, she is faced with the grueling condition of her captivity. She could collapse and give up, surrendering to a fate of being forever beaten down. Or she could turn, sing her blues song, and refuse to give up. Indeed, it is Sophia's songs that Christ presents in the *Pistis Sophia*, paralleling the Biblical Psalms, that constitute some of the most powerful expressions in sacred literature of spiritual longing.

The Curtain Opens

In the *Pistis Sophia* (PS), there are extensive passages where Jesus describes to his disciples how Sophia is going through what could be seen as *metanoia*, a deep change. This is a great turning, where she is both acknowledging her shortcomings and coming to terms with how her abuse is a great injustice.

Knowing that her tormentors are far more powerful than she is without her Light, Sophia sings a number of songs where she grapples with her condition of persecution and suffering. Specifically, she is calling out for her "Light of Lights" (PS) the Christ, her consort. "This is the song of praise which Pistis Sophia uttered..." says the Gnostic Jesus.

"Save me out of the matter of this darkness, that I may not be submerged therein, that I may be saved from the emanations of god Self-willed [Yaldabaoth] which press me sore, and from their evil doings. Let not this darkness submerge me, and let not this lion-faced power entirely devour the whole of my power, and let not this chaos shroud my power. Hear me, O Light [Christ], for thy grace is precious, and look down upon me according to the great mercy of thy Light" (PS:32).

Mary Magdalene, who addresses Jesus far more than the other disciples in the *Pistis Sophia*, says, "My Lord, my indweller of light hath ears, and I hear with my light-power..." whereupon she recalls the Biblical Psalm of David that equates to Sophia's lament.

"Save me, O God, for the waters are come in even unto my soul. I sank, or am submerged, in the slime of the abyss, and power was not. I have gone down into the depths of the sea; a tempest hath submerged me. I have kept on crying; my throat is gone, my eyes faded, waiting patiently for God. They who hate me without a cause are more than the hairs of my head; mighty are my foes, who violently pursued me" (PS:33).[1]

This Sophianic cry is also found in the Song of Songs, where the Shulamite longs for her beloved.

"I sought him, but I did not find him. I called him, but he did not answer me. The watchmen that were going about in the city found me. They struck me, they wounded me. The watchmen of the walls lifted my wide wrap off me." [2]

The *Pistis Sophia* text presents twelve song cycles as Sophia moves through various stages of her repentance, where she reckons with her grief, torment, shame, and rage in the aftermath of this tragic fall. In this way, Sophia is modeling what is called "shadow work," where emotional expressions of the soul's journey into darkness are like the alchemical process of distilling away all that is impure within one's personal being.

In the words of Jesus in the *Secret Book of John*,

"And when the mother [Sophia] recognized that the garment of darkness was imperfect, then she knew that her consort had not agreed with her. She repented with much weeping. And the whole pleroma heard the prayer of her repentance, and they praised on her behalf the invisible, virginal Spirit [Higher Sophia, Pronnoia]" (AJ).

Eventually, after what must have felt like an eternity, after some attempts by the Christ to rescue her, which resulted in even harsher persecution from the lion-faced Yaldabaoth, the fallen Sophia sang her thirteenth repentance.

"Hearken unto me singing praises unto thee, O Light of lights. Hearken unto me uttering the repentance for the thirteenth aeon, the region out of which I have come down..." (PS:57).

So filled with anguish was her call, so fully did she acknowledge the darkness of her embodiment, so far-reaching was her cry, that her call was finally heard.

The Descent of Jesus

In the Sethian Gnostic texts, there is a specific and astounding theme of "descent." This Gnostic Christ describes himself as a high angelic being who, in order to rescue Sophia, descends through the gates of the aeons which are under the control of the archons.

"For as I came downward, no one saw me. For I was altering my shapes, changing from form to form. And so when I was at their gates I assumed their likeness. For I passed them by quietly, and I was viewing the places, and I was neither afraid nor ashamed, for I was undefiled. And I was speaking with them, mingling with them through those who are mine, and trampling on those who are harsh to them with zeal, and quenching the flame. And I was doing all these things because of my desire to accomplish what I desired by the will of the father above" (ST).

Here, Jesus is describing how he descended through the lower regions below the Pleroma and, in order to get past their guards, the archons, disguised himself as one of them. Invoking the theme of the prince's descent in search of the one Pearl, Jesus is referring to his desire to rescue Sophia.

The following is from my first "bardic" presentation of the Gnostic creation story of Sophia in 1998.

"It was the Christ who came to her in the form of Jesus, to meet her on the material plane. She saw him and at first, she was ashamed and she put a veil over her face to hide. But then, when she saw his warmth and the love that he had for her, she ran to him and they embraced. And she looked into his eyes and she knew that he was there to help her. She cried again because of the pain that she had carried for so long and for his help in easing the suffering of her affliction. She was moved. Her emotions moved to where she was no longer bound or weighted by them because this lover of hers had penetrated through her terror and shame" (Morse, 1998).

The Crowning of Sophia

What follows is a very specific action taken by Christ and his helpers in the rescue of Sophia. A crown of Light was placed upon her, which then rendered her immune from the tyranny of the archons. "It came to pass then when Pistis Sophia had finished saying these words in the chaos, that I made the light-power, which I had sent to save her, become a light-wreath on her head, so that from now on the emanations of Self-willed could not have dominion over her. And when it had become a light-wreath round her head, all the evil matters in her were shaken and all were purified in her. They perished and remained in the chaos, while the emanations of Self-willed gazed upon them and rejoiced. And the purification of the pure light which was in Pistis Sophia gave power to the light of my light-power, which had become a wreath round her head" (PS:59).

In this most astounding process, all that had become defiled within Sophia due to the torment of the archons was purified out of her. With Christ's placing on her the crown of Light, her own original divine essence that had been taken from her was restored. This is important to keep in mind when, in Chapter 21 on the Bridal Chamber, we look at how we ourselves can also pursue this process.

Mother Mary then quotes the 19th Ode to Solomon, one of a collection of rare Wisdom scriptures that are referred to in the *Pistis Sophia*. "The Lord is on my head as a wreath, and I shall not depart from him. The wreath in truth is woven for me, and it hath caused thy twigs to sprout in me" (PS:59).

In the *Pistis Sophia*, Jesus described how he came to rescue Sophia. "And my light-power led Pistis Sophia up to the higher regions of the chaos" (PS:58). He said that, at some future time, a command would come from the First Mystery, whereby Sophia can be fully restored into the region he calls the Light Land, equating to the Pleroma. As described in the *Apocryphon of John*, Sophia is lifted up to the ninth heaven, where she is safely out of reach from the tormenting archons, though still not restored to her original place within the heavenly realm. "And he consented; and when the invisible Spirit had consented, the holy Spirit poured over (Sophia) from their whole pleroma. For it was not her consort who came to her, but he came to her through the pleroma in order that he might correct her deficiency. And she was taken up not to her own aeon but above her son [here identified as Yaldabaoth], that she might be in the ninth until she has corrected her deficiency" (AJ).

According to this account, this is where she currently resides. She still has not yet returned to her original place within the Pleroma as she awaits the reclamation of her Divine Sparks. Wisdom calls forth her children, if we have ears to hear. Sophia also awaits the arrival of her bridegroom, the Christ, to the ceremonial bridal chamber, whereupon the restoration of the disrupted Pleroma will finally be accomplished.

The Bible's Song of Songs echoes this archetypal theme of rescue: "My dear one has answered and said to me, 'Rise up, you girl companion of mine, my beautiful one, and come away. For, look! The rainy season itself has passed, the downpour itself is over, it has gone its way. Blossoms themselves have appeared in the land, the very time of vine trimming has arrived, and the voice of the turtledove itself has been heard in our land.'"[3]

So ends the dramatic tale of the fall and restoration of this divinely feminine Goddess. May her example be our guide.

PART III

TRACKING THE DEEP CHRIST

12

Emergence of the Deep Christ

Section I of the Deep Christ – *Via Positiva*

We will now step into an investigation of the Deep Christ, a mystery thriller with twists, turns, and mind-boggling discoveries. To proceed, we will need to step back from the familiar Jesus of the New Testament and look at how he appears in the Gnostic tradition in order to get to the epicenter of the 1st century Wisdom Revelation. Here, our mystery theater is filled with stage fog that makes it difficult to know what is true history, what is mythological spin, and what are valuable archetypal motifs that transcend the confines of history.

I have been asked: Why go into all of this and spend so much time on some long-forgotten story of Sophia? Why bring even more pages to the gazillions of books about Jesus? These are good questions, which I ask myself often. But, as I continue to dig deeper into the enigma of early Christianity, with each misleading story, each name change, each storyline diversion, there is a clue that keeps me on the trail of a treasure, a pearl, that I know is out there, or maybe more precisely, is within.

A classic Christian interpretation of Jesus focuses on his sacrifice that enables our salvation. However, in a strange irony, teachings found within the mysteries of the Spark of Christ Sophia have themselves been sacrificed in the process of creating a theology of the crucified Jesus.

The Gnostic Christ

In the first part of this investigation into the mysterious Deep Christ, we will drop into the position of grace of the via Positiva, where he is associated with the most glorious emanation of creation. There are six primary texts that I will be drawing from: the *Apocryphon* (Secret Book) *of John* (AJ), *Pistis Sophia* (PS), *The Second Treatise of the Great Seth* (ST), *Eugnostos The Blessed* (Eug), *Sophia of Jesus Christ* (SJC), and *Trimpophic Protennonia* (TP).

The *Pistis Sophia* was written sometime in the 3rd to 4th century; however, it is likely a later edition of an earlier text dating back at least to the 2nd century.[1] In the *Pistis Sophia*, there is a long description of the disciples witnessing Jesus's dramatic ascension to heaven. He returns shortly thereafter and promises to teach them the "mysteries."

Here is a synopsis of this ascension story of Jesus taken from the first book of the *Pistis Sophia*.

Jesus's Ascension and Return

For eleven years after the crucifixion, Jesus talked with his followers about the origins of creation. He had shared with them about the great emanation of the feminine Thought, Ennoia, that erupted out of the ineffable Godhead "in the form of a dove" (PS:1).

It was around this time that Jesus was sitting on the Mount of Olives, apart from his disciples, when suddenly, a most incredible light energy came down and surrounded him entirely. It "shone most exceedingly, and there was no measure for the light which was on him" (PS:2). And then, in this radiant light, he was lifted up until he disappeared into the sky. And his followers were incredibly shaken.

About a day and a half later, he returned the same way he left, but he was now shrouded in a Light far more incredible than when he ascended. Attempting to appease their fear, he said to his disciples, "Take courage. It is I, be not afraid" (PS:5). Jesus said that he would now be able to teach them about the unfolding of the cosmos, including the mysteries of Sophia. What is more, much like in the *Hymn of the Pearl*, he said that he had come from the region from whence he originally came, the First Mystery, where he received what he calls his Vesture.[2] "From today onwards now I will speak with you openly from the beginning of the truth until its completion. And I will speak with you face to face, without parable. I will not conceal from you, from this hour onwards, anything of the things of the height and of the place of the truth. For I have been given authority, through the Ineffable and through the First Mystery of all the mysteries, that I should speak with you from the beginning until the pleroma... Hear now, so that I tell you all things" (PS:6).

Significance of this Story

To review, eleven years after the crucifixion, Jesus undergoes a dramatic ascension experience where he receives his radiant robe of Light and, upon being granted permission from the highest levels of creation, he returns, saying that he will now tell his disciples the details of the complex nature of divine reality.

This account of the *Pistis Sophia* is in stark contrast to Jesus's ascension as portrayed in the New Testament. "When he had led them out to the vicinity of Bethany, he lifted up his hands and blessed them. While he was blessing them, he left them and was taken up into heaven. Then they worshiped him and returned to Jerusalem with great joy. And they stayed continually at the temple, praising God" (Luke 24:50-53).

In Luke's Gospel, there is no detail about this ascent, and he doesn't return. That is the end. There are no mystery teachings of complex cosmology, no mention of Sophia.[3] Though there is a brief account in a later edition of Mark, there is no mention of this ascension in the Gospel of Matthew. There are three very general references to this ascension in the Gospel of John, such as: "No one has ascended into heaven but he who descended from heaven, the son of man" (John 3:13).

These are all good examples of how stories in the New Testament appear to be, at times, simpler and possibly reduced versions of more complex original stories found in the Gnostic, and especially the Sethian, scriptures, though the commonly accepted theory is that the Gnostic versions are later corruptions of the pre-established orthodoxy.[4]

This ascension scene from the *Pistis Sophia* also has much in common with the "Hymn of the Pearl," as told possibly by Christ's close associate, St.

Thomas, where the prince returns to the kingdom of his father to receive his Robe of Glory. In this ascension story of the *Pistis Sophia*, Christ returns adorned with his vesture of Light.[5]

This is just one glimpse of how Jesus is described in the Gnostic scriptures. As one looks more into how this savior figure is depicted in a number of these texts, a strange and often unfamiliar image begins to take shape. The following are a few more of the unique ways in which Jesus is portrayed in key Gnostic texts, including the *Apocryphon of John* (AJ), *The Second Treatise of the Great Seth* (ST), and *Eugnostos the Blessed* (Eug). I will present a more comprehensive look at how he is depicted in the Gnostic tradition in Chapter 13.

Apocryphon of John

The *Secret Book of John* was likely the most popular of the Gnostic texts, as three copies survived its 4th-century ban. This particular book evolved over time, and AJ-D differentiates the sections of the writing from what was earlier and what was added later.

The earliest sections of this text include an extensive overview of the creation story of Sophia, which corresponds to other cosmological teachings of the Gnostic Christ. What is missing in this more original first-generation section is Christ being identified as the source of this information. Even with the later addition of Christ speaking in first person, what he says corresponds closely with what he reportedly described in other Gnostic scriptures. It is this *Secret Book of John* that is one of the primary sources for my rendition of this creation story, especially regarding Sophia's descent and her being trapped by the archons.

The Gnostic Jesus speaks to John: "The Monad is a monarchy with nothing above it. It is he who exists as God and Father of everything, the invisible One who is above everything, who exists as incorruption, which is in the pure light into which no eye can look. He is the invisible Spirit, of whom it is not right to think of him as a god, or something similar. For he is more than a god, since there is nothing above him, for no one lords it over him" (AJ).

Here, Jesus is giving a description of the Ineffable-Ein Soph as presented in the first part of the creation story of Sophia. Descriptions of Divine Source are the first teachings that Christ presents to John. He is speaking of a singularity or monad, a most ineffable beginning in this story of origins.

"And his thought performed a deed and she came forth, namely she who had appeared before him in the shine of his light. This is the first power which was before all of them (and) which came forth from his mind. She is the forethought of the All - her light shines like his light - the perfect power which is the image of the invisible, virginal Spirit who is perfect" (AJ).

In this text, Jesus is delivering a profound description of what I call the Great Emanation. This is an explosion of divine Light called Thought, the higher aspect of Sophia, that breaks out of the Ineffable's own self-contained radiance (Ein Soph Or) and pours out into a new creation.

It is quite noteworthy to read this in contrast to the New Testament Gospels, where Jesus provides virtually no descriptions of this level of creation.

Second Treatise of the Great Seth

"Now these things I have presented to you - I am Jesus Christ, the Son of Man, who is exalted above the heavens..." reads the *Second Treatise of the Great Seth* (ST). Of course, any document can claim to be signed by any name, and scholars have not been inclined to attribute this to the pen of Jesus. However, based on its highly unique theology and rendering of historical events, clues suggest that this text is closer to the original teachings of the elusive Deep Christ.

The *Second Treatise* speaks specifically of the Christ Logos becoming connected to the mortal Jesus: "I visited a bodily dwelling. I cast out the one who was in it first, and I went in" (ST). This may be a reference to the concept of a "walk-in," where another soul steps into a body upon the exit of that person's soul.[6] "For he was an earthly man, but I, I am from above the heavens" (ST). Strange as this may be, the Gospel story of Jesus's baptism might be a version of this. This mention that he "visited a bodily dwelling" brings valuable insight into the long-standing debate about whether Jesus was divine or human.[7]

Jesus then describes his participation in the planting of the Divine Spark, which he calls Ennoia (Greek for a seed/spark or thought of consciousness). "I have an Ennoia of a single emanation from the eternal ones and the undefiled and immeasurable incomprehensibility. I placed the small Ennoia in the world, having disturbed the archons and frightened the whole multitude of the angels and their ruler" (ST). Here is a clue to Christ's role in planting the spark of the feminine indwelling presence (Shekinah) into the fabric of this world as part of his mission.

Eugnostos the Blessed

Eugnostos the Blessed (Eug) is one of my favorite texts as it offers powerful descriptions of the unfolding of divine reality and does not include the very difficult material on the archons. This Gnostic gospel is presented in first person by this unknown figure known as Eugnostos. This unique name or title may be shielding scholars from further speculation about who this author might have been.

Whoever Eugnostos was, he seems to be giving firsthand knowledge in great detail about the origins of creation in much the same way as Jesus does in *Apocryphon of John* (AJ), *Trimorphic Protennoia* (TP), *Second Treatise of the Great Seth* (ST), *Books of IEOU* (IE), and the *Pistis Sophia* (PS). What is more, there is a later version of *Eugnostos* known as the *Sophia of Jesus Christ* (SJC). In the Robinson edition of *The Nag Hammadi Library* (1978), these two scriptures are laid out side by side on each page to show what parts of the earlier *Eugnostos* were either added to or changed in the later *Sophia of Jesus Christ* text.

In juxtaposition to how this unknown teacher, Eugnostos, is the one who is presenting this high cosmology, in *Sophia of Jesus Christ,* the speaker is identified as Jesus. Given that *Sophia of Jesus Christ* is a later elaboration on *Eugnostos*, we might deduce that Eugnostos was a name or title, possibly of endearment, used for Jesus. The Greek "eu" is a prefix for good or true. This "eu" is combined with a variation of *gnosis*, a word that is a key signature of the teachings of the Gnostic Christ, a word that Christ himself uses in the *Trimorphic Protennoia:* "It is through me that Gnosis comes forth" (TP).

These *Eugnostos* and *Sophia of Jesus Christ* texts go into great detail about the earliest emanation from the Ineffable-Ein Soph, "He-Who-Is." In addition, Sophia is identified as an equal to the Christ, who the author calls "Immortal Androgynous Man": "His male name is 'Begotten, Perfect Mind. And his female name is 'All-wise Begettress Sophia'". It is also said that she resembles her brother and her consort" (Eug). Here is a rare reference to how this Sophia equates to a feminine aspect of Christ and how, within the structure of this divine realm called the Pleroma, Christ and Sophia are paired in the outermost emanation (aeon) of the Pleroma, the heavenly realm.

Conclusion

To encounter this material for the first time can be perplexing, if not astounding. How could all this be going on with Jesus, and yet this story is barely told? The voice of Christian orthodoxy claims that this is all heresy and is a later creative mythology stirred up in the imaginations of ungrounded mystics. Ironically, however, as we move further into this Mystery Thriller, there is enough evidence to at least raise eyebrows that this material has roots that predate Christianity.

In the four Gospels of the New Testament, there is one fleeting single reference to the trinity, "Father, the Son, and the Holy Spirit," in Matthew 28:19. In stark contrast, in these core Gnostic scriptures, there are numerous instances when Jesus presents elaborate details about the unfolding trinity. This is a classic signature of a Novel Revelation, where more complex, earlier teachings are later reduced or simplified. This is opposed to what we might anticipate, where original teachings develop in complexity over time, such as what I believe has occurred with the Kabbalah.

Clearly, in these texts, we are seeing a more complex Christ, a Deep Christ, who seems to have his finger on the pulse of a vast sweep of a creation drama. Yet, this unique story of a cosmic Christ has been almost entirely wiped from the Christian theological record. What is happening here? This is the question that will be explored in the next chapter.

13

Lost Teachings of the Gnostic Christ

Section II of the Deep Christ – *Via Negativa*

That is not to say that the Jesus of history did not exist, only that the evidence is skewed and that the problem is more complex than many think.

- Robert Eisenman, *James the Brother of Jesus*

These past 2000 years in the processional turning of the ages have been marked by the double-fish astrological symbol of Pisces. As this cycle slowly shifts into the Aquarian age, perhaps we can look back into this past Christian epoch to see that, indeed, something fishy was going on.

In the last chapter of this Deep Christ investigation, the issue of how differently Jesus is portrayed in the Gnostic texts in contrast to how he is depicted in the New Testament was introduced. Regarding this difference, the preeminent Gnostic scholar, Elaine Pagels, posed the question in her book *The Gnostic Paul* (1975): how do we reconcile that St. Paul is celebrated as being a key player in the formation of both Christianity and Gnosticism? In the same way, how do we account for how both the Christians and the Gnostics attribute their inspiration and origins to this man Jesus, who is depicted so differently in these two traditions?

This investigation into these two competing versions of Jesus is not a mere academic exercise but rather gets to the very heart of the New Revelation of Wisdom. Somewhere along the way, I believe, a more original message from this man and his close associates was largely lost. Sophia, a primary clue on this trail, was not the only thing written out of Jesus's teachings. Also expunged was the most central enigma and the greatest buried treasure of this lost tradition, the Divine Spark Within. Recovering what might be perhaps an earlier historical footprint of this savior figure could help uncover the raw materials of these lost mysteries.

As part of the next phase of this investigation into the Deep Christ, we will get down, so to speak, via Negativa, to excavate what is going on with this enigmatic figure known as Jesus. This "descent" includes 1) how he came down to this aeon to rescue Sophia, 2) how he descended from the first century, through the mysteries of gnosis and into the jungle of Christian history, and 3) how he is represented or misrepresented in various theories about the historical Jesus.

I am circling around the 1st century with so-called soft eyes, holding off on making any concrete conclusions. There are too many questions about what happened historically and too many layers of misinformation to get a clear picture of this Jesus story, despite what is written in the Bible. In fact, as we step into this whole enigma of the historical Jesus, as I recommended earlier, it might be easiest to just set aside any prior conceptions one has of this man. This is not to abandon one's own relationship with him, whatever that might be. For the purposes of this investigation, however, I find that it is easier to clean the slate, so to speak, and see how his character and teachings begin to take on a new shape.

Gnosticism is Not a Christian Corruption

Gnosticism grew and developed alongside Christianity in the first few centuries CE. As two separate but parallel religious systems, there were cross-fertilizations between the two.

However, these pre-325 CE "ante-Nicene" Gnostic texts, particularly the Sethian, were specifically not Christian. They were novel and not later corruptions or heresies of the Roman orthodoxy. Though this is counter to the overwhelming consensus of Christian theologians, Pagels quotes Karl Barth at the turn of the century saying quite clearly that the foundational tenets of the Valentinian teaching which were influence by the Sethian texts, were clearly older than Christianity itself.[1] This is why the more original Gnostic texts, such as the Nag Hammadi Library that survived the orthodox Nicene heresy purges, are all the more remarkable and valuable.

James M. Robinson, editor-in-chief of the first edition publication of the 1700-year-old Nag Hammadi Library (1978), posits that instead of Gnosticism distorting and corrupting the more authentically pure Christian themes, rather, the largely independent early Gnostic movement sprang from non-Christian roots and, over time, gradually adopted Christian themes. In his introduction, Robinson underlines that it is impossible to conclude that Sethian themes could have originated from the Christian tradition. In certain texts such as the *Trimorphic Protennoia*, it is clear that a "secondary Christianizing" has been added to a lost, more original, and definitively non-Christian text.[2] Though Robinson is clarifying that the early Gnostic trends were not Christian offshoots, he indicates that Gnosticism came from Jewish roots. Though certainly there are streams of Jewish influence, even today, scholars have not come to any clear conclusions or consensus about the origins of Gnosticism. My thesis on the Deep Christ, with the idea of a 1st century New Revelation that was novel and distinctly non-Jewish, may shed some helpful light on this subject.[3]

From my research, I am proposing a thesis that Gnosticism sprang from a primary source in the 1st century CE associated with a generalized personhood I am calling the Deep Christ. This point of origin provided the raw material upon which both the proto-Gnostic and proto-orthodox Christian systems (proto, meaning formative) began to take shape in the late 1st century.

Does the Jesus of the Gnostic tradition offer a wholly unique and possibly more original depiction of the biblical savior as depicted in the New Testament? If so, what are the implications of these teachings that had greater complexity and presented a more comprehensive cosmological view of human history? Though this question may never find a clear answer, it will be helpful to first sketch a clearer overview of Jesus as he is depicted in the Gnostic texts.

The Gnostic Jesus

As I have outlined in the previous sections on the creation story of Sophia, there are very distinct references to how the main character in these Gnostic scriptures is Jesus, who, through his own narration, gives extensive explanations of the origins of creation.

The Gnostic texts where Jesus is narrating in first person include *Pistis Sophia* (PS), *Apocryphon of John* (AJ), *Second Treatise of the Great Seth* (ST), *First Apocalypse of James* (FstAJ), *Book of Thomas the Contender* (BTC), *Gospel of Thomas* (GT), *Apocalypse of Peter* (APe), *Sophia of Jesus Christ* (SJC), and *Letter of Peter to Philip* (LPP).

In some of these manuscripts, Jesus, being the one who is presenting the teaching, is added to an earlier version of the text, such as in the case of *Eugnostos the Blessed*, the *Secret Book of John*, and I assume, also with *Pistis Sophia*. Some later, more Christianized scriptures found in the Nag Hammadi collection, such as the *Gospel of Truth* (GTr) and *Tripartite Tractate* (TT), are written as a third-person account of Jesus's teachings.

Some scholars suggest that attributions of Jesus that were added to later texts are evidence of how Gnosticism in general did not originate from the original teachings of Christ. However, let's look at a collection of quotes that outline a fairly consistent storyline and range of characteristics attributed to the Gnostic Jesus across the span of earlier to later Gnostic scriptures. Keep in mind that although these might include some later edits to some lost and more original texts, these references still present a consistent and unique tone of how Jesus appears in this Gnostic, pre-Nicene (pre-orthodox) context.

1. The Gnostic Jesus's First Person Voice in the Gnostic Gospels

The following are quotes attributed to Jesus in the Gnostic texts.

"Now these things I have presented to you - I am Jesus Christ, the Son of Man, who is exalted above the heavens…" (ST).

"He said to me, 'John, John, why do you doubt, or why are you afraid?'" (AJ).

"The savior said, 'Brother Thomas, while you have time in the world, listen to me, and I will reveal to you the things you have pondered in your mind'" (BTC).

"Jesus said..." 114 sayings (logions) in *The Gospel of Thomas* (GT).

"And he (the Savior) said to me (Peter), 'Be strong, for you are the one to whom these mysteries have been given...'" – *Apocalypse of Peter*.[4]

"The Perfect Savior said, 'I came from the Infinite that I might tell you all things'" (SJC).

As in the ascension story account in *Pistis Sophia*, Peter is recounting Jesus's revelation appearance on the Mount of Olives. "Listen to my words that I may speak to you. ... I am Jesus Christ who is with you forever" (LPP).

2. The Gnostic Jesus Describes the Cosmology of Origins

The following are quotes from the Gnostic Jesus, where he is describing the complex cosmology of creation.

Jesus said, "The Monad is a monarchy with nothing above it" (AJ).

Jesus said, "This is the first thought, his image; she became the womb of everything for it is she who is prior to them all..." (AJ).

Jesus said, "And his [the Ineffable's] thought performed a deed and she came forth, namely she who had appeared before him in the shine of his light" (AJ).

Jesus said, "It came to pass then, when Pistis Sophia saw me shining most exceedingly and with no measure to the light which was about me..." (PS:29).

3. The Gnostic Jesus Came from "The First Mystery" or the "Great Power"

"...He decided to have his likeness become a great power" (Eug and SJC).

Jesus is describing and performing a eucharist ceremony with his disciples. "The blood on the other hand was for a sign unto me because of the human body [the Anthropos] which I received in the region of Barbēlō, the great power of the invisible god" (PS:141).

In the *Pistis Sophia*, Jesus is frequently referred to as The First Mystery. For example, "And the First Mystery continued again and said unto the disciples..." (PS:70).

4. He Identifies Himself as the Father, the Mother, and the Son

"I am the Father, I am the Mother, I am the Son" – (AJ).

5. The Gnostic Jesus Describes the Region of the Right and the Region of the Left

As part of this cosmology, Jesus describes areas that are both inside and outside the Pleroma. These are called the Region of the Right and the Region of the Left, respectively.

"And if I lead you into the Light-land, that is into the Treasury of the Light, and ye see the glory in which they are, then will the region of those of the Right count for you as the light at mid-day in the world of men, when the sun is not out; and if ye look at the region of those of the Right, it will have for you the condition of a speck of dust because of the great distance the Treasury of the Light is distant from it" (PS:84). (I.e., the high divine beings in the Region of the Right are far closer to the Source/Ein Soph though a great distance from the Treasury of Light which is a location further out but still within the Pleroma.)

"Let all the powers (archons) of the Left go to their regions" (PS:141).

"And it giveth the apology of all the rulers [archons] of all the regions of the Left, -- whose collective apologies and seals I will one day tell you when I shall tell you the expansion of the Universe" (PS:112).

6. The Gnostic Jesus's "descent" through the Regions of the Archons

In these passages, the divine Christ disguises himself during his descent down through the Region of the Left into the mortal body of Jesus to pass through the gates of the archons undetected.

"For as I came downward, no one saw me. For I was altering my shapes, changing from form to form. And therefore, when I was at [the archon's] gates, I assumed their likeness. For I passed them by quietly, and I was viewing the places, and I was not afraid nor ashamed, for I was undefiled" (ST).

"I am the one who was sent down in the body because of the seed which had fallen away. And I came down into their mortal mold. But they did not recognize me; they were thinking of me that I was a mortal man" (LPP).

"And I went into the realm of darkness and I endured till I entered the middle of the prison. And the foundations of chaos shook. And I hid myself from them because of their wickedness, and [the archons] did not recognize me" (AJ).

"The Third time I revealed myself to them in their tents as Word, and I revealed myself in the likeness of their shape. And I wore everyone's garment, and I hid myself within them, and they did not know the one who empowers me. For I dwell within all the Sovereignties and Powers [i.e., archons], and within the angels, and in every movement that exists in all matter" (TP).

"As for me, I put on Jesus" (TP).

7. He Identified the Jewish God YHWH with the Demiurge He Named Yaldabaoth

"'I am God and there is no other beside me.' But I laughed joyfully when I examined his empty glory" (ST).

"And when he saw the creation which surrounds him and the multitude of the (archons) around him which had come forth from him, he said to them, 'I am a jealous God, and there is no other God beside me'" (AJ).

"Now the archon who is weak has three names. The first name is Yaltabaoth the second is Saklas, and the third is Samael. And he is impious in his arrogance which is in him. For he said, 'I am God and there is no other God beside me,' for he is ignorant of his strength, the place from which he had come" (AJ).

8. The Gnostic Jesus was Known as the Christ and Savior[5]

"I am Christ, the Son of Man, the one from you who is among you" (ST).

"The perfect Savior said: 'I came from the Infinite that I might tell you all things'" (SJC).

"It is he alone who came to be, that is, the Christ" (TP).

9. The Gnostic Jesus Came to Rescue Sophia, who was Trapped and Persecuted by the Archons

In this next set of quotes from the *Pistis Sophia*, Jesus is talking to his disciples about the plight and rescue of Sophia.

"...[it was] a lion-faced ruler in the chaos, of which one half is fire and the other darkness, that is Yaldabaoth, of whom I have spoken unto you many times. When then this befell, Sophia became very greatly exhausted, and that lion-faced light-power set to work to take away from Sophia all her light-powers..." (PS:31).

"And the lion-faced power and the serpent-form and the basilisk-form and the dragon-form and all the other very numerous emanations of Self-willed surrounded Pistis Sophia all together, desiring to take from her anew her powers in her, and they oppressed Pistis Sophia exceedingly and threatened her. It came to pass then, when they oppressed her and alarmed her exceedingly, that she cried again to the Light and sang praises, saying: 'O Light, it is thou who hast helped me; let thy light come over me'" (PS:66).

"It came to pass then when Pistis Sophia had finished saying these words in the chaos, that I made the light-power, which I had sent to save her, become a light-wreath on her head" (PS:59).

Jesus said, "The (Father's) kingdom is like a shepherd who had a hundred sheep. One of them, the largest, went astray. He left the ninety-nine and looked for the one until he found it. After he had toiled, he said to the sheep, 'I love you more than the ninety-nine.'" (GT logion 107).

10. He Descended to Save Humanity from the Tyranny of the Archons

"Now I have taught you about Immortal Man and have loosed the bonds of the robbers from him" (SJC).

As quoted earlier, 'Lord, tell us: In what way shall we fight against the archons since the archons are above us?' Then a voice called out to them from the (Savior) saying, 'Now you will fight against them in this way, for the archons are fighting against the inner man' (LPP).

"And when Jesus had finished sealing them with this seal, in that moment the archons took away all their evil from the disciples. And they rejoiced with very great joy because all the evil of the archons had ceased within them"

(IE).[6]

11. He Descended to Rescue the Divine Spark Within Individuals

"I have awakened that drop that was sent from Sophia, that it might bear much fruit through me, and be perfected and not again be defective, but be joined through me, the Great Savior, that his glory might be revealed…" (SJC).

"I am the Light that illumines the All. I am the Light that rejoices in my brethren, for I have come down to the world of mortals on account of the Spirit (epinoia) that remains in that which descended and came forth from the innocent Sophia" (TP).

12. Teaching Lasted Past the Time of the Crucifixion

"It came to pass when Jesus had risen from the dead, that he passed eleven years discoursing with his disciples…" (PS:1).

"Thou hearest that I suffered, yet did I not suffer" (ActJ).

"For my death which they think happened, happened to them in their error and blindness, since they nailed their man unto their death" (ST).

Reclaiming the Story of the Gnostic Christ

This collection of quotes and references attributed to Jesus of the Gnostic texts presents remarkable descriptions of this man in a story which is rarely told. To his disciples, this pre-Nicene Christ describes the complex cosmology of origins that includes great details about the trinity. He says that he came from this First Mystery, or the Great Power, and identified himself as the Father, the Mother, and the Son. He refers to higher and lower regions of the Universe and that he himself descended from the Region of the Right to the Region of the Left, where he disguised himself to go undetected as he traversed the regions of the archons. In a profound insult to his Jewish roots, the Gnostic Christ claims that the God YHWH was the demiurge himself, called Yaldabaoth. He was known as the Christ who came down to rescue Sophia, who was trapped and persecuted by the demiurge. Likewise, he came to rescue humanity from the control of these "princes and principalities" with the reactivation of the Divine Spark Within. Much of this information became known after the event of the crucifixion.

One cannot help but question: are these all just bastardized offshoots of the "true" story of Jesus as found in the New Testament? Why were these highly detailed, textually cross-referenced and unique depictions of the Deep Christ that flourished in some of the earliest Christian traditions that pre-dated the orthodox framework of Christianity so thoroughly persecuted and banished?

A thesis is beginning to take shape: A more original story became overwritten by the now common plotline that has been passed down through the centuries. The following is a very narrow slice of this thesis, of which a more complete analysis would take volumes. In this, I will be attempting to bushwhack my way through the overgrown jungle of early Christian history to find lost clues in this Deep Christ mystery.

14

The Descent – from the Gnostic Christ

to the New Testament Jesus

Section II of the Deep Christ (continued)

In contrast to this unusual Gnostic version of Jesus, let us step back and review the very familiar story of the origins of Christianity.

A Reader's Digest Version of Christian Origins

A recent Cambridge University history of Christianity has taken upon itself to present a more responsible scholastic overview of this religion's shrouded origins. Their goal was to bring more clarity to the dominant narrative that has been largely unquestioned for much of the last 2000 years. This story goes as follows: A simple carpenter received a pure faith teaching that was passed on to his disciples. Having no disagreement between them, the "Apostles Creed" was spread throughout the lands. However, the devil was hard at work spurring distortions of the savior's teachings, called "heresies" that were producing offspring that threatened the purity of his message. With this, Christianity ultimately triumphed with the conversion of Constantine and the creation of the Nicaean Creed.[1]

Though one might wish that Christianity's origins were this simple, unfortunately, this shallow version is obscuring some inconvenient historical truths. Christianity has built an almost impenetrable wall around a dominant narrative and any variations from this needed to be persecuted and eliminated. At the very least, unless we work to bring more scrutiny to the ever-present story of Christianity's origins, then it is easy to just default to this simple version.[2]

It is not by chance that this Reader's Digest rendition of Christian history has been the definitive version for much of the past 2000 years. This was shaped by many hands amidst the social, political, and religious influences of the times. What got lost along the way, however, is that the biblical Jesus may well have started out as a more mystical Gnostic Jesus.

Christian Heresiologists: How Orthodoxy Won the Narrative Game

One of the earliest formidable influences in Gnosticism becoming more "Christianized" was a relatively small group of theologians who were instrumental in narrowing down and defining what they believed to be the orthodox doctrine. These theologians were known as the "heresiologists" because they wrote about what was seen as the corruption or heresy of a more pure and "original" Christian doctrine. They presented the case for a cohesive or "orthodox" religious system by picking apart the "heterodoxic" or diverse theologies that proliferated in the early days of Christianity.

A prominent heresiologist, the French bishop of Lyons named Irenaeus (155–202 CE) embarked on one of the earliest and most rigorous campaigns to dismantle the novel Gnostic cosmology and replace it with a more "exoteric" (meaning known by and available to all), more generalized, and less complex religious system. Irenaeus's own personal story is a fascinating one that Pagels explores in her book *Beyond Belief* (2003).

In a strange irony, these writings from the heresiologists preserved the only record of Gnosticism since the times of their virtual elimination in the late 300s CE, until the discoveries of the Bruce and Askew Codices in the late 1700s. If it weren't for these writings, Gnosticism might have been fully lost to history, being just one more forgotten blip in the array of innumerable sects of that time period.

St. Peter was the disciple who became a figurehead for the orthodox tradition, and, as we will explore, by emphasizing Peter's theology, the

Roman church guarded against the more Gnostic-leaning teachings such as those of St. Paul and St. Thomas.

Clement, who succeeded Peter as the bishop of Rome, a position known as the Pope, opposed "false Gnosis with the true Gnosis of the Christian. By means of good, healthy living, knowledge of the principles of faith and growth in the spiritual dimension, the Christian is able to achieve the status of a true Gnostic, of one who aspires to know God through the Son."[3] Here, a depth wisdom process and individual spiritual empowerment championed by the Gnostics were replaced by moral guidance as accessed "through the Son." Instead of referencing one's own unique spiritual experience (meaning *gnosis* by definition), the Christian is counseled to approach spiritual matters according to a doctrinal and clergical church authority.

The Move to Orthodoxy

It is easy to feel anger at how these heresiologists virtually destroyed the sacred scriptures of gnosis, and this anger is, of course, warranted. However, it is important to understand their work when viewed from within Christianity's fledgling effort to survive through its infancy. The Gnostic system was too complex and too esoteric, with its strange alien beings and a complex creation story, for a "universal" Catholic religion to be adopted by the common man.

The Gnostics were aware of this. Though they had a tendency to become increasingly speculative over time, their intent also seems to have been to systematize their philosophy in a way that could be better understood within the emerging Christian orthodoxy and make these profound teachings more accessible to the general public.

A good example of this is the Valentinian *Gospel of Truth* (GT). This text included later developments in the Gnostic system that contained more "Christianized" concepts, making it less cosmological, with more focus on the savior Jesus than on the epic journey of Sophia. The Valentinians were like a second generation of the earlier Sethian tradition that became more popularized and accessible. If the earlier renditions of this cosmology came from first-hand mystical accounts, later writings tended to be more philosophical than metaphysical, some being blended with the philosophies of Plato. According to Pagels's (1975) analysis, St. Paul sought to write with a cryptic reference to these more esoteric teachings while also packaging it in a way that required less study and could be more readily accepted.

Haar (2003) helps explain why the orthodox tradition took on the role of denouncing the heresies. 1) From its earliest days, Christianity needed clear definition to survive amidst its sprawling and unending variations. 2) Unlike Judaism and other Mediterranean religions at the time, Christianity was not linked with a particular ethnic group and hence had less legitimacy. And 3) Christianity needed legitimation because, as was necessary, it was unable to trace its roots to religious movements from the distant past.[4]

Given Christianity's need for uniformity in order for it to survive past infancy, it is clearly a tragic loss that the whole of the Gnostic system had to be discredited and marginalized for this to happen. The following is an example of how this gradual conversion took place.

Marcion as an Example of How Orthodoxy Conquered Gnostic Motifs

Marcion of Sinope (85–160 CE), a wealthy shipowner from northeastern Turkey, became involved in the formation of early Christianity in Rome. Marcion is notable for three very significant accomplishments.

First, he compiled what arguably became the first prototype of the New Testament, including a collection of Paul's letters as well as the Gospel of Marcion, which has many similarities to the four Gospels. Some scholars, like Matthias Klinghardt (b. 1957), believe that Marcion's gospels were *the* original gospels which the emerging Roman orthodox architects then edited into their own versions.

Secondly, Marcion developed an extensive network of churches in Asia Minor that, like his bare-bones New Testament, became a prototype for how Christian congregations began to be organized.

And lastly, Marcion had core assertions which, according to his detractors the heresiologists, were clearly Gnostic. He believed that Paul was the sole inheritor of the true teachings of Jesus. Marcion worked with the famed Valentinus in Rome, and both rejected the theory of the Jewish roots of Jesus's teachings. To him, Jesus descended from a higher place than this lower god called Yahweh, a figure he equated with the famed Gnostic demiurge. He completely rejected the notion that Jesus was a fulfillment of the Jewish Messiah but rather asserted that he was coming from a novel, specifically non-Jewish new revelation, which included a rejection of the Jewish God as opposed to the true God, referred to in some Gnostic texts as "the Ineffable." Like Valentinus, Marcion was denounced as a heretic and expelled from the emerging orthodox Christian tradition that was beginning to take firm hold in the 2nd and 3rd centuries in Rome.

The heresiologists did to Marcion what they did to Gnosticism in general: they discredited and buried his teachings, turning him from a valuable early Christian pioneer into a villain. The heresiologist Tertullian was particularly masterful in making sure that Marcion's writings were seen as a corruption of the Gospels and of Acts, rather than what some scholars believe was the opposite: that Marcion was coopted by these later New Testament writings (Tyson, 2006).

A prominent German scholar, Ferdinand Christian Baur (1792–1860), was one of the first to attempt to untangle the head-tilting orthodox version of Christian history. He argued that Eusebius, a key heresiologist and close associate of Emperor Constantine, rewrote early Christian conflicts so that the proto (meaning formative) orthodox Christian model, as opposed to the Gnostic system, might be seen as the original version that came straight from the teachings of Jesus.

It appears that Marcion carried forward Paul in a similar way that Paul carried forward the Gnostic Jesus. Both took the more esoteric teachings and tried to work them into the dominant religious culture of the first two centuries CE. In both cases, however, their Gnostic teachings were eventually dissolved and Jesus was no longer the sage of mysteries but rather the one who taught in parables. As Marcion's religious system was rejected by the proto-orthodoxy that was forming, so were Paul's Gnostic leanings subsumed into the less esoteric teachings of Peter, which became the apostolic foundation upon which the new Roman religious institution was built.

In 325 CE, Constantine gathered bishops from across the land and locked in the core belief framework in what was to become the orthodox Christian tradition. The Nicene Creed was a big nail in the Gnostic coffin, further compounded by Athanasius's proclamation in 367, which forbade possession of any non-canonical texts.[5] Christianity was left with one baptism, not the multiple baptist rituals of the Gnostics; just Jesus with no Sophia; just God the Father and the now neutered Holy Ghost, without that messy cosmology of origins.[6] By 380, the Roman Emperor Theodosius I made Nicene Christianity the national religion of its vast empire, a move whose motivations were as political as they were religious.

One intention for bringing more uniformity to the Christian doctrine was to establish a quality control system of institutionalizing the church through "apostolic succession" from its head office in Rome. Starting with Peter, this centralized system established a standardized orthodoxy to guard against endless variation (heterodoxy). There was a great diversity of the early Christian sects from Britain to Babylon, with no anchor of coherence between them. The Roman orthodox system sought to overcome this by maintaining a uniformity within the religious doctrine.

There was also the need to foster people's dependency on this central savior image as well as on the church itself, both being promoted as necessary intermediaries with the divine. The church as an institution, by its very nature, required people to depend on it to grow, and grow it did — into a vast complex of one of today's most powerful, wealthiest, and influential organizations on Earth.

The Gnostics, having little chance in the face of what ultimately became a Roman state-supported religious system, became increasingly suspect and the focus of ridicule, censorship, and persecution. Those who saw value in their books, such as the Nag Hammadi collection, resorted to desperate measures like burying them in large clay pots in the desert in hopes they might survive.

The Fog of the Historical Jesus

I have come to suspect that a clear understanding of this strange Gnostic portrayal of Jesus has been virtually impossible for even modern scholarship to attain from the now numerous ancient Gnostic scriptures. There appears to be an almost unconscious urge to want to complete the image, a gestalt in the mind's eye, that the Gnostic Jesus is simply another way of looking at the biblical Jesus and just leaving it at that.

Theaters both old and contemporary have used artificial fog to create a mood or obscure a scene. As we begin to become more familiar with this Deep Christ character in our Sophianic Mystery Play and try to make sense of how differently he is portrayed in the New Testament, we have to slowly drag our way through the fabricated fog in the theater of Christian history.

Jesus was a real man who lived in the early part of the 1st century in the area we know now as Israel. I was surprised to learn that many modern-day Gnostics in fact do not believe this. Instead, they subscribe to the idea that he was a spirit who had direct contact with his disciples and that his teachings were delivered from a disembodied state. This is a doctrine known as Docetism, where Christ is believed to have been an etheric being and not an actual physical person. Christ-as-spirit harkens back to the age-old debate that plagued Christian theology for centuries about whether Jesus was human or divine or some combination of the two.

The Docetist view is found in later editions of some of the Gnostic Gospels, such as the *Pistis Sophia* and the *Books of IEOU*, with references to the "voice of Jesus" coming to the disciples. This is due, I believe, to great confusion that surrounds the historical event of the crucifixion (as I will explore in the Appendix). According to Gnostic scholar John Turner (2001), the Sethian Gnostic school, one of the earliest of the various traditions, rejected a Docetist explanation of Jesus, believing that this great masculine counterpart to the Divine Sophia was indeed human.

To be clear, I subscribe to the idea that Jesus was a mortal, living, breathing man and that he was clearly at the epicenter of the origins of a new religion. However, his story is so shrouded with smoke and mirrors that it is hard to find the historical ground where he stood in the world.

As many who have investigated this religious figure have found, there are only slim correlations between the biblical stories of Jesus and non-biblical written accounts of the day, such as from the most prominent and significant historian of that time and place, Josephus (37– c. 100 CE).[7]

Included in Josephus's writings were detailed descriptions of characters we are familiar with in the Bible, such as Pontius Pilate and the Herods. In 44 CE, for example, Josephus describes how two brothers, who were players in the Jewish zealot uprisings against the Romans, were crucified. However, apart from one very questionable exception, there is no authentic account of Jesus's crucifixion to be found in Josephus. The paragraph that describes Jesus's crucifixion, known as the *Testimonium Flavianum*, is written so differently than the rest of Josephus's writing that it was undoubtedly added in a later edition of his works. The structure and tone of it are highly similar to the way that the orthodox writers also fostered the emerging storyline.[8]

There is, however, one reference to Jesus in Josephus's writings, and this is a fleeting mention that he was a brother of a figure of historical significance to Josephus, known as James. For Eisenman, this is the single most important piece of evidence that, in fact, there was a savior in 1st century Palestine known as Jesus.

"Festus was now dead, and Albinus was but upon the road; so he assembled the Sanhedrin of judges and brought before them the brother of Jesus (who was called Christ), whose name was James, and some others, and when he had formed an accusation against them as breakers of the law, he delivered them to be stoned...."[9]

Here Jesus is identified as a brother of James, an awkward pairing clearly mentioned in two of the four Gospels (Mark 6:3 and Matthew 13:55). If Jesus had such a dramatic presence and impact in this time period, why did he not get more contemporary press?

Every theory under the "Son," so to speak, has been written about this. Was Jesus a Jewish zealot (Aslan, 2013), a wand-wielding magician (Smith, 2014), or a character who was recreated as a Pagan God from a Greco-Roman mystery cult (Freke, 1999)? Did he go to India and Tibet in his missing years? Was he a creation of the late 1st century Flavian attempts to conflate Titus with a messianic Jesus (Atwill, 2011)? How does the highly problematic Yeshu ben Pandera, "the sorcerer" of the Talmud, written centuries after the historical events, fit into all of this?[10] Was he a construct of late 1st and 2nd century theologians who superimposed a "Christ of faith" into "historical accounts" of early and mid-1st century, known as the Christ Myth theory? Or, as many scholars seem to conclude, was he simply a Jewish apocalyptic prophet who spoke of a coming new age of salvation? This debate will unfortunately never be resolved for "there is no physical or archaeological evidence for Jesus; all existing sources are documentary."[11]

However, I have stumbled onto a most phenomenal theory about the historical Jesus that has remained hidden for the past 2000 years.

I am not a peer-reviewed scholar in the same way that established academic scholarship requires. Rather, I am a storyteller at heart. As an artist, however, I am striving as much as possible to honor the first- or second-generation historical and textual resources from which this story has been gathered.

That being said, I have found no other way to present a backdrop to a profoundly unsettling and even outrageous thesis. This is not easily grasped, and yet, like finding a missing puzzle piece, suddenly, the whole picture starts to make more sense.

The thesis is simply this: the familiar New Testament version of Jesus is a toned-down, almost storybook version of a more complex, more original historical figure.

Introducing...

Up until now in this series, I have been holding back on bringing in a key figure in the mysterious origins of both Gnosticism and Christianity. I have been circling around him without mentioning him because he deserves a place on the stage that is not cluttered by all of the preliminaries that were needed to get to this point in our story.

The extent to which the character of this man has been completely destroyed by Christian orthodoxy is equal to the extent to which Gnosticism has been wholly discredited as well, so key was he to the origins of Gnosticism.

It is with great pleasure to introduce a new lead character in this Deep Christ Mystery Thriller: Simon Magus.

15

Introducing Simon Magus

Section III of the Deep Christ – *Via Creativa*

Simonianism is the first system that, as far as our present records go, came into conflict with what has been regarded as the orthodox stream of Christianity... I believe that Simon has been grossly misrepresented, and entirely misunderstood, by his orthodox opponents...

> -   G. R. S. Mead, *Simon Magus*

Simon Magus is a lead character in the Sophianic Mystery Play, who, as a nearly exact peer and contemporary of Jesus, has for the past 2000 years been shrouded in theatrical and theological fog. Clearly, as we will see, it was history as written by the victors that relegated him to barely a minor role. Or maybe, being far ahead of his time, he has been waiting to come back into the spotlight, where he can be applauded at last for the enormous role he has played in this story.

This chapter will focus on reclaiming a more accurate portrayal of this spiritual master from the torrent of misinformation that has been written about him through the centuries. The significance of who this man was and how he relates to the bigger picture of this Deep Christ investigation will be addressed in the next chapter.

Seen at face value as he appears in the Bible, it is easy to conclude that this man was a shady swindler with a bad messiah complex who tried to pay his way into attaining spiritual gifts — a sin known to this day as Simony. Like a shadow image of the much more glowing Jesus, he is depicted as the very archetype of a pseudo-Christ. However, in following the trail into this Deep Christ mystery, I'm not buying it. The very fact that he has sustained an unrelenting campaign of character assassination for two millennia suggests that something is going on here beyond just the Church's effort to marginalize what they believed was a theological bad apple.

Though I am bringing pieces together that rest on the shoulders of esteemed scholars in the field, very little can be proven here about this person Simon. Mead (1892) writes, "We must always remember that every single syllable we possess about Simon comes from the hands of bitter opponents, from men who had no mercy or toleration for the heretic."[1]

Thanks to some Christian historians like Ferdinand Christian Baur and Robert Eisenman, we are learning how to see through the orthodox Christian strategy of what Eisenman calls "historical obliteration and transformation," "neutralizing and deflecting" as a means of spinning the narrative in a desired direction, regardless of the historical accuracy. When falsehoods are told often enough, they become true, and efforts to try to find one's way through this confusion within early Christian history is an uphill struggle. However, as the strategies of disinformation become more clearly seen, it is easier to get to the bottom of what really happened. And thanks to the scholarship of Mead (1892) and Haar (2003), a much clearer and less biased description of this man Simon is available.

Simon Magus was likely a real person who appeared throughout the Middle East in the 1st century CE, from Rome to Syria and beyond. There are prominent writings about him in the first few centuries CE which offer important clues as to who he might have been. His appearance in (Luke's) Acts in the New Testament is arguably the earliest surviving written record of him.

"A man named Simon had previously practiced sorcery in that city and astounded the Samaritan people while claiming to be somebody great. They all paid attention to him, from the least of them to the greatest, and they said, 'This man is called the Great Power of God!'" (Acts 8: 9-10).[2]

These two sentences speak volumes. As I will explore, this link between

Simon and what is called the "Great Power" has an uncanny resemblance to descriptions of Jesus in the Gnostic texts, who was also said to have come from the Great Power.

Pseudo-Clement's *Homilies, Recognitions,* and *Kerygmata Petrou*[3] were writings that influenced the formation of Christianity in its earliest days. Called "romance literature" because of their loose attachment to historical accuracy, these writings included extensive efforts to destroy Simon's reputation by staging dialogues between him and St. Peter, where Peter shines through as having the superior theology.

Eisenman (1997) believes that Acts was created from a lost earlier rendition of these romance pieces.[4] He pointed out that Acts took great liberties to create a storyline that steered toward a proto-orthodox rendering of the origins of Christianity, leaning away from both a Jewish and a heterodox (multifaceted) view. I believe, more specifically, that this trend in Acts appears to coalesce around demonizing a Simonian influence during the construction of an orthodox-endorsed Jesus.

Simon the "Sorcerer"

Finding out who Simon really was will take much digging through the rubble of Christian disinformation. Like the very word "Gnosticism," the name Simon Magus carries indelible impressions of darkness that are hard to see past. This is no accident.

The word "sorcery" and its dark connotations may well have been deliberately used in Acts to denounce the advanced skills that this man appears to have possessed. In the published version of his Ph.D. dissertation titled, *Simon Magus: The First Gnostic?* (2003), Haar offers some context for the use of the word magus, from the Greek *magoi,* as related to the highly regarded lineage of Persian, Babylonian, and Greek spiritual traditions of that time.[5] To the Greeks and the Romans from the 7th century BCE to well into the first centuries CE, these Magoi were a particular tradition that was recognized and honored by Zoroaster, Pythagoras, and Plato. Like Daniel and Joseph, they interpreted dreams and studied the synchronicities that only made sense from outside the standard and concrete frameworks of knowing. They accessed higher divine wisdom for guidance and, like indigenous shamans, acted as intermediaries between humans and the divine. To be called a sorcerer, on the other hand, was a way to denounce a man with spiritual gifts, for as Haar concludes there is no justification in Acts rendition of Simon to conclude that he was a selfish practitioner of dark magic.[6]

Simon the First Gnostic

The 2nd-century French bishop named Irenaeus, one of the most prominent and influential heresiologists, made a remarkable claim. Irenaeus wrote in ~185 CE, "Now the sect of the Samaritan Simon, from whom all sorts of heresies took their origin..." and "...being called Simonians, from whom the Gnosis, falsely so-called, derives its origins, as one can learn from their own assertions."[7] Though he didn't agree with this claim, Irenaeus was reporting what he knew to be true: that Simon's followers considered him to be the first to introduce what might be the original teachings of Gnosis.

This is astounding when fully considered. According to this claim, we can infer that Simon was the first to bring forward the complex creation cosmology that is the very signature of the Gnostic system. Furthermore, as we will see, it is Simon himself who appears to play a leading role in the whole Gnostic creation story. We are now hot on the trail of this Deep Christ mystery.

If, as I indicated in Chapter 14, we look at how thorough the architects of the Roman orthodoxy were in burying the Gnostic tradition in order to promote their own theology, this begins to make sense. Simon's connection to the origins of Gnosticism may have factored into why he was purposely marginalized, obscured, and practically erased from history.

Fortunately, some of his invaluable writings managed to survive past the purges, and nearly two centuries ago, there was a most dramatic discovery. Hippolytus of Rome (170–235 CE) was an important early Christian theologian who wrote ten volumes against the Gnostics called *Refutation of All Heresies*,[8] of which only one survived. In 1842, however, with great excitement to students of early Christianity, seven more of these books were discovered at a Greek monastery on Mount Athos. In Book VI,[9] Hippolytus sought to denounce Simon by including extensive quotes from a document he believed was written by Simon, called the *Apophasis Megale*, or the *Great Revelation* (GR). Though there is no way of proving that these words came from Simon himself, it is significant that Hippolytus believed that they did. It is also significant to note that the earlier Irenaeus also wrote about Simon using phrases that correspond word for word to this *Great Revelation*.[10]

"This is the writing down of the declaration of voice and name from thought, which is the Great Power, the Boundless," begins Simon in a clear invocation of this idea of the Great Power. He is writing his revelation (gospel) from "Thought," the feminine aspect of the original trinitized expression of the Ineffable, the Holy Spirit or Higher Sophia.

His description of the first burst of creation is dense and difficult to grasp, but we might envision it like this: out of nothing (the Ineffable silence), there is a Great Emanation. This emerges in a dual fashion where there is a masculine "mind" and a feminine "thought." It is the masculine who remains in the heavenly Pleroma while the feminine extends out into creation, "giving birth to all things" (GR).

These two came together to form a third, a manifested "father" — or, in Gnostic terms, sometimes called the "Son," the Logos, the Anthropos, the Image, or divine form. Simon calls this the "Middle Distance" between the masculine "Mind" and the feminine "Thought," identified as "He Who Stands."

At this point in Simon's story, something happened that was a crisis of great significance.

Simon and Sophia

"And to this manner did the fire assume both male and female forms, the one from above and the other from below, as each did mature into perfect conformity with the Heavenly Power [the ineffable silence] whose likeness and the image they were. And when they appeared in the midst of the rushing water of the realm of becoming, the female Thought was set upon and defiled by the angels and lower powers...." (GR).

Simon is describing how Thought (the higher Sophia) descended outside of the Pleroma into "the realm of becoming," where she was captured by the "angels and lower powers." If this revelation came from Simon Magus in the 1st century, then this would have preceded the later edited version of this story, presented by the Gnostic Jesus, as documented in the *Pistis Sophia* and the *Apocryphon of John*. In this long-lost and forgotten manuscript, Simon's

Great Revelation, this may well be the first appearance of the story of the "fall" of Sophia.

Simon himself claimed to be the "Standing One," as Hippolytus affirms — a title equated with the third in the Trinity, the Christ. According to another heresiologist named Epiphanius (~310 to 403 CE), Simon appeared "under the name of Christ,"[11] who came down from the highest levels of creation, the Great Power, to rescue Sophia. To come to this dimensional location (aeon), he would have had to pass through the regions of what he called the "Left," which were controlled by what later Gnostics termed archons. To traverse down into this earthly realm into his mortal body, he disguised himself so that they wouldn't notice his true identity and block his entrance. He says that as the great horse of Troy was used to infiltrate behind enemy lines, "So did her (Thought/Sophia's) yoke-mate Mind (Christ/Logos), the male, gain entry to the realm of her captors by appearing in the likeness of their creatures as a man" (GR). These are all nearly identical claims made by the Gnostic Jesus in his *Second Treatise of the Great Seth*.

Unlike how Sophia shows up in the Gnostic system in general, Simon believed that Sophia/Thought inhabited one human bodily incarnation after another, being trapped in successive mortal bodies by the demiurge who stripped her of her divine power. One of the lives into which Sophia was incarnated, according to the *Great Revelation*, was of an orphaned girl who was found abandoned in a large city in the 1st century CE. "After these things, when her body was exchanged by the angels and powers, she was exposed in the streets of Tyre in Phoenicia as an infant, taken up by a brothel master, and raised in a brothel, where she knew no other life save that of degradation" (GR). Simon found this woman he called Helen and paid "ransom" for her freedom. Simon considered Helen of Troy to be one of the incarnations of Sophia and this might have inspired Simon to name this orphaned girl Helen. "And I sought her out," writes Simon. There are accounts in the heresiologist writings of this famous couple being traveling companions, renowned lovers, and teachers of the "heresies."

Simon's version of the incarnated Sophia might have been changed by later Gnostic variations to highlight a more archetypal divine Light being. If this is the case, then one incentive for this change might have been to downplay the controversy that surrounded Simon and Helen's royal connections, such as accounts of them appearing before the courts of Nero and Claudius.

Justin Martyr, a 2nd-century Christian theologian and the earliest heresiologist, wrote cynically of Simon's enormous popularity, where he performed "mighty acts of magic" in the city of Rome during Claudius's rule. His statement, "And nearly all the Samaritans, but few among the rest of the nations, confess him to be the first god and worship him,"[12] gives a clue to the specifics of his popularity. He wrote that Simon had a female companion, a former prostitute who Simon considered was his "first Thought."[13]

To Simon, Sophia is identified as the "lost sheep" in a metaphor that resembles Jesus's parable (Matthew 18:10-14 and Luke 15:1-7). "It is Thought who is the lost sheep of the parable and mind [*Logos*] who seeks her out at the cost of abandoning all his goods. For she passes from body to body, ever abiding in the forms of woman and ever does she hurl the powers of the world into confusion, pitting the one against the other, by reason of her superlative beauty, as of the heavens themselves" (GR). The magnitude of this divine heavenly beauty is so great that she throws the "powers (archons) of the world" into turmoil. "And she suffered every kind of indignity at their hands to prevent her reascending to her Father, even to being imprisoned in the human body and transmigrating into other female bodies, as from one vessel into another" (GR). This description of how the archons prevented her from returning to her home in the heavenly realm constitutes a primary theme of the entire *Pistis Sophia*, the longest of the surviving Gnostic texts.

Sparks of the Latent Fire

Even more significant in this Deep Christ investigation is that Simon refers to Helen's rescue as a microcosm of what he is doing to humanity. "Thus I wrought the ransoming of the human race, recalling to myself the sparks of the latent fire...." (GR).[14] Here might be one of the earliest references to the quintessential Divine Spark theme found in the proto-Gnostic tradition. What are these Simonian sparks, and what did he mean by this?

He explains in his *Great Revelation*, "Man, here below, born from blood, is the dwelling, and the Boundless Power dwells in him." Though difficult to decipher, I believe that Simon is explaining that this Great Power, which he clarifies is "fire," is both manifest and "concealed" or unmanifested. "… In the concealed side of fire may be found all that is conceived and that is intelligible, even if it surpasses the senses, or that which one is unable to conceive." In other words, the latent fire carries within it the endless possibilities of what can become manifest. These Divine Sparks are the very substance of the original Light emanation, which, perhaps like quantum stem cells, are found in latent form within us. As Simon explains, this requires a specific focus of consciousness to bring this latency into a transformational manifestation.

The Tree-Fruit Metaphor

In his *Great Revelation,* Simon presents extensive and highly obscure theology, much like a Jewish midrash interpretation of the Hebrew Bible. One of these teachings points to a great jewel of this Deep Christ mystery. He writes,

"The Fire, which is above the heavens, is the treasure-house, as it were a great Tree, like that seen by Nabuchodonosor [Nebuchadnezzar in Daniel 4:4-8] in a vision, from which all flesh is nourished. The manifested side of the Fire is the trunk, branches, leaves, and the bark surrounding it on the outside. All these parts of the great Tree are set on fire from the all-devouring flame and destroyed. But the fruit of the Tree, if its imagining has been perfected and it takes the shape of itself, is placed in the storehouse, and not cast into the Fire. For the fruit is produced to be placed in the storehouse, but the husk to be committed to the Fire; that is to say, the trunk, which is generated not for its own sake but for that of the fruit" (GR).

This metaphor seems parallel to the prince's pearl hidden in the lower world to be reclaimed. Is Simon pointing to this meta-question of what it is we are being asked to Bring Forth with dire consequences if we don't? "If he matures to perfection," then he will be "one and the same" with the Boundless Power (GR). Simon is saying that man is the dwelling for the Boundless Power, and it is this inner divine self that we are being asked to mature to perfection for this to become manifest. "…If it remains in potentiality only, and it never attains unto its proper image, then it is doomed to vanish…"

Displaying what must surely have been inspired by a Greek education,

Simon argues that this would be like failing to use one's knowledge of grammar or geometry, which results in the loss of those abilities. If the divine inner man remains only latent and not used, it will atrophy to extinction.

I believe that here, we are moving very close to the epicenter of this Novel Revelation of Divine Wisdom.

This tree and fruit analogy, allegedly passed down from the 1st century, may have preceded a similar motif that appears in the synoptic Gospels. "For now the ax is set at the root of the tree. Every tree that fails to bear good fruit is chopped down and flung in the fire" (found in both Matthew 3:10 and Luke 3:9). Here, the Gospels focus on the potential failures of the tree to produce fruit that will then fall to the ax. Might the Simonian emphasis on the fruit being imagined to perfection, which brings immunity from the ills of this mortal world, have been an earlier, more original, and frankly more theologically significant application of the tree and fruit analogy than in the later, distinctly non-Simonian version in the Gospels?[15]

The Human Simon

As a flesh and blood person in this world, little is known of Simon's origins. He may have been born in Cyprus and was, at times, referred to as "Simon the Cypriot." Other accounts say he was from Gitta in Samaria (near modern-day Nablus), which was likely a central location for his teaching in that region, at the base of the Samaritan's holy mountain, Mt. Gerizim.

Simon was highly educated and engaged in extensive esoteric studies that likely included Egyptian, Greek Eleusinian, Essene, and Jewish mysteries, as well as Persian Zoroastrian Magi and Asian sacred traditions. He did apparently use magic, which was astounding to those who witnessed it. He could have acquired these abilities in Egypt and may have even used a wand. Legends of Jesus's use of magic come to mind here, as Houston Smith discusses in his book *Jesus the Magician* (2014).

He may also have been an advanced student of John the Baptist, as is noted in the Pseudo-Clementine *Recognitions*.[16] Though this text is clearly designed to denounce Simon, there are elaborate details that may dovetail with actual historical accounts. When John the Baptist was killed by Herod out of fear that John would lead a popular uprising against the Herodians,[17] an early Gnostic and student of John's named Dositheus, claimed that Simon had been killed (a theme discussed in the Appendix) and took over John's ministry for a brief time. Soon after, upon returning from Egypt, Simon assumed this leadership position based on the merit of his superior spiritual mastery.[18]

John the Baptist introduced some of the earliest themes of 1st century gnosis, and his role in helping to spur this new Revelation of Wisdom deserves more research beyond Mead's valuable contribution to this in his book *Gnostic John the Baptizer* (2012). That Simon allegedly was the successor to John's ministry, not Jesus, is information that is hard to ignore.

Based on the *Great Revelation* as well as how he is presented in the romance texts, one can deduce that Simon showed mastery in the Greek debate method known as dialectic. For example, there are pages upon pages of discourse between Simon and Peter in the Pseudo-Clementine literature that were designed to prove that Peter's theology was superior and that Simon's views just didn't add up. It is possible that this romance literature was a reworking of some of Simon's lost writings and speeches.

Mead draws from the heresiologists to reference a book believed to have been authored by Simon called *The Four Quarters of the World*.[19] This may have had some associations with the Gnostic concepts of the Region of the Right and Left and even predated the fourfold Gospel model of Marcion. Mead quotes a rare heresiological reference. "Those traitors (the Simonians) fabricated for themselves a gospel, which they divided into four books, and called it the 'Book of the Four Angles and Points of the World.' All pursue magic zealously, and defend it, wearing red and rose-coloured threads round the neck in sign of a compact and treaty entered into with the devil their seducer."[20] This red thread reference is curiously associated with Mary Magdalene[21] and may suggest a connection between her and Simon. The idea that Simon may have authored an original collection of four gospels is something that the Christian orthodox architects must have gone to great lengths to bury.

Simon founded the first of the Gnostic sects called the Simonians. Like Irenaeus, the earliest of the heresiologists, Justin Martyr (~ 100 - 165), reported that followers of Simon, his successor Menander and also Marcion, all called themselves "Christians." Though Justin argued that this was not a true claim, reports that his students called themselves Christians in the 1st century are highly intriguing.

According to Justin Martyr, almost all Samaritans and some from other nations worshipped Simon as the "first god." Haar's analysis of pre-Lukan oral tradition is that Simon was "highly respected as a specialist in all religious matters." And "the powers of Simon [were] considered to be without peer."[22] These identifications are astonishing given that Simon was a near-exact contemporary of Jesus, who crossed paths with some of the same key players, including John the Baptist and Peter.

The Samaritans were a different Jewish sect from the Jews of Judea, and they were often at odds. The Samaritan spiritual center was Mt. Gerizim, next to today's Nablus, where they believe Moses's chosen successor, Joshua, successfully conquered this territory and built a holy temple on this sacred site. Simon may have been considered a fulfillment of the Taheb, the long-awaited Samaritan Messiah, the new Joshua/Yeshua, who returned to bring resolution to the plight of their people.

Simon and Paul

Though the relationship between Simon and St. Paul is incredibly difficult to ascertain, my sense is that Paul had a lot more of a connection with Simon than any written record attests. Ferdinand Christian Baur came to the conclusion that the two were so closely aligned that he believed Simon was a character created to obscure the deeper teachings of Paul — a thesis that scholars have since concluded is untenable. However, what might be more accurate is the possibility that the esoteric Paul was cryptically and enthusiastically trumpeting the voice of Simon.

The following description in Acts (13: 6-12) of an encounter that St. Paul had with a "magician" on the island of Cyprus can easily be seen as an obscured reference to Simon Magus, as Eisenman has postulated.[23]

"When they had gone through the whole island as far as Paphos, they met a certain magician, a Jewish false prophet, named Bar-Jesus. But he was with the proconsul, Sergius Paula, an intelligent man, who summoned Barnabas and Saul and wanted to hear the word of God. But the magician Elymas, for that is the translation of his [Bar-Jesus'] name, opposed them and tried to turn the proconsul away from the faith. But Saul, also known as Paul, filled with the Holy Spirit, looked intently at him and said, 'You son of the devil, you enemy of all righteousness, full of all deceit and villainy, will you not stop making crooked the straight paths of the Lord? And now listen—the hand of the Lord is against you, and you will be blind for a while, unable to see the sun.' Immediately mist and darkness came over him, and he went about groping for someone to lead him by the hand. When the proconsul saw what had happened, he believed, for he was astonished at the teaching about the Lord" (Acts 13: 6-12).

This is a shining example of how Acts works to contort Simon into a devilish enemy and steers the divinely inspired Paul toward being the true carrier of Christ's message. This passage is similar to the defamation of Simon during his dialogues with Peter in Acts as well as in the Pseudo-Clementine literature. That he was called "Bar-Jesus" (meaning son of Jesus) adds even more strangeness to this passage.

The theme of blindness that shows up in Acts may have been a way of contorting and even ridiculing Simon's claims in the *Great Revelation* about the Greek poet Stesichorus (c. 630–555 BC).[24] The poet famously became blind when writing harshly about the Sophianic Helen of Troy. The poet's sight was restored, however, after he wrote praises to her.

The same play on the theme of blindness might have been used by Luke in Acts in the famous account of Paul becoming blind on the road to Damascus (Acts 9: 1-19) upon his encounter with the risen Jesus. This scene might be an embellished romance version of the earlier and more likely genuine, profoundly spiritual "ascension" experience that Paul hints was his own, as Eisenman suggests. "I know a man in Christ who fourteen years ago was caught up to the third heaven. ... And I know that this man, whether in the body or apart from the body I do not know, but God knows was caught up to paradise and heard inexpressible things, things that no one is permitted to tell" (2 Corinthians 12:2–4). The *Apocalypse of Paul* (APa) found in the Nag Hammadi library may be an account of this ascension experience.

The *Acts of Peter* (AP) is designed to promote Paul and Peter over Simon and completely destroy anything associated with Simon. "There is only one God, the God of Peter" (AP). This text also presents Peter's test of Simon's true faith by having Simon prove that he can magically fly, leading to one of many accounts of his death. Haar notes that as soon as Peter comes into the picture, the degradation of Simon begins.[25]

Simon's presence in Jerusalem in the mid-first century may have placed him amidst the battle between the Jewish nationalist movement and the Roman occupiers. Like the Gnostic Jesus, Simon also had a disdain for the Jewish god YHWH, equating him with the Region of the Left. This must have put him at great odds with the Jewish leaders in Jerusalem, as well as how he was seen as a spiritual saint in the eyes of the Samaritan populations who were hated by the Judean Jews.

His close connections with Roman authorities bring even more confusion into his identity as a revered mystic. Josephus, in his Jewish Antiquities, spoke of a figure called Atomus, who, as a "Jewish Cypriot magician" is presented very much like Simon. Here, the famed spiritual leader, if this is the same person, which Eisenman believes he is, gave counsel to Antonius Felix, the Herodian governor (procurator) in Caesarea. Felix sought Simon's help in convincing Herod Agrippa II's sister Drusilla to divorce her husband so that Felix could marry her. Simon, as many legends report, may well have rubbed shoulders with the nobility of Palestine and Rome. It is difficult to fathom how this advanced spiritual adept might have been an advisor to the Judean Felix, a corrupt Roman financier famous for his insatiable appetite for taking bribes. Such is the enigma of trying to understand this man not as a mythologized savior but as a mortal, complex, and even flawed historical person.

Simon and the Heresiologists

Simon sustained an unrelenting campaign of character assassination within an extensive body of hereseological romance literature, from Pseudo-Clementine to *The Preachings of Peter*[26] (*Kerygmata Petrou*). It is apparent, for example, that descriptions of Simon engaging in ridiculous uses of magic were intermingled with his spiritual cosmology in a way that served to discredit any validity of his teachings.

In what was likely a contortion of Simon's magic, the Pseudo-Clementine *Recognitions* seemed to be making fun of his extraordinary abilities. "I shall change myself into a sheep or a goat. I shall make a beard to grow upon little boys. I shall ascend by flight into the air, I shall exhibit abundance of gold. I shall make and unmake kings. I shall be worshiped as God, I shall have divine honors publicly assigned to me, so that an image of me shall be set up, and I shall be adored as God."[27] This portrayal of him being a pompous showman with a big appetite for praise likely served to discredit any reputation he might have had as being a genuine holy man.

The *Acts of Peter and Paul*[28] presents a story that weaves what were likely some historical events with embellishments that were clearly designed to diminish Simon, raise the holy status of Peter, and bring Paul away from Simon and into Peter's camp. In a scene describing Simon, Peter, and Paul appearing before Nero, this text includes a long piece of fiction where Peter tries to prove that he knows what Nero's thoughts are, showing that Simon is unable to do so. This is a clear reduction and denouncement of Simon's concept of Thought, the Ennoia, the Light of Sophia. The text then goes on to describe Nero challenging Simon to build a great tower and show that he can fly — that ends, yet again, in Simon's death.

Scene of Simon Magus before Nero, where Peter is proven to be more holy than Simon and where Paul joins with Peter against Simon. Mural at the Palatine Chapel, Palermo, Sicily, Italy (1140–1170). Story drawn from the 5th century Acts of the Apostles Peter and Paul.

A good depiction of how Simon appears in the Pseudo-Clementine Romance literature is portrayed in an old movie called *The Silver Chalice* (1954), which is based on a 1950's New York Times bestseller by the same title. It is a terribly campy movie with scenes of Jerusalem and Nero's otherworldly palace in Rome. It is also a most notable movie not only because it was Paul Newman's first (which he later said was embarrassing) but because the story takes place during the post-crucifixion stage of early Christianity in the 1st century. What is more, the main characters in this movie are none other than Simon Magus and his consort Helen.

This movie does a good job of depicting how this enigmatic figure, Simon, was demeaned and ridiculed in the subsequent accounts of him. The script draws from a number of sources in early Christian writings, including the heresiologists and the romance literature of Clement of the 4th century and the *Acts of Peter and Paul* of the 5th century. Here, Simon is depicted as a messianic imposter and Christ wannabe.

Conclusion

This chapter has sought to provide an introduction to Simon for those who have had no idea of, let alone appreciation for, who he was. Though he may be a strange character in certain ways, I have gone to some lengths to bring a more comprehensive look at this man and his teachings to fill in the gaps in common knowledge about him. As the details of his life and teachings begin to take shape, it is impossible to overlook the uncanny resemblance he has to the Gnostic Christ. The next chapter will outline this correlation.

16

Simon Magus and the Gnostic Christ

Section III of the Deep Christ (continued)

I am circling around this 1st century drama with an open mind, holding off on making any focused conclusions, at least for now. Despite what much of the New Testament would have us believe, there are just too many questions about what happened historically and too many layers of misinformation to get a clear picture of the story of this man Jesus. That said, we are now quite deep into this mystery investigation of the Deep Christ, and the implications are profoundly unsettling.

When we strip back the false leads in this case and look past the agenda of complete character assassination perpetrated by history as written by the Christian victors, Simon Magus shows an extensive and uncanny resemblance to how Jesus is portrayed in the Gnostic gospels.

Parallels Between the Gnostic Jesus and Simon Magus

Here is an overview of the parallels between the Gnostic Jesus and Simon Magus. Both went into lengthy descriptions of the cosmology of origins (cosmogony). They both identified their higher self as "Christ," who came from the Great Power and the divine trinity of Father, Mother, and the Son. They both equated the Jewish God YHWH with the lead archon, the demiurge. They both claimed to have descended through the Region of the

Left in disguise to pass undetected by the archons. They both described how Sophia descended from the heavens, became trapped and was persecuted by the archons. They both came to this region to rescue Sophia and the Divine Spark within humans, thus seeking to save humanity from the grip of the archons.

Text References to these Parallels

The following are textual references that draw these parallels between the Gnostic Jesus and Simon Magus.

Both the Gnostic Jesus and Simon Magus:

1. Describe the cosmology of origins.

Gnostic Jesus: "The Monad is a monarchy with nothing above it. It is he who exists as God and Father of everything, the invisible One who is above everything, who exists as incorruption, which is in the pure light into which no eye can look" (AJ).

Gnostic Jesus: "And Its thinking become a thing. She appeared. She stood in Its presence in the brilliance of the light; she is the power which is before the All. It is she who appeared, she who is the perfect Pronnoia of the All, the light" (AJ).

Simon: "From the universal aeons spring two shoots, which are without beginning or ending, stemming forth from a single root, which is the invisible Power, unknowable silence. Of the two shoots, one appears from above. This is the Great Power, the Universal Mind that sets all things in order, being male. The other appears from below. It is the Great Thought, which is female and brings forth all things" (GR).

2. Claimed that they came from "The First Mystery" or the "Great Power."

Gnostic Jesus: "...he decided to have his likeness become a great power" (SJC).

Simon: "He came from the Great Power of God" (Acts 8:10). (Also referenced in Justin Martyr, Irenaeus, Hippolytus, and Epiphanius).[1]

3. Identified themselves as the Father, the Mother, and the Son.

Gnostic Jesus: "He said to me... 'I am the Father, I am the Mother, I am the Son. I am the undefiled and incorruptible one'" (AJ).

Simon: "I was manifested to the Jews as the Son, in Samaria as the Father, and among the gentiles as the Holy Spirit, and I permitted them to call me by whatever name they pleased" (GR).

4. Identified the Jewish God YHWH with the demiurge from the Region of the Left.

Gnostic Jesus: "Now the archon who is weak has three names. The first name is Yaltabaoth, the second is Saklas, and the third is Samael. And he is impious in his arrogance which is in him. For he said, 'I am God and there is no other God beside me,' for he is ignorant of his strength, the place from which he had come" (AJ).

Simon: according to the heresiologist Epiphanius, "He pretended that the [Jewish] Law is not of God but the law of the left-hand Power..."[2]

5. Descended into the Region of the Left disguised to pass by undetected by the archons.

Gnostic Jesus: "For as I came downward, no one saw me. For I was altering my shapes, changing from form to form. And therefore, when I was at [the Archon's] gates, I assumed their likeness. For I passed them by quietly, and I was viewing the places, and I was not afraid nor ashamed, for I was undefiled" (ST).

Simon: "But as the poet recounts the stratagem of the Achaians whereby they infiltrated the fastness of Troy inside a great toy horse, so did her yoke-mate Mind, the male, gain entry to the realm of her captors by appearing in the likeness of their creatures as a man. The angels who governed the world were corrupt by reason of their lust for power, and so I appeared to set things right, transforming myself and making myself like unto the dominions, principalities, and angels, so that I manifested myself as a man, though I was not really a man" (GR).

6. Describe how Sophia became trapped and was persecuted by the archons.

Gnostic Jesus: "…it was a lion-faced ruler in the chaos, of which one half is fire and the other darkness, –that is Yaldabaoth, of whom I have spoken unto you many times. When then this befell, Sophia became very greatly exhausted, and that lion-faced light-power set to work to take away from Sophia all her light-powers…" (PS:31).

Simon: "And when they appeared in the midst of the rushing water of the realm of becoming, the female Thought was set upon and defiled by the angels and lower powers who made this world of matter" (GR).[3]

7. Came to rescue Sophia.

Gnostic Jesus: "It came to pass then when Pistis Sophia had finished saying these words in the chaos, that I made the light-power, which I had sent to save her, become a light-wreath on her head" (PS:59).

Gnostic Jesus: "The (Father's) kingdom is like a shepherd who had a hundred sheep. One of them, the largest, went astray. He left the ninety-nine and looked for the one until he found it. After he had toiled, he said to the sheep, 'I love you more than the ninety-nine'" (GT, Logion 107).

Simon: "It is Thought who is the lost sheep of the parable, and Mind who seeks her out at the cost of abandoning all his goods" (GR).

Simon: he came to rescue Helen, known as First Thought, Ennoia (Sophia). (Justin Martyr, Irenaeus, Tertullian, Hippolytus, Epiphanius, Pseudo-Clementine).[4]

8. Descended to save humanity from the grip of the archons.

Gnostic Jesus: "Now I have taught you about Immortal Man and have loosed the bonds of the robbers from him" (SJC).

Simon: "The angels who governed the world were corrupt by reason of their lust for power, and so I appeared to set things right..." (GR).

9. Descended to rescue the Divine Spark within individuals.

Gnostic Jesus: "I am the Light that illumines the All. I am the Light that rejoices in my brethren, for I have come down to the world of mortals on account of the Spirit (spark) that remains in that which descended and came forth from the innocent Sophia" (TP).

Simon: "The angels who made the world issued whatever laws amused them, thinking thus to enslave all of humanity. Thus I wrought the ransoming of the human race, recalling to myself the sparks of the latent fire which the angels used to order their creation, and this must issue in the dissolution of the world, but equally in the redemption of all who believe in me" (GR).

10. Ministries lasted for years past the crucifixion.

Gnostic Jesus: "It came to pass when Jesus had risen from the dead, that he passed eleven years discoursing with his disciples..." (PS:1).

Gnostic Jesus: "For my death which they think happened, happened to them in their error and blindness, since they nailed their man unto their death" (ST).

Simon: there are Pseudo-Clementine accounts of him appearing before the royal courts of the Roman Emperors Claudius and Nero, well past the time of the crucifixion.

Conclusion

Clearly, there is a near direct correlation between Simon Magus and Jesus of the Gnostic texts. The links are undeniable. Simon and the Gnostic Jesus have distinctly similar cosmologies, an almost identical story of an intervention, and uncanny parallels in their relationships with Sophia. That Irenaeus in the 2nd century reported that Simon was known to be the founder of these traditions of gnosis and that the Simonians were the first of the Gnostic movements in the 1st century who called themselves "Christians" suggest that he was a key source of this Novel Revelation of Wisdom.

A question inevitably arises: was Simon Magus the actual personhood of Jesus as depicted in the Gnostic texts? Was it Simon who not only authored the *Great Revelation* but also a follow-up gospel, the *Second Treatise of the Great Seth*? Admittedly, I am only able to present an initial overview of a Simon-

Gnostic Jesus identity thesis which would require far more excavation from the 2000 years of misinformation surrounding this. Though the resemblance is impossible to ignore, this is an outrageous thesis given how Simon has been painted as a sort of anti-Jesus. For it to be taken seriously within fields of academic research would require an almost complete reevaluation of the roots of both Gnosticism and Christianity itself.

Short of this, in this Deep Christ mystery investigation, significant questions are raised. What is the relationship between the Simonian Gnostic Jesus and the biblical Jesus? How do we make sense of the vast difference between the two? Could it possibly be that Simon was the figure who inspired the later design of Jesus as found in the orthodox Christian tradition, as clues in this mystery thriller suggest? At least one thing is clear; the Jesus we are so familiar with, as found in the Bible, is radically different from how he appears in the Gnostic texts which raises fundamental questions about the accuracy of historical accounts of this man.

The unique theology of both Simon and the Gnostic Christ has been obscured and persecuted since its historical origins. With the resurgence of Gnostic studies in the late 1970s due to the publication of key lost texts, it is now even more apparent how this radical theology has been downplayed for centuries, contributing to the all-too-common instinct to blur the distinction between the Gnostic and the New Testament Jesus. So deeply entrenched is this demonization of both the Gnostic Jesus and Simon Magus that an immense theological and historical bulwark of protection has been built up to guard against the possibility that Jesus Christ was, first and foremost, Simonian. As Mead has documented, we must never forget that everything written about Simon comes from the "hands of bitter opponents" and, with the help of St. Peter's victorious religious model over Simon's, the vast majority of what was written was designed to obliterate this non-orthodox Christ from history to firmly establish not only the theology but the very identity of the orthodox Jesus.

At least, outlining the links between Simon Magus and the Gnostic Jesus provides a historical context to this thesis of a 1st century Novel Revelation of Wisdom. It was over a decade ago when I first began to consider that Simon Magus may have been the original source for the creation story of Sophia and the seed teachings that spurred the development of the Gnostic tradition. It gradually came into focus as a key missing piece of the puzzle, where the whole picture of the origins of Gnosticism and Christianity began to make more sense. It has been the goal of this book to present, at the very least, an introduction to what this picture might look like.

I must caution the reader against the temptation to get side-tracked and even lost in the historical intrigue around a Simonian Jesus identity, such as what has happened, for example, with the theories of Jesus's bloodline. Though I will consider some further lines of inquiry of this thesis in the Epilogue and Appendix, the real treasure found here is not in the questionable personhood of Jesus but rather in his message that provides a key to the Sophianic mysteries: the gift of our hidden potential that longs to be reawakened.

PART IV

THE DIVINE SPARK WITHIN

17

Sparks of the Hidden Light

Section I of the Divine Spark Within – *Via Positiva*

I move in everyone and I delve into them all. I walk uprightly, and those who sleep, I awaken... And I am inviting you into the exalted, perfect Light.

-   The voice of Sophia (TP)

It is a mystery; it is unrestrainable by the Incomprehensible One. It is invisible to all those who are visible in the All. It is a Light dwelling in Light. (TP)

In following the clues of this word "Sophia" through the ancient texts of gnosis, there are fleeting references to the Divine Spark motif that appear on the pages like fireflies in the night. Indeed, the holy mystery of the Divine Spark Within flickers so imperceptibly that it has gone largely unnoticed for much of human history. Though invisible to the naked eye, according to the Gnostic scriptures, these sparks are the stuff of original creation and are also found in the deepest regions of the human form.

In exploring this phenomenon of the Divine Spark Within, in these next three chapters, I will be exploring this enigma according to the four paths of Creation Spirituality. This chapter, via Positiva, highlights this Divine Spark as our birthright — something essential and inherent within what could be called our spiritual biology. We do not have to create it or earn it. Rather, we have only to find it or relax enough for it to emerge within us, though this is no easy task.

In *The Hymn of the Pearl,* the prince left his home to find the one most precious pearl guarded by a ferocious dragon. The prince was able to rescue this pearl and return to his home, where he once again received his Robe of Glory.

What does this pearl signify? It can easily be passed off as a symbol of beauty or one's life purpose, but as we work to mine the complex creation story of the Gnostic tradition, this pearl, I believe, like the Divine Spark, is nothing short of a holy mystery to be discovered.

The Gnostic Society Library is the most comprehensive and academically sound collection of online texts of the Gnostic tradition. In their *Introduction to Gnosticism and the Nag Hammadi Library,* they describe this central motif found amongst the various texts. The Gnostics called this by a number of names, including the uncreated self, "the divine seed, the pearl, the spark of knowing: consciousness, intelligence, light." What is more, this seed-spark is made of the very same substance as God. This realization that we have within us the very substance of original creation is the doorway to true freedom.[1]

The Divine Light of Christ Sophia

As spoken of by the Deep Christ, this Light theme appeared at the earliest stages of creation, including the creation of the third, the archetypal being of Light, Anthropos, the Standing One. "S/he (Barbelo, the Mother Great Emanation and the Father who Stands) begot a spark of light with a light resembling blessedness. But it does not equal his/her greatness. This was an only-begotten child of the Mother-Father which had come forth; it is the only offspring, the only-begotten one of the Father/Mother, the pure Light" (AJ). "It is a hidden Light, bearing a fruit of life, pouring forth a living water from the invisible, unpolluted, immeasurable spring, that is, the unreproducible Voice of the glory of the Mother, the glory of the offspring of God..." (TP). These two primary Gnostic texts speak of the sparks of the hidden Light, using language that has an uncanny resemblance to Simon Magus' sparks of the latent fire.

As has been outlined previously, Sophia, the female companion to the

Christ Logos, was a carrier and bringer of this Light into the outer regions. The Gnostic mythos tells of her coming into this world from the heavenly realm, the Pleroma, possibly with an intention to create "bodily dwellings" (a species?) in which these archetypal divine beings could reside. But her mission was "aborted," and her Light was captured by Yaldabaoth. Sophia became trapped in the matrix of matter. In his rescue mission, her consort, the Christ, brought this same divine Light to her, whereupon she became free from the tyranny of the archons.

As will be presented in the next chapter, this spark is the Light of Sophia within us and is there if we can only slow down enough to see it. This is a shard of what Christ calls the Great Power, and it has the potential to be life-transforming.

From the creation story as brought forth by Simon Magus, this Light is the substance of the original energy of the emanation from the source that dwells within us. "Man, here below, born from blood, is the dwelling, and the Boundless Power dwells in him, and it is the Universal Root" (GR). Simon is saying that our mortal bodies are the dwelling for the most fundamental "root" or source energy of All That Is.

Simon spoke of his coming to rescue humanity from the oppression of the "angels" (archons). His reference to reclaiming the "sparks of the latent fire" points to a glorious theme that equates to the Luriac Kabbalist concept of Tikkun, the regathering of the sparks. This is a process of repair within the spiritual dimensions of matter, where both these sparks of Sophia, as well as the divine potentials of our souls, can be restored.

I want to be clear about this pair, Light and matter. Typically, this tradition of gnosis is passed off as "dualistic" with references to a higher and lower God, the body viewed as being wholly inferior, and the indelible split between spirit and matter. However, I believe that this is an unfortunate reduction of some of this esoteric system's profound teachings. This is not about "escaping" material reality or ascending out of the hardship of being in a body. Rather, from all that I can gather, it is our task to bring heaven to Earth, to awaken this Divine Spark here and now, within our bodies, within this moment, within this world. From this place, we can then reach to the heavens.

The Divine Spark Within: Metaphor or Real

Like many parts of this Sophia Christ story, the lines between archetypal expression and concrete reality are often blurred. Is this Divine Spark a real phenomenon within the human form, or is it simply a metaphor?

Like the word "soul," the inner spark is sometimes referred to, in general terms, as the creative impulse, a burst of inspiration, or unbridled artistry. The archetypal mythologist Michael Meade (2018) and Jungian psychoanalyst, Donald Kalsched (2013) both invoke this metaphor of the Divine Spark to mean something so fundamental to our personhood though it is largely intangible. It represents a fire of passion deep within us, a "birthright" associated with our seed self, our inner child. It represents our potential that is there from our beginnings and can be distilled down to one key concept: the light of the mysterious center of our being which equates with the concept of our soul.[2]

Meade seems to use the term "Divine Spark" both metaphorically and literally. Similarly, instead of seeing the spark as either a symbol or physical reality, I prefer to see it as a combination of the two. As I will now explore, this spark motif points to the energy of creative inspiration that is part of a greater process of reclaiming our more original divine nature.

The Divine Spark in the Esoteric Wisdom Traditions

In the medieval Jewish Kabbalah of Isaac Luria, Shekinah is a type of code word that refers to a similar type of divine indwelling presence. Though this word appears often in the older, more traditional Hebrew Torah, according to Scholem (1991), it was only later that it became identified with an inner divine radiance that was specifically feminine.[3] This is the Light that emanates from the Ein Soph which is immanent within the very fabric of our being. In the Kabbalah's model of the Tree of Life, the Sephiroth, this Holy Light is indwelling in the farthest extensions of the divine emanation, called Malkuth, associated with the material world. This Shekinah, like Sophia, is both the high Light of the Holy Spirit and the younger, the daughter, who has come into this world as radiance from the distant Source.

As we will explore, the knowledge or gnosis of this inner Light has been shrouded from us, either out of our own ignorance or because it was deliberately deflected from our awareness by the lower gods, much like how the Light of Sophia was kept from her. Indeed, the reclamation of our inner spark is one of the great acts of liberation and one which can become more available to us as this puzzle of our own latent power comes closer to being solved. In Chapter 21, I will be presenting a specific meditation process called the Bridal Chamber that works with the phenomenon of this Divine Inner Light.

The idea of a great seed of Light is not only found in the Gnostic and Jewish mystical traditions but is found across many esoteric systems. There is an extremely rare Chinese alchemical text discovered by Richard Wilhelm called *The Secret of the Golden Flower* (1962). This text became the firm ground that Carl Jung landed on after crossing the treacherous psychological waters following his break with Freud. This little book is a rare window into this mystery of the awakening of our inner spark. "The Golden Flower is the light. What colour is the light? One uses the Golden Flower as a symbol. It is the true energy of the transcendent great One."[4] Contrary to the natural impulse to look outside of ourselves for solutions, this text gives a very specific technique on how a meditator can work to cultivate the inner Light that fosters the differentiation of our body of Light from our physical being. This is the ultimate fulfillment and expression of the small spark.

Henry Corbin delves extensively into this theme in his book *The Man of Light in Iranian Sufism* (1994). This is a thrilling investigation that offers even more insight into these Gnostic and Simonian themes as they weave through Persian Sufi mystical writings.

In medieval alchemy, which was so rigorously investigated by Carl Jung, the motif of the philosopher's stone is another reference to this ultimate inner potential. It also corresponds to the theme of the holy grail, the sacred vessel, the carrier of the divine energy that is suggested in the Arthurian legends.

In a more contemporary reference, this spark is known as *The Sophia Code* (Kaia Ra, 2016). This book works on many human and spiritual levels, bringing fresh insight to the nuance of how this code works in us. Through this Sophianic seed, we can reclaim our truer original nature, as Sophia had intended for us from the beginning. Indeed, the "Divine Spark Within" is a ubiquitous subject and metaphor found within innumerable spiritual traditions.

This Divine Seed of Original Light Embodied Within

How do we come into synchrony with this inner potential? How might we dial the focus of our consciousness to this subtle, invisible, yet unfathomable energy? This appears to be the main task of the Sophianic process.

According to the story I will share in the next chapter, Sophia planted this light inside of us, we humans, at our inception. This seed is of such high energy that the archonic overseers of this world, some say, fear it more than anything else, as they themselves do not have this gift. Much to their advantage, we continue to be docile and disempowered as we are subsumed within their control system, and this divine seed within remains largely inactive.

It is a key challenge to identify within ourselves that which shrouds us from our inner spark. Many emotional and mental processes of self-preservation act to shield us from this deeper core of ourselves which thus protects us from further trauma. In my work as a psychotherapist and in my personal healing work, I have become more aware of emotional, mental, psychological, and somatic constrictions that are rooted in coping strategies developed earlier in life in response to a harsh outer world. As Kalshed (2013) describes, it is the ingenious ability of the psyche, in the face of traumatic experiences, to create ways of preserving what he calls the innocent core and our inner spark. The psyche will initiate spiritual processes that serve to protect this core Self at least until the traumatic impact of a disconnection with this embodied seed self can once again be restored.

Formed earlier in life, it is possible for us to unhook ourselves from these internal barriers, especially as we become aware of a whole other emotional neural network of consciousness lying outside of this system of tension and defensiveness.[5] As we increasingly bring our attention to the immensely solid and powerful core of our being, this Pearl Self, in time, gains more traction in our consciousness, and the whole system of emotional and mental defense patterns can slip away.

The Deep Christ said that if we don't bring forth what is within us, what we don't bring forth will destroy us. This is an inner fire that smolders within us in its latency, that needs to come alive. Instead, we fill the void with mimics of this true inner inspiration. Addictions, regrets, and endless distractions keep the air of our spirit from blowing on our inner spark, causing smoke but no fire. Indeed, the inability to bring to fulfillment our soul essence into this world is a significant cause of human disease and even death, as St. Thomas's quote forewarned.

This un-constricted inner fire of passion that is our birthright is the central theme and most important boon of the whole epic drama of Christ Sophia. Like the Simonian fruit on the ephemeral Tree, this is our heritage to claim, if only we are able to imagine it into perfection. Sophia has sent forth her children and is now waiting for our return. May we calm ourselves enough to allow for this spark to be experienced, and may our hearts awaken to new levels of radiant joy.

Prelude to the Next Act of the Mystery Play

At this point in the Sophianic Mystery Play, there is an extensive Act which features the story of Adam, Eve, and the demiurge. This complex version of the story is rarely told, being so different from the common tale found in the Book of Genesis. The few times that I presented a bardic rendition of the creation story of Sophia, I would get to this strange Gnostic version of Adam and Eve and find that there was little attention span left in the audience after having already gone through the complex tale of Sophia. But the more I work with this material, the more I find that this part of the story is key to what matters most to us, to who we are, and what our potential may be.

18

Adam and the Sophianic Eve:

The Creation of Humans and the Planting of the Divine Spark Within

Section II of the Divine Spark Within

Via Negativa

Introduction to the Gnostic Story of Adam and Eve

The biblical version of the story of Adam and Eve, commonly portrayed in the mystery plays of medieval Europe, is one of the most familiar tales in the Old Testament. However, beginning around the 1st and 2nd centuries CE, long after the Genesis story was locked into the Hebrew Bible, a very different version of this story began to appear from the tradition generally known as Gnostic. This is the story of the fall of the divine-human form into the matrix of this material world. What is more, a gift, planted into us at our inception, is known as the Divine Spark Within.

This version of the tale is little known and it is difficult to extract a coherent narrative from the spare fragments that survived from the time of the Gnostics. I believe this story has important links with this man I call the Deep Christ. In the *Second Treatise of the Great Seth*, a text that seems closely related to Simon Magus's *Great Revelation*, it is written, "For Adam was a laughingstock, since he was made a counterfeit type of man by the Hebdomad (archons of the lower seven aeons), as if he had become stronger than I and my brothers. We are innocent with respect to him, since we have not sinned" (ST). This is a glimpse of the Deep Christ's contention that, with both his and Sophia's intervention, humans are undergoing an upgrade from the initial experiment of the creation of Adam and Eve.

Simon Magus and the Story of Adam and Eve

Simon Magus speaks of the creation of man in his *Great Revelation*. He does not talk about Eve having sinned and causing the downfall of humans, nor does he speak of God's instructions for them not to eat from the Tree of Knowledge of Good and Evil. Rather, he analyzes the first five books of the Hebrew Bible in a way that deciphers a broader cosmology, one that extends beyond the "angels" who created the world. Like the analogy of the fruit, he writes how the "merest spark" is there from our earliest beginnings as an embryo in utero and that it "will increase to mature protection and expand till it becomes an infinite power, immutable, equal in power and alike in form to the Immutable Aeon…" (GR).

Simon spoke of how the "angels" (archons) used the spark of divine "Thought" (the higher Sophia) in the creation of man and that it was his mission to reclaim this world from their grip, a prophetic vision in some future time that he calls the "dissolution of the world" (GR).

I suspect that the Gnostic versions of the creation story of Adam and Eve are later versions of those presented by Simon Magus. Because so little remains from Simon's original writings, this link between Simon and the Gnostic tales of Adam and Eve requires greater deductive exploration. I will therefore present a rendition of the story of Adam and Eve as derived more from the Gnostic texts, especially the earliest Sethian texts such as the *Apocryphon of John*.

A Review of the Christ Sophia Story

As this story rides the edge between archetypal myth and history, it helps to review the first sections of the Sophia mystery drama as described in Chapters 8, 9, and 11. According to the Gnostic mythos presented in those chapters, Sophia "fell" from the Pleroma, the heavenly realm. The lead archon, called Yaldabaoth stole Sophia's divine Light and imprisoned her in our local dimensional world of matter. Prior to the advent of Adam and Eve, Christ underwent a descent from his place in the Pleroma, where he rescued Sophia and raised her safely out of reach of the tormenting archons.

I find it helpful to entertain this tale of human origins through the lens of archetypes. Because these supposed events all took place outside the limited framework of our third-dimensional space and time, it is best to read this with an open-ended mythological lens. This is not to say that these events are mere myths with no historical basis; rather, they point to phenomena of creation that are impossible to grasp according to a logical timeline. This is especially helpful when considering what appears to be Christ's rescue of Sophia having taken place before the creation of Adam and Eve.

As described in the *Second Treatise of the Great Seth* (ST), Sophia and what are called the "sons of light" had intended to seed a divine luminous being into this realm, but their project went awry. Yaldabaoth and his legion of archons then strutted around as overlords to this world, showing off the stolen Light of Sophia, which they were unable to upload into their own dark and nefarious bodies. The failure of the original Sophianic plan to plant the divine Anthropos (Greek for human template) into this quadrant of the Universe resulted in a Plan B to infuse the Divine Spark into Adam, which was initiated by Sophia from her perch in the 9th heaven.

The Mystery Play now continues.

The Creation of Humans

1. Seen in the Waters

The Gnostic text called the *Hypostasis (Reality) of the Archons* (HA) includes important Sethian Gnostic elements, including the creation of Adam.[1] It begins by referencing St. Paul (as quoted in Ephesians), who said, "Our contest is not against flesh and blood; rather, the authorities of the universe and the spirits of wickedness."[2] This text reads as if being delivered by a teacher who is clarifying questions about this enigma of the archons. It is therefore likely a synthesis of prior texts that may have included the *Secret Book of John*.

"A veil exists between the world above and the realms that are below" (HA). This boundary is also identified as "the waters." "As incorruptibility looked down into the region of the waters, her image appeared in the waters; and the authorities of the darkness became enamored of her" (HA).

Remember that Sophia is sitting in the 9th heaven, not having been fully restored to her original place in the Pleroma but safely out of the reach of the archons, while she waits for her full return to her original place in this heavenly realm.

Yaldabaoth was outside of the Pleroma. He did not know of the existence of the Ineffable monad, which in the Valentinian tradition is called the Deep. Yaldabaoth could not see the distant, dark face of the Deep. Meanwhile, Thought/Pronnoia, the higher Sophia, looked through this window of the waters at the tragedy of this failed seeding.

The more common version of this story is found in the first lines of the Bible: "In the beginning, God created the heaven and the earth. And the earth was without form, and void; and darkness was upon the face of the deep. And the Spirit of God moved upon the face of the waters" (Genesis 1:1-2).

A case can be made that the Gnostic version of the tale offers a more detailed account of the creation story as seen from outside the lower regions and includes greater complexity and specificity to these themes of "spirit," "darkness," and "the Deep." We will likely never know whether the version in Genesis is simply presenting a more limited view of this or even whether this Old Testament text was presenting a cosmology as seen from the perspective of the demiurge.

The Holy Spirit of God is here equated with the Epinoia, the Sophianic divine Light of creation, who seems to have projected the image of her divine creation in the waters as seen from below. "And of the waters which are above matter, the underside was illuminated by the appearance of his image which had been revealed. And when all the authorities and the chief archon looked, they saw the whole region of the underside which was illuminated. And through the light they saw the form of the image in the water" (AJ).

Yaldabaoth saw the image of Adamas or Geradamas, the divine-human template, the Anthropos. This may well have been what Sophia had originally intended to bring to this lower region, a being who was created in the image of the Ineffable-Ein Soph. Instead, upon seeing this, it was the *demiurge* who then decided to create a man in *that* image.[3]

2.   The Creator Gods (Archons) Made Man in that Image

In the *Apocryphon of John*, the Gnostic Jesus recalled the lead archon, Yaldabaoth's declaration, "Come, let us create a man according to the image of God and according to our likeness, that his image may become a light for us" (AJ).

And so, he created angels (archons) to help him, and, perhaps in an oddly simplified description, the many "creator gods" took part in the formation of this being called Adam. One created a left foot, another made the brain, and one created the chest until Adam was gradually assembled (AJ). But he was not alive. He was just a body, a dead corpse. There was nothing alive in him.

3.   Sophia's Light Was Breathed into Adam, and He Became a Luminous Being

Sophia requested help from the First Mystery to trick Yaldabaoth into blowing her stolen light into Adam. And so, these non-archonic angelic beings that were sent down to him, "Said to Yaltabaoth, 'Blow into his face something of your spirit and his body will arise.' And he blew into his face the spirit which is the power of his mother; he did not know (this), for he exists in ignorance. And the power of the mother went out of Yaltabaoth into the natural body, which they had fashioned after the image of the one who exists from the beginning. The body moved and gained strength, and it was luminous" (AJ).

Yaldabaoth was tricked into blowing the Divine Spark into Adam. When this happened, he not only became alive, he became a luminous being. The Hebrew Bible is less specific about this: "Then the Lord God formed a man from the dust of the ground and breathed into his nostrils the breath of life, and the man became a living being" (Genesis 2:7).

All of this sounds like mythology describing the fanciful work of the gods. To even consider this as real is to stand with some Christians who throw their full faith behind the literal tale of Adam and Eve. Or maybe it suggests the idea of "intelligent design," where there was some knowing hand behind the creation of our species that was not just the haphazard result of Darwin's natural selection. This begs the question: what if there were (and even are) higher dimensional beings who were vastly superior to us in their evolution and who had the ability to work with the very building blocks of life itself: DNA? This is one way in which the Gnostic creation story is valuable. In attempting to describe a vast cosmological sweep of historical events, it ingeniously does so as a creation story which can more easily be fathomed without getting too caught up in the scientific proof or otherworldly strangeness of what is being presented.

Getting back to the story, it is at this point where things start to go really badly for this new being, Adam. He was a luminous being with a quality of Light that the creator gods did not have themselves.

4.   The Archons became Jealous of Adam

"And in that moment the rest of the powers became jealous, because he had come into being through all of them and they had given their power to the man, and his intelligence was greater than that of those who had made him and greater than that of the chief archon. And when they recognized that he was luminous, and that he could think better than they, and that he was free from wickedness, they took him and threw him into the lowest region of all matter" (AJ).

5.   Adam Undergoes a Second Modeling that Shrouds his Luminosity

As this Adam was a luminous being, Yaldabaoth could only see him by his shadow. They brought Adam out of the "shadow of death," so that he could then be molded out of the material elements, a creation process which was wrought with ignorance and greed. The brigands remodeled the body with the sinew of forgetfulness. And he became a living human being.[4]

6.   Sophianic Eve

At this point in the story, Eve was seen in an opposite way from how she is depicted in Genesis. Eve was sent by Sophia to remind Adam of the luminous essence that the archons were trying to hide from him. Instead of

Eve being the cause of Adam's downfall, she was identified as Sophia's daughter, who was sent to be an ally to Adam to help him understand how he had descended from divinity but whose physical body had been formed by a jealous god. "And he (the First Mystery) sent, through his beneficent Spirit and his great mercy, a helper to Adam, luminous Epinoia which comes out of him, who is called Life (Zoe)" (AJ).

Delivered from inside Adam *is* the Divine Spark, the indwelling Eve, called the Luminous Epinoia. She was sent from Sophia to be planted within him so that he might remember the true divine nature that had been originally blown into him when he was first created. The demiurge only pulled a mere physical shadow of this luminous Epinoia spark out of Adam (fashioned from his rib, according to Genesis 2:21-22) as "god" was not able to grasp this light essence. This is the mortal Eve, who, like Adam, in her physical body, is a mere echo of her true luminous self. The *Apocryphon of John* describes this in more detail:

"Then the Epinoia of the light hid herself in him (Adam). And the chief archon wanted to bring her out of his rib. But the Epinoia of the light cannot be grasped. Although darkness pursued her, it did not catch her. And he (Yaldabaoth) brought a part of his power out of him (Adam). And he made another creature, in the form of a woman, according to the likeness of the Epinoia which had appeared to him. And he brought the part which he had taken from the power of the man into the female creature, and not as Moses said, 'his rib-bone.' And he (Adam) saw the woman beside him. And in that moment the luminous Epinoia appeared, and she lifted the veil which lay over his mind. And he became sober from the drunkenness of darkness. And he recognized his counter-image" (AJ). As we shall see, this flips the biblical story of Adam and Eve in the garden on its head.

7. The Female Divine Spark, Epinoia, Appeared as the Snake Who Instructed Eve

Adam and Eve were in the lower regions of matter whereupon the "female spiritual principle" (HA), the luminous Epinoia appeared to them as an instructor in the form of a snake. In contrast to the portrayal of the snake as a seducer in Genesis (3:13), Eve knew that "god" the demiurge told her not to eat the fruits of this tree because of his jealousy. This female principle of light (the snake) urged Eve to eat from this Tree of Knowledge so that she would become awake to the difference between archonic enslavement and acting according to the impulse of the luminescent spark within. Upon this instruction, Eve shared this with Adam, and they both then became sober to the reality that had been thrust upon them: that they were spiritual beings who had become bound within dense material bodies, naked as animals, stripped of their divinity.

This sculpted image from Notre Dame Paris may be cryptically depicting this unusual Gnostic narrative of the (possibly cunning but) compassionate "female spiritual principle" (HA), the Epinoia, who, in the guise of the snake, encouraged Eve to eat the fruit that revealed their true divine nature.

When Yaldabaoth learned that they had thus become aware of their divine nature that was more advanced than his own, he threw them out of the garden and into the lower regions of material reality. "...They threw mankind into great distraction and into a life of toil, so that their mankind might be occupied by worldly affairs, and might not have the opportunity of being devoted to the holy spirit" (HA).

This reinterpretation of the creation story in Genesis is highly significant with regard to how the Gnostic model sees "God" as Yaldabaoth, which then makes the Genesis story more understandable with regard to his jealousy and anger toward the First Couple. It is also profoundly ironic that Eve and all of womankind have been blamed for, what Augustine interpreted as, humanity's "Original Sin." Instead, according to this Gnostic tradition, Eve was a heroic emissary of Sophia, having been sent to help Adam in the face of the tragedy of the loss of his divine luminescent form.

8. Cain and Abel

Though this seems to be an outrageous claim, it is clearly stated in this Gnostic version of the story that Eve was "seduced" (or raped?) by Yaldabaoth, which resulted in the birth of her first two famed offspring. "And the chief archon seduced her and he begot in her two sons" (AJ). As is laid out in the Book of Genesis, Cain eventually seized upon Abel, killing him.

9. Adam and Eve Give Birth to Seth, the Carrier of the Divine Spark into Humanity

After Abel was killed, Adam and Eve gave birth to Seth, their first offspring, who then escaped the direct hand of archonic molding to which Adam had been subjected. This figure Seth is a most significant character in the Mystery Play as he is the one who carries the message, the Divine Spark itself, into history as it unfolded from the time of Adam and Eve.[5] He is like Neo in the movie, *The Matrix* (1999), who holds a key to human transformation but moves onto the streets of this world in a way where he is of the people without losing his spiritual power.

There are a number of texts that are either attributed to Seth or are in praise of Seth. *The Revelation of Adam* (RA) is an extensive end-of-life message that Adam delivers to his son Seth. The text *Allogenes* (Allo), meaning "stranger," is thought to be a text presented by Seth, the stranger in a strange land, to his son, Messos. There are allegedly three stone tablets that are reported to have been written by Seth himself, described in the *Three Steles of Seth* (TSS), in praise of 1) the Holy Pronnoia (Higher Sophia), 2) his father Adam, and 3) the "pre-existent one," the Ineffable monad.[76]

What is more, multiple references suggest that Jesus himself was an incarnation of this figure Seth. Others suggest that Seth, being the Son of Adam or the Son of Man, was part of the higher consciousness that spoke through the man Jesus.

10. Eve Gives Birth to Norea, the One Who Expressed Holy Anger in Response to the Tyranny of the Archons

Despite how prominent Seth is in the whole Gnostic creation story, it is astounding that in the last section of the *Hypostasis (Reality) of the Rulers* (HA), Seth is eclipsed by his sister, the daughter of Adam and Eve, called Norea, who courageously stood up against the archons. In this text, the demiurge did not like Norea's youthful free will and said to her, "You must render service to us (as did) also your mother Eve." The text continues. "But Norea turned with the might of ... (the next phrase is broken off in the text, darn!) and in a loud voice she cried out to the holy, the god of the entirety, 'Rescue me from the rulers of injustice and save me from their clutches - immediately!'" (HA).[7]

The power and conviction of her holy anger must have reached the heavens because one of the four primary angels known as Eleleth, "Who stands in the presence of the holy spirit," came to Norea: "I have been sent to speak with you and save you from the grasp of the lawless. And I shall teach you about your root... And these authorities cannot defile you and that generation; for your abode is in incorruptibility, where the virgin spirit dwells, who is superior to the authorities of chaos and to their universe" (HA). Here, a high angel is telling Norea that she is immune from the tyranny of the "lawless" ones because her human form contains a Divine Spark, here called the virgin spirit, which has powers greater than those of the archons.

Norea appears like an embodiment of Sophia, who is in this world and refuses to comply with the rule of the archons. Perhaps Eleleth's answer to her cry is a prophetic preview of times to come when these tyrannical overlords will one day be ushered off the world stage so that the originally intended seeded beings of Light can truly be made manifest.

Conclusion

This rendition of the origins of man is complex and profound. If the more familiar Genesis version of this story is portrayed through the eyes of the demiurge, as the Gnostics and even Simon seem to suggest, then this version may offer a glimpse of our heritage from outside the encompassing archonic world. At least, the view that we are bound within a God universe that is less than altruistic is perhaps one of the great messages from this Sophianic Deep Christ New Revelation.

Though she is a lead character in this mystery play, I hesitate to present artistic depictions of Sophia as she is beyond form in many ways. However, this image, from a 16th century Dutch Anabaptist mystic named David Joris (1501 – 1556) encapsulates the greater themes of the Sophianic Eve. Here, in graphic depictions, she emerges from a higher dimensional field of Light into this material reality, where the archonic death program is tamed and overcome.

Sophianic Eve image by David Joris from his "Wonder Boeck" (1542, 1551).

A key to this Gnostic story of Adam is that Sophia was responsible for the latent Divine Spark being planted into him and hence, into us, the Adamic species. This meta-view of our origins can help lift humanity up "by our own bootstraps," so to speak, by awakening this indwelling divine Light, rather than forever beseeching relief from (and losing our power to) an external authority. In this way, the Gnostic Christ calls Adam a "laughingstock" (ST), a failed initial creation to which the Christ came as a new Adam to help us reclaim our true nature.

In many of the early icons and paintings of Christ, he is holding up two fingers. This is often interpreted as being a sign of a teacher or as him giving a blessing. However, as Tabor[8] has indicated, according to St. Paul, Christ came to correct the failure of the first Adamic man and introduce to humanity the "new spiritual body" that we were unable to put on at the time of Adam.[9] Hence, as indicated by his two-fingered sign, Christ is the second Adam, the new human form which was originally intended for us.

Salvator Mundi, attributed to Leonardo Da Vinci (c. 1500).

With this, maybe our task is not so much to simply pray to God for salvation but rather, like Norea, refuse to stay bound within the sophisticated multidimensional confines of the archonic control system and recover the seed spark of our higher nature.

19

Retaining the Childlike Spark – My Story

Section III of the Divine Spark Within

Via Creativa

As has been explored thus far, one interpretation of how Christianity eventually took shape was that it developed as a regimented orthodoxy that pushed aside this theme of the Sophianic spark within. Instead of encouraging us to stay rooted in this inner fire in the pursuit of gnosis, it established the church and the priest as intermediaries which became the authority over the subtle alchemy of our spiritual process. But this investigation into Sophia and the Deep Christ shows something different. If we are to take seriously how we humans, as offspring of Adam, Eve, Seth, and Norea, were planted with the Sophianic Light, then we are tasked with taking on the enormous responsibility of being creative, self-emanating beings.

This overview of the spirituality of gnosis found in these pages is best approached by a seeker who enters it through the portal of his or her own experience. Especially when it comes to the enigma of the latent spark, it is through the nuance of our own highly specific inner process where this can be accessed. No priest nor guru has the goods on this one. Rather, it is you, it is me, it is each individual who holds the key to the precision of consciousness that can rescue our inner pearl from the sleeping dragon. A plant's flowering comes from its own roots, and so, following the thread of one's subjective historical predisposition is ultimately how these mysteries can come to fruition. In this way, I would like to share how this Christ Sophianic mythos has been working in my own life.

My Story

I must admit that I have not experienced many knee-dropping or eye-popping revelations in my life, and I am quite ordinary in this way. However, I have regularly experienced inspiration, insight, and profound experiences of open awareness. These have been invaluable in my process of living a life of depth and meaning. One doesn't need to have profound awakening experiences to court this inner fire but rather merely follow the twists and turns of one's inner sense. And so, I share this story of my traversing these mysteries in my quest to bring it forth.

It was during my 60th year that the elements of this book were largely crafted. This writing project is the outgrowth of a long trajectory of Sophia and her Epinoia moving through me. Years before I became aware of the Gnostic creation story, the very name Sophia brought me a strange sort of guidance. When I was 18 and in the throes of a life crisis of meaning and direction, I entered what became a unique and highly personal doorway into the mysteries of Sophia. But the ground had been set long before that. It all started when I was a child.

The Childlike Inner Spark: Via Positiva

"I suspect that a child plucks its first flower with an insight into its beauty and a significance which the subsequent botanist never attains" - Henry David Thoreau.

As a child, I was intimately in touch with this inner fire, experiencing full-body ecstasy and profound levels of excitement that came with the smells of the seasons and the immensity of the world around me. There was an aliveness and a reaching curiosity that was not held back by self-consciousness. They say play is the language of children, and I was fortunate to have an abundance of it growing up. Diving to catch the ball, crashing down the snow mound as a fallen soldier, tackling my friends in play, and running with sheer delight were all hints or maybe premonitions of this obscure inner spark. My life was not yet clouded by the filter and psychological defense of thought, much less anxiety and shame.

Before its descent into the complexity of adulthood, the child-self carries an unfiltered rawness of this latent fire. Though this might seem cliché, we only have to take in the sounds of an elementary school playground that is filled with unrestrained yelps of passion and delight to sense its reality. There is an evident purity and immediacy in children's aliveness, in their uninhibited play.

That said, I am not promoting an unreal fantasy of a magical child-land. I had the good fortune to have worked as a psychotherapist with three- and four-year-old children in preschool class settings.[1] I often observed huge swings of emotions and many behavioral challenges in a room filled with kids with varying degrees of impulse control and home challenges. But still, the rawness, authenticity, and genuine desire expressed so often in these little people is more the rule than the exception.

As Joseph Chilton Pearce (1977) claimed in his book *Magical Child*, a child's squeal of delight is connected to the impulse or intent that moves out into the world with a highly personal curiosity. In many ways, this is obvious and also clearly evident in most young animals that display an exuberance typically less seen in adulthood. The uninhibited experience of joy that comes so often in little children is evidence of this soul fire that kindles within. At least, this is what I was aware of at a time when I still had a foot in the child's world.

The Descent of the Childlike Spark: Via Negativa

The natural feelings of joy I felt as a child seemed to hit a wall at the transitional stage of puberty. At age 12, I found myself being thrust into a more impersonal school system and peer culture, where the childlike *esprit* was becoming more complicated. This was not the time for uninhibited play. School and life, in general, were getting more serious.

This is not easy to unpack as we are certainly developmentally and biologically programmed to eventually set aside childish ways. I am aware of the risks of this line of thinking being used to justify a shallow way of staying in a dreamy childlike state to avoid the demands and responsibilities of being an adult. However, I am convinced that this inner pearl, the uninhibited awe that is hard-wired to play, dance, and otherwise riff off the creative improvisations found in nature, need not be outgrown or sacrificed in the name of maturity.

Over time, I became increasingly aware that this adolescent transition was a developmental crux through which my original exuberance was becoming more clouded. Thick layers of socialization and identity contortions seemed to be building up around me, causing this childlike inspiration to grow fainter. During my late adolescence, this impulse of innocence became my reference point to what I eventually understood was an expression, if not just a hint, of this inner spark.

Even worse than the systemic prejudice against women in a patriarchal culture is the manner in which the thoughts and feelings of children, being at the bottom of the social pecking order, are readily dismissed. As a psychotherapist, most of the adults I see present mental and emotional afflictions that relate back to a mal-attuned parental or social environment that has caused some form of psycho-emotional injury during the most sensitive stages of childhood. In adolescence, struggles in relationships with parents, peer groups, and schools can also be intensely taxing on this childhood spark.

Amidst the confusion of my high school years, I read a poem that affected me profoundly.

Crushed

He always wanted to explain things.
But no one cared.
So he drew.
Sometimes he would draw and it wasn't anything.
He wanted to carve it in stone or write it in the sky.
And it would be only him and the sky
And the things inside him that needed saying.
And it was after that he drew the picture.
It was a beautiful picture.
He kept it under his pillow and would let no one see it.

And he would look at it every night and think about it.

And when it was dark, and his eyes were closed, he could still see it.

And it was all of him.

And he loved it.

When he started school he brought it with him.

Not to show anyone, but just to have it with him like a friend.

It was funny about school.

He sat in a square, brown desk

Like all the other square, brown desks

and he thought it should be red.

And his room was a square, brown room, like all the other rooms.

And it was tight and close.

And stiff.

He hated to hold the pencil and chalk,

With his arm stiff and his feet flat on the floor.

Stiff.

With the teacher watching and watching.

The teacher came and spoke to him.

She told him to wear a tie like all other boys.

He said he didn't like them

And she said it didn't matter.

After that they drew

And he drew yellow and it was the way he felt about morning.

And it was beautiful.

The teacher came and smiled at him

"What's this?" she said. "Why don't you draw something like Ken's drawing?"

"Isn't that beautiful."

After that his mother bought him a tie.

And he always drew airplanes and rocket ships like everyone else.

And he threw the old picture away.

And when he lay alone looking at the sky,

It was big and blue and all of everything.

But he wasn't anymore.

He was square inside

And brown,

And his hands were stiff,

And he was like everyone else.
And the things inside him that needed saying didn't need it anymore.
It had stopped pushing.
It was crushed.
Stiff.
Like everything else.

(This poem was written by a high school senior. Two weeks after handing it in, he committed suicide).[2]

I remember shedding tears over this poem, not only for the tragedy of its author but because it was foreshadowing what my life could become if I didn't protect against these square, crushing, brown erasures of my own unique personhood.

Carrying the Spark into Adolescence: Via Creativa

I was increasingly aware of what my inner child life force was facing, both in my effort to tend to it and also in guarding against the forces that might consciously or unconsciously trample over it. In my senior year in high school, I started an "underground newspaper" that featured articles related to youth rights and served as an outlet for my increasing internal crisis. This triggered a months-long legal battle between our editorial staff and the local school committee to defend our first amendment right to distribute our "unauthorized" paper on school grounds.

With the wonderful help of the ACLU, we were ultimately victorious. However, the school adopted an extensive student publication distribution policy that had previously been ironed out in the courts, exposing what I saw as an underlying architecture of control that was an invisible and unrelenting foundation to the whole educational system. This became the strategy by which the school system was able to allow "free speech" while at the same time ensuring that wayward students were kept in line. Though I was aware of what the School Committee had to juggle, I nevertheless saw their policy as a final insult against the intent of our publication to champion the creative inquiry and expressions of youth. To me, this was just one of the many personal battlefronts of my non-school-sanctioned expressions of creativity that were desperately trying to keep that inner flame from becoming snuffed out. In our final issue of the paper, we quoted a great advocate of children's rights, A. S. Neil, in his book *Summerhill* (1960): "New generations must grow in freedom. A bestowal of freedom is a bestowal of love. And only love will save the world."[3]

So, when I was finally able to get temporary relief from what could be called the initiatory stage of adolescence, I stumbled out of high school, dazed and emotionally exhausted. Putting off college for a year, in 1978, I went on a sort of walkabout, where I finally had the time, space, and freedom to try to grapple with how my personal consciousness and individual deep self might keep its inner fire alive.[4]

As a child, Carl Jung (1989) had a secret pencil box that he kept hidden in his attic, containing a cloaked manikin carved from a wooden ruler that had numinous significance to him, though to anyone else, it might look like just a silly figure. I, too, had my coveted special thing; though, in my case, it was not a box but a simple name. I felt like I had to define what I was wrangling with before it all faded from conscious awareness. The name became like a seal of my commitment to stay connected to my childlike inner flame. I called it the Sophia Project.

The Sophia Project

Throughout my young adulthood, the Sophia Project was personal and very private. I had few associations with the name Sophia other than that she was a female figurehead and Goddess of Wisdom. In my imagination, she served as a sort of obscure deity of encouragement. This name identified an endeavor, a vague map of sorts, that would guide me as I stepped further away from my "magical childhood."

Neil Douglas-Klotz[5] once asked students in a class of his how many of us had a personal religion when we were young. More than half of us raised our hands.

Though this wasn't a "religion," this Sophia Project served as a personal contract to never forget or abandon this inner child spark, and I took it very seriously. Through my tumultuous twenties, I would periodically remember, "The Sophia Project! Ah, I almost forgot!" Am I moving into the world from a place that is in connection to this sense of exuberance, joy, and curiosity? If not, I would make little or even big changes in my life to steer myself back on track. Am I falling into a slumber of routine? Am I going down a path that will lead me further away from my inner inspiration? If the answer was yes, then it was time for a course correction.

Before dropping out after my first semester at Hampshire College in 1979, I wrote a paper that was a sort of personal manifesto called "Youth Oppression and Liberation." The whole idea of retaining the inner-sourced inspiration to which I had committed myself in the Sophia Project was becoming harder to hold on to as my childlike exuberance was increasingly out of place. This paper was one way I sought to bring more of a theoretical foundation to my personal contract to keep that inner flame alive.

After moving to Berkeley from Massachusetts a few years later, I engaged in youth rights organizing, but with time, working within the political sphere felt too limiting, eventually leading me into a more psycho-spiritual approach.

I soon discovered that the preservation of childlike wonder actually has a biological imperative, a phenomenon called Neoteny.[6] Ashley Montague's book *Growing Young* (1981) helped me to see that the retention of child-like traits carries a profound evolutionary significance. This theory corresponds to a chapter in my college paper titled "Youth Liberation and the Maturation of Consciousness" looked at how the retention of these inherent qualities of childhood was vital in enabling humanity as a whole to attain its untapped developmental potential.

A theory of "age dialectics" posits that the basic reality of a child-spark (thesis, Positiva) is countered by the demands of adulthood (antithesis, Negativa), where the urge, the intention, the spark of the inner creative self is tasked with pushing up against this limitation (Creativa), resulting in a new outcome (synthesis, Transformativa), where the adult is not staid but rather carries with him a mature and yet still childlike aliveness.[7] This Hegelian model of the dynamics of change in age difference was a sort of life-saving lens that helped me make some sense of these key formative years. This was my own form of descent and fall into matter, where, like Sophia, the task was to cry out, to reach out, and to push against the enticing lure of giving up.

To be clear, youth liberation is not about being free from parents or school. Rather, it is about freeing the inner exuberance from the layers of psycho-emotional contortions that arise in order to survive the effects of overbearing socialization and trauma. In this way, maintaining the childlike spark is an ongoing process, much like Sophia's efforts to free her Light from an enforced lockdown into materiality.

Years ago, in a journal entry I wrote when in the full throes of fatherhood, I recalled my fascination with the name Sophia. "I established a very personal endeavor called The Sophia Project that I desired would embody the magic I so longed to maintain, the inherent grace that I knew I had, but that struggled to hold up against the eroding force of acculturation."

Little did I know that the same year I started this project, the name Sophia had broken onto the world stage in a much more dramatic fashion with the publication of a vast stash of strange 1700-year-old texts called the Nag Hammadi Library.

The Gnostic Sophia Project

In the mid 1990's, the Gnostic Sophia finally caught up with me. I stumbled on a book from one of my old storage boxes called *The Gnostic Religion* by Hans Jonas (1962), the copy my father had read for a Unitarian book study group. This was the volume that opened my naïvely personal relationship with Sophia into her vast cosmological story.

Here, Sophia was no longer a vague Goddess of Wisdom. Instead, she sprang out from ancient texts as a key figure in a complex story of creation. She had qualities that exemplified those of youth, irresponsibly leaving her post in the Pleroma to fly to the source of Light, with awe and folly drawing her toward it. In time, I would learn that Sophia carried with her sparks of Light that made their way into humanity and which remain within us with vast though largely untapped potential.

As I became increasingly familiar with this Gnostic goddess, I saw that my Sophia Project had some resemblance to the much larger cosmic drama, both involving a fall, struggle, and a process of liberation. It then became my personal affinity with the simple name of Sophia, with all of her significance regarding my will to stay fresh, that fueled a rigorous investigation into the mysteries of Sophia's grand project.

In 1998, I presented a "Bardic Recalling of the Myth of Sophia" for a master's project at the University of Creation Spirituality (Morse, 1998). This and later presentations included live music, a dancer, and the hope of bringing this old, forgotten tale to life.[8]

During my counseling master's degree at the Pacifica Graduate Institute, I learned about Jung's psychological journey that drew on the obscure traditions of alchemy and Gnosticism. In their library, I found a first edition copy of Marie-Louise von Franz's *Aurora Consurgens* (2000) that interprets a rare ancient manuscript as being the last testament of Thomas Aquinas. According to von Franz, this document is a transcript of the Christianity-bound cleric who, though he dabbled in alchemy, had his psyche cracked open with the appearance of a Sophianic Queen of the South. It was after this that, as he famously reported, all his writings "were like straw."

During two trips to France in 2009, I began to notice how stone images featured on the earliest gothic cathedrals seemed to hint at this story of Sophia (which I will introduce in the Epilogue). This has brought me growing inspiration and insight from these motifs in the years since.

Through these last few decades, I studied, facilitated spiritual gatherings, and wrote and played music, all fueled by my youthful curiosity for this grand creation story. This investigation continues to spur from my own often uncertain but steadfast commitment to the reclamation of the Divine Spark Within.

The Sophia Project Currently

At a critical period of my life a couple of years ago, when it felt like my inner Light was fading, I had the good fortune to run into Michael Meade. Telling him of my woes, he mirrored back to me the idea that I was now entering what he called the Third Act, where everything that was leading up to this point could now more fully come to fruition. Don't fall back, he said, rather take it to the next level! It was from his impetus that I went full throttle to writing this current volume.

My whole investigation into these mysteries is connected to that time in my adolescence when I committed to staying rooted in the curiosity and wonder I knew as a child. I do not want to be in the audience of some worn-out Christmas play. Rather, I want to be a part of the living Mystery Theater, an agent of remembering, a flint upon which more sparks can fly.

And so, I sit here on the stage of my Third Act. Strewn on the floor around me are piles of books, notebooks, and oversized three-ring binders stuffed with writings, articles, and sprawling analyses of the myth of Sophia.

Beside me is the cow-headed djembe drum I restrung after having pounded my way through the goatskin. With zither, dulcimer, guitar, trumpet, and electronic looper, I am embarking on the next phase of this journey, working to keep a steady pulse of the unyielding positivity of this story's message, with an ear leaning toward the music of the Deep.

In a recent dream, pointing my open hand toward this Sophia Project, I was saying, "This, this was my garden." In another dream, I was holding up a Bic lighter like at a rock concert and flicking it. As it would not light, I raised it up in celebration of the holy sparks.

"Youth is a gift of nature, but age is a work of art," the beloved poet, Doug von Koss, said years ago. This is a work in progress. In my spiritual practice, I hold meditative space that invites my Christed inner self, who is seeking to become more embodied. I work to disengage from patterns of limitation that result from a pervasive and largely invisible archonic control matrix. Fine-tuning my consciousness (as I will describe in Chapter 21), I court my inner spark, where doors to new wonders might open. Recently, I caught a glimpse in my mind's eye of what I was like free from all neurotic and addictive patterns. This Dan held stature and was quite exuberant. To the unknown archonic forces that seek to gain from my weakness, my exalted self declared emphatically: Be Gone!

Trauma and The Divine Spark Within

Just before going to press with this volume, I went on a backpacking trip to the North Cascade mountains, returning to a place where, 40 years ago, I was in the tumult of my nineteenth year and in the earliest stages of the Sophia Project. As memories flooded back to me of that time, I began to read a book on trauma that seemed to take my excavation of these mysteries to a new level.

Donald Kalshed is a Jungian depth psychoanalyst and a pioneer in the field of trauma. In his book *Trauma and the Soul* (2013), he describes how a child lives between two worlds, being in the outer physical world and in the inner, magical "mytho-poetic" world of the imagination. If a child sustains some form of an overwhelming threat to its being, this trauma can interrupt the interplay between these two worlds. There can be a disconnection between them that in fact serves to protect the core seed self which Kalshed equates with the concept of "soul." He also described this as St. Thomas' pearl and the inner spark.

On this wilderness adventure, I began to see a new angle to how my whole Sophia Project, as it related to specific childhood traumas, served to protect my inner state of soul innocence. One sustained childhood trauma was largely invisible to me for much of the first half of my life though it was nevertheless hugely impactful, affecting my body as it was in relation to others in this world. As a result, my creative inner world became somewhat detached from what could have been a healthier more integrated development had there not been this abuse. Instead, as an adolescent, I embarked on a numinous but at times disembodied decades-long investigation into this meta-story of creation where my inner imagination was filled with the mysteries of Sophia.

This spiritual search has not necessarily been negative nor "dysfunctional" per se, rather it had everything to do with the survival of that part of me that the Sophia Project as well as the teachings of Sophia and the Deep Christ were all seeking to reclaim: the divine inner Self.

As a nineteen-year-old, the whole fragile connection between my basic ego consciousness and my Great Self was in dire risk of becoming severed. I desperately clung to new spiritual understandings and filled many journals with an evolving theory of age dialectics which kept me in visceral touch with this inner seed self. However, during this recent backpacking trip, as I absorbed the pages of Kalshed's writing, it was as if a spell was being broken. This trauma was now ready to be more integrated and I was letting go of something that all along involved some form of dissociation.

On the last night of the wilderness trip, I had a dream where I was being told that I needed to let go of "her", which I felt referred to my infatuation with the Sophianic mysteries, to allow "her" to go her own way. In the dream, we were both crying with bittersweet sorrow at this realization. I now needed to retract how I had been holding this material in a way that was being kept more within the imbalanced world of spirit apart from my body's guardedness against its fears of being further traumatized. At the same time, I needed to let this material stand on its own, not tied to my own overly zealous attachments to it.

Now as I write this, though this whole Project is all just as significant, there is less of a numinous glow I feel in relation to this Sophia material. However, I am also dropping into deeper feelings and sensations in my body that were not as present for many of the long years on this Sophianic journey. Here, in these more mundane corners of my physical being and relationships, as Kalshed discusses, is the ground upon which my divine inner spark has descended and been tempered in the ordeal of lived experience. This has led to a more mature innocence which is better integrated and less elusive. I believe that the course of writing this book has helped me to get to this point, to where I am now even more capable of working with the jewels of wisdom found in these mysteries.

I share this autobiographical review to encourage you, the reader, to both own and share your story. Where are you on your life's adventure in search of the pearl? How are you showing up amidst humanity's shift from an adolescent cockiness to conscious maturation? And how can we each attain our fuller potential and become more grounded and sustaining on this most precious planetary home?

The next and final Part of this volume will bring a culmination of all that has been written up to this point. Because what follows is densely concentrated material, it might help the reader to go slowly or use it as a reference over time. This is not light reading though I offer it as nourishment to stay on track with what the ancient alchemists called the *Magnum opus*, the Great Work.[9]

PART V

A TIME FULL OF MARVELS

VIA TRANSFORMATIVA

20

Overcoming the Counterfeit Spirit

In 1911, shortly before their famed split, Sigmund Freud wrote to his colleague and younger protégé, Carl Jung, the following sentence: "I have unearthed strange and uncanny things and will almost feel obliged not to discuss them with you. But you are too shrewd not to guess what I am up to…"[1]

In response, Jung wrote a highly cryptic clue into his own strange and uncanny discoveries: "I… have the feeling that this is a time full of marvels, and, if the auguries do not deceive us, it may very well be that . . . we are on the threshold of something really sensational, which I scarcely know how to describe except with the Gnostic concept of Sophia…"[2] This was a rare hint of what Jung was tracking at that time though not a word more was mentioned of this in his letters to Freud.

What did he mean, "This is a time full of marvels?" What did Jung's familiarity with the mysteries of Sophia tell him about the times ahead? I believe that the investigations presented thus far, with their many clues, points to what Jung suspected and even championed in his own life: that we are entering times of immense revelation and change.

To explain this further and help bring this "Gnostic concept of Sophia" into more focus, let's first review the grand creation story as presented by the Deep Christ.

The Creation Story of Sophia Synopsis

The Great Emanation of Holy Light sprang from the singularity, the Ineffable. From there, the aeon pairs of the Pleroma rippled out, Sophia being the last. Along with her consort, the Christ, Sophia was part of a plan to create vessels for the Children of Light to become embodied within the "chaos" that lies far outside the Pleroma. In the first stage of this project, when Sophia set out to lay the groundwork for this, she was misled and trapped by these egoic gods called archons, who stole her divine Light essence and threw her down into the lower regions of the material world. The high Christ came to rescue her, though as presented in the *Pistis Sophia*, this was only achieved after Sophia went through a metanoia process of soul reckoning. A crown of Light was placed over her, which shielded her from the torment of the archons, and she was lifted up to a higher region just below the Pleroma, out of the reach of the archons but not yet fully restored to her original place in the heavenly realm.

Meanwhile, the archons saw the "image" of this divine form in the "waters" as they looked up at the boundary of the Pleroma. It was from this that they decided to create man "in his image." They cobbled him together, but he was lifeless. Sophia sent angels down to Yaldabaoth who "blew" this Light into Adam and he became alive. The gods, having been tricked into planting this inner spark, realized that this Adamic creation, now a whole Light being, was greater than themselves. Despite Eve being sent by Sophia to help Adam awaken to his true nature, both she and Adam were thrown out of their divine state and into a matrix of matter, much as they did with Sophia. This divine Light that was originally planted within this Adamic creation, though latent, is still within our human form, having been carried into humanity by Adam and Eve's offspring, Seth and Norea.

The Relevance of this Story for Our Present Time

This Gnostic mythos of origins is an attempt to describe a history that is far more complex and multi-dimensional than can be captured in words or stories. Though Christianity proper has written this all off as being corrupt fiction conjured up by elitist psychonauts, however, what is more likely is that this unique creation story provides a rare cosmological context for understanding our latent human potential that the Church sought to marginalize. Stephan Hoeller, one of the most accomplished modern-day

Gnostic priests, believes that it is through our awareness of these historical mythos that we can better pursue "gnosis," or divine transformational insight. "The experience of Gnosis… receives expression in the Gnostic Mythos which allows the Gnostic to amplify and assimilate the experience of Gnosis and also makes further experience of Gnosis possible."[3]

Michael Meade spoke of the Greek word *mythos* as having two meanings: "The story itself, the why it is, the way it is, the how it went, aspect of the world, and the telling or retelling of the story which becomes the recreating of the myth in the moment. The power of myth resides in both these aspects, in the symbolic narrative itself which makes meaning of the world, and in the art of telling the story again, and thereby directly opening deep levels of consciousness."[4] It was from Michael's encouragement to me that this story is being retold in these pages as a mythos that is alive in the now of this moment in time.

If Sophia is emblematic of this unique story of our origins, why was Jung so excited about these times to come? I believe it is this: having been dumbed down by the strategies of lower gods, a more original model of our human form is on the verge of being renewed. Indeed, the whole Sophia Christ drama is fundamentally about the restoration of humanity to its originally intended potential. In order to get to this, first it is important to try to understand the effects that the archons are having on us.

I encourage the reader to remain cautious and discerning when entering into this material. Unfortunately, it is easy to be swept up by this and lose one's bearings while navigating the whole topic of the archonic control system. My recommendation is that this phenomenon is best approached with so called "soft eyes" where one doesn't become too myopic in the face of its many complex layers. Indeed, even entertaining the idea that there is a non-terrestrial influence that is pulling meta-strings of control with key points of power in our civilization can easily be seen as being absolutely crazy and anyone who thinks this is viewed as crazy too. I therefore greatly encourage the reader to approach this whole discussion carefully and in a way that does not cause one to lose one's grounded-ness of living life in the world.

The Counterfeit Spirit and Archonic Control of Humanity

As I have described in Chapter 11, it is virtually impossible to locate and identify who or what these archons are. But the big question arises: how do the archons affect us? As it turns out, the Deep Christ gave a profound and detailed description of this.

The archons are described in the Gnostic system as dominating the lower regions that equate with the seven planetary systems. From Christ's teachings in the *Pistis Sophia* as well as in the *Secret Book of John* (AJ), we learn that when a soul enters into a body during conception and birth, passing through the lower regions, the archons lodge onto our souls a false self which Christ calls a "counterfeiting spirit." As was done to Adam, the archons first "breathe into that soul, and there cometh out of them a portion of my power [Divine Spark] ... And the portion of that power remaineth within the soul, so that the soul can stand."[5] Then, "They put the counterfeiting spirit outside the soul, watching [the soul] and assigned to [the soul]; and the rulers bind [the counterfeiting spirit] to the soul with their seals and their bonds and seal it to [the soul] ... so that [the soul] continually doeth [the archon's] mischiefs and all its iniquities, in order that [the soul] may be [the archon's] slave always and remain under their sway..." (PS:131).

What is being said here is that, first and foremost, we have a soul. Some believe this is the consciousness that joins with us when we are born into this world and leaves our body upon death. I like to call this our Great Self. Normally, our souls have strong connections with higher consciousness, greater ranges of non-physical perception, and even, as some suggest, a connection with "past lives" into which our souls have incarnated.

However, aside from the descent into a body, whereupon there is a veil of "forgetfulness," the egoic gods called archons sew around our souls a sort of sheath or etheric chaperone that interferes with our soul's connection with higher consciousness. This counterfeit spirit becomes like a mimic of our soul that pulls us into fulfilling the needs of the archonic control system. Given that this is happening at the soul level, which is generally outside our normal waking awareness, we remain ignorant of this subtle but profound dynamic between our real and manipulated selves.

It is my understanding that one of the most important tasks we have as conscious beings on a spiritual path is to differentiate between these two aspects: to move away from the counterfeit spirit and move ever more deliberately toward the soul, our true Self. There are innumerable ways in which our thoughts, emotions, relationships, and behavior patterns can be caught in the web of the manipulated counterfeit self.

Various systems and technologies generate forms of internalized oppression that continue to keep us dumbed down. The dopamine thrills of social media, the lure of corporate advertising, deeply entrenched systems of economic inequality, and trances of consensus reality as sustained by corporate-influenced media are just a few modern-day examples of this.

Certain foods and eating habits are some of the most persistent ways that I am pulled back into the mindset of my counterfeit self. From a very early age, instead of eating for physical nourishment, I learned to turn to food consumption as a way of finding security and solace in the face of heightened anxiety. Consistently, when I go through a period of psychological opening and emotional clearing, it is like there is something that prevents me from staying there, and so I resort to old eating patterns, and my experience of soul opening quickly diminishes. Though this is a classic psychological defense process, it is also a good example of how the counterfeit spirit works.

As a psychotherapist, I help people who have endured some form of relationship wounding called "attachment trauma," resulting in long-standing patterns of distress. Working psychologically and emotionally to recover from this trauma and shift out of self-destructive behaviors is immensely valuable, and yet, there appears to be another factor at work here that goes beyond one's family and biographical histories. Many clients experience a persistence of this trauma over time, which may be in part due to the way the counterfeit spirit guards against and sabotages the healing of these wounds at the deepest levels of our being, the soul level. According to the Deep Christ, some sort of etheric or nonphysical technology interferes with sustained spiritual advancement. It may even be that our general emotional distress, anxiety, depression, bouts of anger, and shame provide the very food by which these parasitic archons are being fed.

It is, of course, not an easy solution to just try to overcome our deeper, soul-level challenges using sheer will, which can lead to what is called a "spiritual bypass." Just ignore the bad thoughts or feelings or, if they persist, get over them, and all will be well. This is a trap that brings about only superficial change that is disconnected from our deeper selves. Rather, I believe that we have to work with our souls in the classic depth psychological sense of the term. "Soul work" involves immersing oneself in the dark well of our being, which often involves reckoning with difficult emotions and troubled relationships. These challenges are opportunities to be faced rather than avoided, as they help us grow and become more consciously aware within our given life circumstances.

Yet, ultimately, we have a choice. By being aware of how our self-destructive impulses, negative thoughts, and toxic emotions are being encouraged by this control tool of the archons, we can then become aware of another option. The counterfeit spirit, as Christ described in the *Pistis Sophia*, is not able to be "healed." Rather, it needs to be released of its grip on us to where our true self, our soul, is increasingly allowed to flourish unhindered.

A House Divided

This is explained specifically in the *Pistis Sophia* by Mary Magdalene. In her extensive dialogue with Jesus during the time after the crucifixion, when he was speaking of the mysteries, she referred to something he had earlier told as a parable:[6] "Think ye I am come to cast peace on the earth? Nay, but I am come to cast division. For from now on five will be in one house; three will be divided against two, and two against three. This, my Lord, is the word which thou hast spoken clearly" (PS:116). Mary is referring to Jesus's parable of a house divided, found in the Gospel of Luke.[7]

Mary explains that what Jesus meant by this was that, through his novel baptismal rituals, Christ brought to this world a way we can dislodge the counterfeit spirit from its parasitic grip on our souls. The "two" in the house represent those aspects of ourselves that are connected to our higher nature: our soul and what the Gnostic Christ calls the "power" or that shard of original divine Light essence within us. "…The inner power stirreth the soul to seek after the region of the Light and the whole god-head" (PS:111). The "three" are part of a lower nature that is caught in the matrix of archonic manipulation. These include: 1) the counterfeit spirit, 2) something Christ calls "destiny," which pulls us toward death, and 3) our physical body.[8] Mary explained, "It hath separated the counterfeiting spirit and the body and the destiny into one portion; the soul and the power, on the other hand, it hath separated into another portion; that is: Three will be against two, and two against three.' And when Mary had said this, the Saviour said: 'Well said, thou spiritual and light-pure Mary. This is the solution of the word'" (PS:116).[9]

For myself and many on the spiritual and healing path, this requires a significant reorientation from what it means to heal and to recognize that 1) this soul-level control technology even exists, 2) that it is debilitating in subtle and at times not so subtle ways, and 3) the object is not to heal it but to disconnect from it. Initial healing work is important for our soul growth and development, but at some point, it comes down to owning our original, authentic, and intended nature. It is up to us to shed as much as possible those beliefs, behavior patterns, repetitive negative emotions, and body energy blocks to allow our truer selves to emerge. This involves setting boundaries against the soul-depleting technologies of the archons.

The ritual and soul-level processes described in the *Pistis Sophia* are highly advanced and are likely related to material found in the Egyptian *Book of the Dead* (Evans, 2015). Though quite esoteric, it gives us invaluable insights into our growth and transformation. Deep and lasting transformational change can occur, to some extent, through the psychological, emotional, and even somatic healing processes, and yet, ultimately, as long as we are blind to the phenomenon of the counterfeit spirit, we will continue to be bound by it. Because of the "power," that droplet of Light that the archons themselves lack, and with divine help, we have the capacity to unhook ourselves from their mechanism of control.

The next chapter will present a process for how this can be pursued.

The Minions of the Archons

The Deep Christ is credited with presenting information in the *Pistis Sophia* about a group of select humans who have interbred with these archons to become their agents or minions in this world. This group was given special privileges and great wealth that secured them with positions of power within the culture. This likely relates to a long history of the priest and royal classes since the time of Sargon the Great (24th century BCE), an early historical figure who may have had some direct access to these higher dimensional overlords. To step into all of this is to open the door to a bottomless rabbit hole of ancient history and "Illuminati" intrigues where one can easily get lost. Yet, like fish in water, this phenomenon of archonic control may be so omnipresent that it will require a significant paradigm shift to step outside of it.

The Gnostic Christ explains in the *Secret Book of John*: "They created a counterfeit spirit, who resembles the Spirit who had descended, so as to pollute the souls through it. And the angels [archons] changed themselves in the likeness of their mates [the daughters of men], filling them with the spirit of darkness, which they had mixed for them, and with evil. They brought gold and silver and a gift [of] copper and iron and metal and all kinds of things. And [their minions] steered the people who had followed them into great troubles, by leading them astray with many deceptions. [The people of humanity] became old without having enjoyment. They died, not having found truth and without knowing the God of truth. And thus the whole creation became enslaved forever, from the foundation of the world until now. And [the archons] took women and begot children out of the darkness according to the likeness of their spirit. And [the people of humanity] closed their hearts, and they hardened themselves through the hardness of the counterfeit spirit until now" (AJ-W).

This is highly disturbing and, though Christ is saying this was happening up until his incarnation 2000 years ago, it may well point to activities that are occurring in some of today's most powerful echelons of society. This material is so dark that it requires anyone who looks into it to have a strong anchor in one's Divine Spark "power" so as not to become overcome with horror. "And thus the whole creation became enslaved forever, from the foundation of the world until now."

Kaia Ra, author of *The Sophia Code* (2016), has revealed publicly[10] that for years as a child, she was a victim of the most severe abuse imaginable from within elite circles. Her account and similar stories told by others are a tribute to the power of the human spirit to overcome such unimaginable trauma. It also raises many questions about what nefarious contracts and crimes against humanity are occurring in the highest tiers of the world of finance, multinational corporations, the medical system, and the military. Whether or not the individuals involved in these dark cults are themselves, victims of such serious criminal abuse, they nevertheless continue to exploit their enormous wealth, power, and privilege, which sets them essentially above the law. But, if I am reading this Deep Christ teaching correctly, these minions will not be able to sustain their charade.

Christ came to rescue humanity from this and not, as Augustine declared, from Eve's "original sin." Much like Jung's "auguries," the angel Eleleth, who came to help Norea, told her, "Do you think these rulers have any power over you? None of them can prevail against the root of truth; for on [this root of truth's] account he [Christ] appeared in the final ages; and these authorities will be restrained" (HA).[11]

Clearly, there is no underestimating the profoundly devastating impact that these elusive and barely recognized nefarious overlords have had on humanity's development. That we have been kept from knowing, or at least, have not yet recognized this "root of truth" within us, makes Norea's example of how we, too, can practice defiance, voicing loud commands for divine assistance in the activation of our spark of divinity that lies outside their control.

The Human Liberation Movement

The idea that humanity could be liberated from the insidious control and manipulation by some advanced but nefarious deities is an outrageous idea. However, this idea has been widely popular in our modern culture, particularly in the world of science fiction.

The cult-favorite movie *The Matrix* (1999), for example, has parallels to the Gnostic worldview and the idea that we are unwitting captives of an exploitative system of manipulation. In this movie, the human race has long been controlled by a cold, soulless world of machines and artificial intelligence. The reality of this is not seen because we are kept within a simulated consciousness zone, a "matrix," where it is all just business as usual.

This movie has often been referred to as a point of reference to what some believe is our dystopian world. Indeed, science fiction might be a helpful lens to better understand what the Deep Christ was talking about. Are we living in an artificial reality orchestrated behind the scenes by invisible overlords?

This is difficult material that can turn the stomach of even the most ardent science fiction fans. However, I urge the reader to remember here that although there are layers of control that keep us disempowered, we have human potential as part of the very fabric of our DNA that offers us the possibility for immense transformational change. The irony is that, although we have this inner spark, we have been led to believe that it doesn't exist.

Instead of seeing Neo (played by Keanu Reeves) as a Messianic figure called "the One," it is helpful to see him rather as an archetypal figure who represents the potential in all of us, in so far as we are able to step outside of the conditioning and manipulations of our captors. Rather than praising Neo as a gravity-defying ninja superhero, he is an example of Everyman, coming into a realization and the manifestation of his true potential, with Wisdom and Love being his greatest weapons.

The phenomenal movie *Intersteller* (2014) might come closer to the truth of this "Gnostic concept of Sophia," showing that we, as higher dimensional Children of Light, are the ones who are here to help we humans to step into the next phase of our evolution.

Struggles for equality and justice are being waged between various sectors of our culture, such as within race, gender, and economic class. However, in the big scheme of things, according to these mysteries, it is humanity as a whole that is struggling to not only rediscover but liberate our dormant sparks from an age-old quarantine. This strategy of keeping us dumbed down within economic and cultural systems where we are pitted against each other has been operating in innumerable ways for much of our civilization's history.

The more I become aware of this bigger picture, both in the world and in my own personal life, the more I see how this is an epic struggle, a liberation movement for all of humanity. This is a vision that sees beyond small-scale reforms that keep us stuck in the same old game. It points toward an evolutionary leap of our latent potential that can come to fruition within higher levels of consciousness and cohabitation. As Nina Simone sings, "A New World is A'Comin'."

In this next and final section in this investigation, I will look at specific processes that can help to fully embrace our true nature and, in Jung's words, step over the "threshold of something really sensational."

21

The Bridal Chamber

Let the Sunshine In!

-    The Fifth Dimension

As the song from the musical *Hair* foretold, this is the dawning of the Age of Aquarius, a time full of harmony and understanding. These 2,160-year increments of the precession of the equinoxes[1] are slow-moving, with occasional dramatic human advances. In the Vedic system, it has been told that we are coming out of the dark Kali Yuga and into the Satya Yuga, the Golden Age. In the Lurianic Kabbalah tradition, creation is moving toward a great return called Tikkun Olam,[2] where the original scattering of Light from divine source will be regathered. Many indigenous cultures are pointing to a Great Purification and the return to a life far more in balance with our home, this living planet Earth.

In the Christian model, this equates with what has been called the Second Coming. Many, including myself, feel that this is not about the return of a messiah but rather the emergence of a new human, where we no longer need to give our power away to a savior figure but rather welcome the Christ nature within ourselves.

Transitions are not easy, however, and the shift out of the Piscean Age, exemplified by the Christian symbol of the fish, is no exception. There are numerous overwhelming threats to life on this planet, such as global climate change that is causing rising sea levels and threatening coastal nuclear power plants. Other unstable global systems of economics, international relations, and management of natural resources, for example, contribute to ever-increasing levels of anxiety in our collective awareness. These are symptoms of human egoic dominion over nature, where the task given by God to man, as described in the Book of Genesis, has led us to the brink of environmental collapse.

Such is life in the liminal zone, the betwixt and between. This threshold period is not an easy place to be, and, like any initiatory passage, it requires great focus if we want to move through it rather than remain stuck within it. This is like a birth canal where humanity is being contracted and pushed to move to a new level.

The jewels of wisdom found in the creation story of Sophia and the teachings of the Deep Christ offer direction and guidance through this treacherous crux in our evolution. The material presented in this volume, though far-reaching and complex, has powerful implications for our current times. How does this all apply in real terms, in the here and now of our lives?

With this in mind, I will now lay out a framework for an inner process of transformation as suggested by these teachings.

A Holy Tone: Vibrating our Inner Resonance to the Exact Frequency of the Great Power

Frequency coherence is a concept developed by the Institute of HeartMath[3] that is a helpful model for understanding the core transformative teaching of the Deep Christ. This research organization has designed ways of monitoring the energetic signals given off by various systems and organs in our bodies that have certain frequencies and qualities of vibration. It is astounding, for example, that the heart generates an electromagnetic field that is 60 times greater in amplitude than brain waves.[4] Based on their research model, I would like to offer a four-part framework for working with frequency coherence as it relates to our inner Divine Spark and the radiance of Source Ein Soph.

1. A Coherent State of Inner Frequency: By dropping into a state of deeper relaxation as found within a sense of gratitude and peacefulness, our hearts, as the organ of our emotional state of well-being, can settle into a positive frequency. On the other hand, if we are feeling anxious or upset, for example, then this creates a disturbance in the wave patterns of our hearts. The HeartMath research found that negative emotions such as anger, anxiety or frustration can result in disordered, non-coherent heart rhythms. During the experience of positive emotions such as love and compassion, heart rhythms become ordered and coherent.[5]

2. A Synchrony Between Different Internal Systems: We can also work to bring our heart frequency into "synchrony" with our thoughts and our bodies. The word synchrony, like coherence, refers to how the heart, mind, and physiology are in synch so that there is a compatible common flow between them. If there is a lack of coherence, then this dissonance can interfere with a positive sense of overall well-being.

3. Synchrony between Two People: The dance of energetic synchrony between two people is a focus of the HeartMath research. They found that sympathetic attunement between two people, such as with empathy, occurs in a sort of mirroring physiological synchronization.[6] When one person experiences distress resulting in an increased heart rate, for example, then this is matched by a similar change in heart rate in the other person. This is not automatic per se but does require the ability to be attuned empathically to the other person. Through the bridge of interpersonal frequency coherence, some of the most important aspects of the human experience, deep relationships and love, are enabled.

4. Synchrony between Our Inner Coherence of Frequency with the Divine Realm: In the same way, our inner energetic of peace and love can come into sympathetic resonance with what the Deep Christ called the Great Power, that supernal Light that radiates from the Ineffable Godhead. When this occurs, this can usher in an experience of sacred union and profound new levels of human spiritual experience.

Sympathetic resonance is best described by using a musical instrument. When the string of a guitar, for example, is tuned to the exact frequency or note of another string on the guitar, then when plucking one string, the other will begin to vibrate in sympathetic resonance. Likewise, a wine glass will shatter as it vibrates in sympathetic resonance to the diva's high note.

This is the principle that seems to be at work with the activation of our

Divine Spark Within. To bring our inner light into synch with the Great Power, I believe, is a fundamental human goal that affects all other aspects of our personhood and society. The task is not necessarily about working to fix the world of its problems, for example; rather, it is about first being in a state of inner peace and gratitude that then opens up a vast resource of universal and inexhaustible Power. From this place, one's ability to bring peace into this world can be far more effective.

The Dramatic Testimonial from the X7 Group

A profound and quintessential example of this was when a small group of men achieved this state of union with their divine nature. This occurred in, of all places, one of Stalin's brutal labor camps during the 1950s. Deep in a Siberian salt mine, a group of seven prisoners began to work with their inner vibrations until they came into exact frequency attunement with the emanations from the great Source.

This phenomenal story began in 1945 when a psychic medium named Anne K. Edwards met Peter Caddy, a founder of the famous Findhorn community in Scotland. With the dawning of the nuclear age, Edwards, as well as Caddy, were looking for guidance as to how humanity might avoid committing global nuclear suicide. Toward this goal, Edwards was in contact with what she referred to as the "Network of Light," comprised of various groups from around the world who were linked up telepathically. One of these groups, code-named "X7," was located in one of Stalin's dreaded labor camps. In the book, *The Mysterious Story of X7* (Anonymous, 2010), Peter Caddy (who also claimed to have had psychic contact with this group), Robert Sardello, Sir George Trevelyan, the publishers of Findhorn Press, and others all corroborated these "transmissions" received by Edwards. Here is an excerpt from this group's first entry that was received in 1953.

"We begin: Out from the very heart of the Universe, the great potential Power, deified as the Supreme Being, come the great radiations, vast in quantity, endlessly increasing in degree and potential as awareness of them becomes an integral part of the beings receptive to them."[7]

This sentence encapsulates the main theme of the teachings of this group: that as we increasingly come into synch with the divine energy of Light, it awakens within us that same Light essence that underlies our very being. As we tune our consciousness to the specific radiations of the Great Emanation, this same dormant divine Light can awaken within us. They referred to the inner light as an "indwelling presence," a term that corresponds to the Luriac Kabbalah term, Shekinah,[8] as well as to the Gnostic divine inner spark. "We have found such radiances (for lack of a better word) to be in form a substance that contains an inner glow visible only to the eyes of those prepared to receive the Inner Light."[9]

The maxim "as within, so without," is clearly outlined in these teachings. "…Harmony exists as reality in the upper levels of consciousness, and man must reach those levels by means of his thought processes before he can experience harmony and manifest peace as a result. Peace then is a vibrational state of being. It has color-tone, rhythm, and balance. It has knowledge of itself as a quality of being, and from it all harmonies proceed."[10]

The transformation that these prisoners went through constitutes one of the great portrayals in mystical literature of our higher human potential. This X7 group's achievements occurred under the harshest of conditions, in the direst circumstances of oppression, supporting the idea that most if not all people who exist within easier life circumstances can engage in this consciousness and spiritual work as well.[11]

X7 used language such as "great potential Power" that corresponds closely to the teachings of the Deep Christ. In fact, this anonymous group attributed their spiritual awakening to an etheric presence who guided them in their work and identified himself as Christ. "He told us that his earthly life, as recorded in the New Testament, was to prepare man for this test two thousand years later. He also told us that the New Testament record was incomplete, partial…".[12] As I have explored in these pages, it was within the consolidated orthodox system of Christianity where the Gnostic Paul placed hints of the deeper teachings, perhaps to be deciphered at a time when humanity was mature enough to be able to understand and incorporate them. This group, as well as many other contemporary thinkers, believe that this time is now.

The testimony of the X7, I believe, offers a model of the ultimate potential of where the teachings of the Deep Christ are pointing. Their process involved bringing their thoughts to an "exact attunement" to frequencies of what they called the Solar Substance, which may correspond to the radiations from Ein Soph. This then became their source of nourishment on many levels.

Here are just some of what the X7 group experienced. 1) They developed highly sensitive perceptual capacities that allowed them to communicate with each other without spoken words. 2) They used their attunement to the "radiance" of the Great Power as a sort of multi-sensory internet in which they communicated across multiple life forms, much like how underground mycelium creates an interconnecting web between living plants and trees in a forest. 3) They required very little food as this "Eternal Substance" gave them extraordinary nourishment. 4) They had almost inexhaustible energy as if having been fed by a "life-giving elixir." This allowed them to do the hard labor by day, followed by long hours of spiritual practice at night. 5) They reported having dramatic physical healings, such as one person's sight being restored from blindness. 6) Their accomplishments came only with the hard work of inner reckoning, purifying within themselves all that was not in synch with the frequencies of the great potential Power.

This account is the closest I have found to what happens when one truly answers the call of Sophia, where the deep self can emerge as a Child of Light. Uncovering this latent potential and attaining this level of spiritual mastery is, of course, not only incredibly difficult, it is also extremely rare. However, these are interesting times, and we might be at a tipping point where far greater human capacities could become more easily available to us.

Though it is unlikely that the degree of spiritual mastery that this X7 group exemplified will be achieved on a mass scale in the near future, any movement in this direction, such as noticing subtle experiences of this sympathetic resonance with the divine, can draw us forward. Small hints of this potential are available to us in each moment: in a breath, a rush of emotion, a gesture of love, or in the words of a poem. I urge the reader not to let this grand possibility for our human evolution, as unattainable as it may seem, distract from the simple small steps that we can take each day. We are in transitional times where we are being asked to Bring it Forth, and I believe that these teachings offer a map to help us find our way forward.

The Bridal Chamber

The *Gospel of Philip* (GP) from the Nag Hammadi library is comprised of key ideas found in a later, second-generation Gnostic movement of the 2nd and 3rd centuries associated with Valentinus (c. 100 – c. 180 CE). This text refers to a ritual called the Bridal Chamber.[13] In the *Gospel of Philip,* it is written, "The Lord did everything in a mystery, a baptism and a chrism and a eucharist and a redemption and a bridal chamber" (GP). Little is publicly available regarding what the ancient Gnostic Bridal Chamber ritual entailed. From my research, I believe it involved a mystical ritual process that served to facilitate the marriage of the indwelling Light of Shekinah with the Light of the Great Power.

As described by the X7 transmissions, this group was able to bring their inner selves to an exact frequency of equanimity, which then allowed them to be ushered into the mystery of the radiations that emanate from the Divine Source. It is possible that this Christ-presence was presenting to the X7 prisoners the same system that he also taught his disciples, described in the Gnostic texts as the Bridal Chamber.[14]

A Bridal Chamber ritual creates a space where our energetic frequencies that are dissonant and out of synch with that zone of exquisite love are purified. This requires being deep in one's soul and not in the rational mind. This is where we can stand within our most exquisite selfhood, dressed in our finest emanations of thoughts and emotions.

An initiatory process facilitates the bride or bridegroom to hold a strong and deeply rooted declaration of, "Yes, I am this being that is a vehicle for the flow of divine Light." This is where a resounding "No" holds up the boundary of the Chamber, and, like Norea, calls can be made for assistance to end the tyranny of the archons "immediately!"

This is a quintessential ritual process that can be done alone or in a group.

The following is an example of how a Bridal Chamber ritual can be created with the help of an Aramaic version of the Lord's Prayer.

The Deep Lord's Prayer and a Holy Light-Tone Meditation

This process of attuning our attention to the Light emanation of Thought-Sophia for that same Light within us to become activated is found in the Aramaic translation of the Lord's Prayer. Neil Douglas-Klotz (1990) famously translated the Lord's Prayer using the more open-ended language of Christ's original tongue, Aramaic. Inspired by Douglas-Klotz's translation,[15] my version of the first two lines corresponds closely to what I have found in the cosmology of the Deep Christ. (I had the opportunity to run this translation by Douglas-Klotz, who said it was true to the spirit of his Aramaic translation).

Abwoon D'washmaya, Nethqadash Shmokh

"Oh, Source of All! Mother-Father of the Cosmos [Ineffable-Ein Soph]

With Radiant Light that bursts forth from you, [Oh, Great Emanation]

We tune our hearts as instruments of your Holy Tone."[16]

Here is a way of working with this version of the Lord's Prayer as a Bridal Chamber meditative process.

Step 1 is to bring yourself into a state of calm peacefulness, being as fully relaxed as possible, drawing back to yourself all distractions and entanglements of the day. In Step 2, focus your consciousness on the Sophianic Holy Spirit or the Great Power. Calling it by name can be helpful. "Oh, Source of All! Mother-Father of the Cosmos. With Radiant Light that bursts forth from you." In many of the sacred texts of Gnosis, they begin with praises to the Unfathomable. Starting with this may help the practitioner to become anchored with this Source and help guard against any number of lower dimensional interferences. Though this may sound obscure, at least being aware of a model of this Divine Source Emanation is helpful.

Step 3 is to invoke the inner Divine Spark of the Shekinah. This is not about thinking it but rather experiencing a felt sense of inner radiance by being open and receptive to its presence within. Another way of explaining this is that there is a divine Light deep within us that can become known once we tune our consciousness to that frequency. This is not about *willing* it to be felt. Rather, it is about quieting our minds and opening our subtle perceptual abilities so that the unique emanations of the Great Power and our inner Light can finally get our attention.

Step 4 is to bring focus to both the universal Holy Light and also on the small Light within, where these two can gradually come into exact resonance or coherence. This is when the doors to the world of the Hidden Light open as the X7 group so eloquently described.

This technique is not easy and can take time and perseverance to cultivate. In a sense, this attunement is an ultimate goal that may take a lifetime to achieve.

One way of looking at this is like if a hole were to appear in a submarine deep in the ocean, the water would automatically come rushing in and wouldn't hold back. In the same way, the Great Holy Power is ever available if we only open up to it. As Sophia beckoned, "Dearly beloved! I have called you so often and you have not heard me, I have shown myself to you so often and you have not seen me."[17]

The X7 group spoke of the radiance of divine Light being perceived as both hues of color and also as tone, including music of magnificent celestial quality. In meditation, seek to allow for the pure tone of your deep nature to resonate, free from doubt and anxiety. The inner frequency can then come into sympathetic resonance with the tones of the Great Emanation.

"We tune our hearts as instruments of your Holy Tone."

The Body of Light

The Bridal Chamber process, like the ritual of the Mystery of Forgiveness of Sins (IE), is profound and ultimately leads to the awakening of what the X7 group calls the "Body of Light." This is not to say that the physical body is necessarily turned into a non-physical etheric light being; rather, one's more original archetypal nature, known as the Anthropos or Adam Kadmon, becomes differentiated from the physical body and emerges from within it. The body is not secondary to this process but is instrumental in bringing our divine nature more into this material reality. "…We had to accept our physical bodies as a very real part of our being and learn to use them in accordance with the principles of the Body of Light. They could not be cast aside because it was through them that the great manifestation of the powers within the Body of Light must be made."[18]

The relationship between the physical body and the Light Body corresponds to what the Simonian Deep Christ was referring to when he talked about the analogy of the fruit of the tree. In the *Great Revelation* (GR), he spoke of how the tree (the body) is here to generate its fruit (the Light body). This is the most quintessential part of our nature that can exist within the divine realms.

"All these parts of the great Tree are set on fire from the all-devouring flame and destroyed [physical mortality]. But the fruit of the Tree, *if its imagining has been perfected* and it takes the shape of itself, is placed in the storehouse, and not cast into the Fire" (GR). The storehouse equates to the Pleroma, called the "Treasury of Light" in the *Pistis Sophia*, the region from where both Sophia and the Christos came.

As the X7 group described, "The mind of the individual and the field of consciousness to be explored must be attuned to an exact degree before release of radiation can take place...."[19] This requires precision of consciousness, a tuning of one's heart and mind to specific frequencies with distinct color hues and sound tones. When this happens, when the "imagining has been perfected," our latent inner spark can vibrate in sympathetic resonance with the Great Emanation and a whole new world opens its doors to us.

If we hold within ourselves energetic qualities of victimhood or anger, for example, these will prevent the doors into this world of Light from opening. Great humility is required to be able to have access to this divine energy. In this way, these heroic survivors of Stalin's brutal gulags cultivated their desire to be of service to humanity, despite enduring deadly conditions of imprisonment. Like an alchemical process, the elements of selfishness and greed were distilled out. With remarkable purity, they crossed the threshold into a world of divine Radiance, or, in the words of the Deep Christ, the "living waters."

This process of distillation corresponds to Sophia's laments and appeals to her Light of Lights, as Christ described in the *Pistis Sophia*. She went through twelve song cycles, all of which were unable to open the door for this supernal Light to be opened to her. Only when she was finally able to clear those elements of shame and false pride in her thirteenth song was she finally rescued from her oppressors.

This is a universal spiritual teaching that transcends any one tradition. In the Vedic system, the famous Gayatri Mantra equates most beautifully to the Aramaic Lord's Prayer.

Tat Savitur Vareniyam: "The One God (Goddess) of Light that is The Most High [Ein Soph],

Bhargo Devasya Dhimahi: Oh, Divine Luminous Radiant One, who Flows like Sacred Waters [Great Emanation],

Dhiyo yo nah Prachodeyat: Ignite our Being with your Light."[20]

In the ancient tradition of alchemy, which sprang up during the time of the Gnostics,[21] this is known as the Great Work and the mysteries of the philosopher's stone. Here through the process of purification, our numinous nature can emerge from the confines of corporal matter.

Jung's work with alchemy focused on the process of finding a union of opposites. Duality is a feature of this third-dimensional world of physicality: light-dark, hot-cold, male-female. A process of union is to shift one's focus out from the limits of polarization to a field that could metaphorically be understood as being of a higher frequency, where the opposites are not separate but are seen as part of a whole. I use the metaphysical term "fifth dimension" for this, which equates with what could be called the unified field or Christed consciousness.[22] As the X7 group described, this involves an ability to work with the zone of divine Light both within oneself and in the external world of matter.[23]

I personally engage in this ritual using prayer, meditation, sacred tone, the invocation of sacred names, and using a right brain awareness process[24] to recognize this subtle energy of the supernal Light as my consciousness becomes better attuned to receive it. This is a constant process of coming back to it after frequent relapses into distraction.

A Magnificent Union

As is described in the entire sweep of the Gnostic creation story, Sophia's epic journey now steps onto the threshold of a grand conclusion. The bride Sophia awaits her consort, the Christ. She is dressed in her finest radiance, having prepared herself to come into union with the Light of Lights (PS).

This is celebrated in a *Wedding Song of Sophia*, found within a Valentinian text, the *Acts of Thomas*.

"The Maiden is Lights Daughter;
On her the Kings' Radiance resteth.
Stately her Look and delightsome.
With radiant beauty forth-shining.
Like unto spring-flowers are her Garments,
From them streameth scent of sweet odour" (AT).

Sophia has purified her being from archonic afflictions. She is ready to enter the Bridal Chamber as she awaits the arrival of her Beloved.

There are also references in these Gnostic texts to how, through this ritual, the separation of Eve from Adam's rib by the demiurge can once again be restored. Eve, known as the Luminous Epinoia or luminous Thought, sent from Sophia to help Adam's encounter with this lead archon, the demiurge, ended with a portion of Eve being pulled from Adam's side. This was a separation that has haunted the Adamic species since our inception. However, when there is a union between the feminine and masculine aspects of our Great Selves, then this split is mended, and we can finally find peace or literally "rest." "The Children of the Bridal Chamber have just one name: rest" (GP). This suggests that when this union occurs, we come into such a state of inner relaxation and peace that the long sweep of struggle humanity has faced living within the auspices of this archonic world might finally be over. "The powers [archons] do not see those who are clothed in the perfect light, and consequently are not able to detain them. One will clothe himself in this light sacramentally in the union" (GP).

To separate that which is dissonant within our mental, emotional, and physical fields is to become more refined. This is the alchemical process of dissolution, where that which is unable to enter into a fifth-dimensional field is separated. The fruits of this labor, our divine being, can then graduate from the cycles of incarnation and be placed in the Treasury of Light, that sanctuary within the Region of the Right.

Preeminent Gnostic scholar Kurt Rudolph (1983) sketches a profound summary of the outcome of what he calls the "perilous journey" of the Gnostic, or Child of Light. After all of the turmoil and inner sufferings, what awaits her is referred to in various Gnostic texts as a spiritual marriage and the wearing of the celestial garment. When this happens, the sojourner, now balanced in masculine and feminine aspects, can rest in herself because the soul has found her place of resting. There, she will become immersed in the bridal bedsheets of silence. Having found nourishment from the immortal food and come to the resting end of her labors, she will have no more need for speaking or to finding mental constructs to explain things. All will be light "which does not need to be illuminated."[25]

Sophia and the New Earth

What does this all look like beyond the transformation on an individual level? Being able to look at this dark legacy of enslavement that the Christ-

Sophia plan sought to rescue us from can open us up to the possibilities that lie outside this archonic control system. This is a vision of a New World that many are beginning to look toward, a civilization that has truly entered the Aquarian age. Perhaps the "promise" that Christ spoke of is that people will have attained advanced spiritual development through the activation of our inner Divine Spark in humble, sympathetic resonance with the Light of source creation. With this, individual physical, psychological, emotional, and spiritual accountability will enable us to live in ways in which abuse of power will no longer be tenable. New systems of social self-organization will be possible as people will be far more able to work through conflict and collaborate more easily towards local community endeavors. Gone will be the ceaseless exploitations of precious earth resources designed to feed us with short-lived consumptive pleasure that benefits the few. Advanced technological solutions to problems of energy and food production, pollution, health, and transportation, which many have witnessed as being viable and currently available, will no longer be held back by the hoarders of these gifts. Indeed, looking beyond the veil of the matrix, perhaps we are on the verge of "a time full of marvels," where a far more glorious arena of life awaits us.

Of course, this is a dream that will not be easy to manifest. However, as we begin to catch glimpses from beyond the invisible cage bars of archonic control, visions of a new Earth can entice us forward through these transitional times. Perhaps this evolutionary leap begins by taking seriously these mysteries of Sophia which are not only real but are here for us to awaken to.

A Musical Accompaniment

In 1954, near the end of his prolific writing career, Jung (2010) wrote his seminal *Answer to Job*, which Henry Corbin (2014) said was Jung's "Sophianic" book.[26] In a correspondence with Corbin, Jung remarked that this manuscript "came" to him during a fever as a piece of music. It was as if it was accompanied by the performance of a powerful musical composition written by a great composer.[27]

While working on this chapter, I've been listening to some old music that I recorded over the years, with melodies and song lyrics swirling through my head and heart. This is the Sophia Project continuing to work through me.

Perhaps, like Jung, it is music that accompanies themes whose gnosis cannot be gained by words alone. What follows is a musically inspired grand conclusion to the final stage of this book's journey, via Transformativa.

The Final Curtain to the Mystery Play Opens

From the balcony, Sophia is waiting to return to her original home in the Pleroma. She was rescued by the Deep Christ but only lifted up to the regions outside the grasp of the archons, for she has not yet completed her grand cycle of fall and return. She is waiting to enter the Bridal Chamber with her consort, the Christ, whereupon they can once again step into their home as the celestial lovers they once were. The bridegroom is waiting for her. But Sophia is not ready.

Sophia needs us.

This is one of the final great mysteries of Sophia. She has planted her sparks of Light inside of us, and she is waiting for us to rise to meet her. "Wisdom sent forth her children," and she now beckons us to return. Sophia looks down from her place above the archons, enticing us to meet her. The Gnostic Reverend Steven Marshall wrote, "We must recover that pearl of consciousness that Sophia sowed in us in the beginning…"[28] and when we do, we will be welcomed back to the arena of great love that permeates all of creation.

Songs of Sophia: Closing Melodies

Thunder, Perfect Mind (Nag Hammadi Library)

"I was sent forth from the power, and I have come to those who reflect upon me, and I have been found among those who seek after me. Look upon me, you who reflect upon me, and you hearers, hear me. You who are waiting for me, take me to yourselves" (TPM).

Christ, Thank You

Oh, vast Christos, you man of great mysteries, who are you really? Where did you come from? We hear a faint and distant echo of words that you spoke long ago. May the broader scope of your wisdom teachings be known once again.

To reclaim a more original historical and theological footprint of the Deep Christ from the New Testament version of Jesus is to be inspired by a more specific and, I believe, more empowered example of our human potential. That said, a person's adoration of Jesus is highly personal and subjective. Love for Jesus has inspired countless people through the ages, with songs and hymns from most cultures around the world sung in his honor, bringing hope to lives often filled with struggle. Whatever longstanding relationship a person has with him does not have to disappear with the advent of the Deep Christ. Let the gospel songs of love and devotion ring for this man whose mysteries continue to unfold.

Christ's Word

Here is a scriptural improvisation on the Word spoken by the "Living Jesus," as presented in the very early Gnostic text called the *Great Logos According to the Mystery* (IE). Here, his Word, which came from Thought (the feminine emanation) which came from Mind (the Ineffable Godhead), also seems to equate to this metaphor of the inner spark.

"The Word existed in heaven before the earth came into existence ... when you know my Word, you will bring heaven down, and it will dwell in you. Heaven is the invisible Word of the Mother/Father; but when you know these things you will bring heaven down. As to sending the earth up to heaven, I will show you what it is, that you may know it: to send the earth to heaven is that (a person) who hears the word of gnosis has ceased to have the understanding of a wo/man of earth, but has become a wo/man of heaven. Their understanding has ceased to be earthly, but it has become heavenly. Because of this, you will be safe from the archon of this aeon" (IE).

Bring heaven down, and it will dwell in us. This is called the descent. Once this is activated, we can then reverse the process and bring Earth to heaven. This is called the ascent. A most intriguing phrase from a sacred Gnostic hymn puts it this way: "The way of ascent is the way of descent" (TSS).

May we acquire heavenly consciousness as sons and daughters of the Light.

A Simple Melody

For someone less familiar with this musical style, like jazz, perhaps, it can take time to appreciate. But the simple melody can be heard. We have heard it before. "If you bring forth what is within you, what you bring forth will save you. If you do not bring forth what is within you, what you do not bring forth will kill you." Bring forth the inner spark because this will be what saves you. If you do not bring this out, if you do not "imagine it to perfection," then the fruit of our Great Self might never ripen, our true potential left to die on the vine.

Simon Magus wrote, "The image [the Anthropos, the archetypal form that we truly are] is that Spirit hovering over the water which, if it does not mature into its true form, perishes along with the world since it has lingered in potentiality and never attains unto actuality" (GR). This is our mandate: to finally fulfill our true potential as homo sapiens — Sophianic Man.[29]

A Pure Tone

Setting aside the complexity of these mysteries, I invite the reader to stay rooted in one's own creative flow. As Rumi says, "Don't open the door to the study to begin reading, take down the dulcimer." Put down the distraction, the electronic screen, and bring forth any simple expression that contributes to the beauty of this world. A poem, a song, a movement, a watercolor, a conversation, a stroll down the street, a whistle to that bird in the tree. "Let the beauty we love be what we do. There are hundreds of ways to kneel and kiss the ground."

As the clutter of so much detail in this book recedes, and, as if vibrating from a sacred bell forged in the fires of some great Tibetan adept, may the resonance of a pure inner vibration ring true. "We tune our hearts as instruments of your Holy Tone."

Rejoice and Seek the Light

The awakening of the Sophia Christos inner Spark is like a beacon that draws us forward through the confusion of these transitional times. Sophia sings to her beloved,

"Now, therefore, O Light, which is in thee and is with me, I sing praises to thy name, O Light, in glory. May my song of praise please thee, O Light, as an excellent mystery, which leadeth to the gates of the Light, which they who shall repent will utter, and the light of which will purify them. Now, therefore, let all matters rejoice; seek ye all the Light, that the power of the stars which is in you, may live" (PS:32).

Epilogue

Thesis Implications and Areas of Further Research

This book might raise more questions than it offers answers, but so it is with mysteries. At the very least, my wish is that these pages might inspire others to investigate the lost treasures of Sophia, the liberating teachings of the Deep Christ, and the implications of a spark of original Light hidden within us. By driving these three thematic pillars into the muddied historical ground of early Gnostic and Christian theology, perhaps a better scaffold of research can be built so that the real significance of a Novel Revelation of Wisdom can be more easily accessed.

A goal of this writing project has also been to delve into these mysteries in a way that can help open the doors for personal and collective transformation. This book can be used as a resource not only for the texts and storylines but to inspire more creative processes where the real-world applications of these teachings can be found. Michael Meade often asks: where do you find yourself in the story? How might your soul journey be recognized within the broader mysteries of gnosis?

In light of this, there are so many questions raised and I will use this Epilogue to provide some additional insights and follow through which can only scratch the surface of fathoming the implications of this material. Here are some key ideas as presented in this book that deserve further research and inquiry.

The New Testament Jesus and Simon Magus

The Deep Christ thesis presented thus far portrays a strong correlation between the enigmatic identities of Simon Magus and Jesus as he is depicted in numerous Gnostic texts. Furthermore, it is extraordinarily difficult to fathom how the New Testament Jesus might have been a later redaction of a more original Deep Christ who, evidence suggests, was a prime originator of the complex Story of Sophia.

Attempting to go against the tide of 2000 years of Christian history by considering a broader view of the historical Jesus is not easy, nor is it intuitive. Imagine, for example, that Moby Dick was actually a land-based monster. How would one even begin to reimagine Captain Ahab's plight? Shifting one's understanding of Jesus from a New Testament to a Simonian or, at least, a Gnostic context can be as difficult as imagining Moby Dick stalking the streets of Nantucket. This is why I have suggested cleaning the slate of prior associations one might have of Jesus for a broader identity to be considered.

This need not detract the reader from the rich overlap between the Gnostic and orthodox Christian Jesus. Perhaps some may want to simply continue to blend these two Jesuses or to generalize a composite figure that doesn't necessitate such a dramatic theological shift in the story of this man. Certainly, the wellspring of the archetypal significance of this Christian hero will never go dry, and there will always be much to be gained from the rich biblical stories told about him.

To propose that the New Testament Jesus and a Simonian Gnostic Jesus are two versions of the same person is intuitively preposterous, and yet, it is an inquiry that I think deserves more attention than I can adequately present in this book. Short of the due diligence that a Simonian Jesus thesis requires, here are just a few clues to consider.

Early descriptions of Jesus, especially from those who strongly disliked him, sounded very much like descriptions of Simon Magus. In 372 CE, for example, St. Jerome documented Jewish denunciations of Jesus as "a Magus demon-possessed, and a Samaritan!"[1] This description of Jesus that comes from outside of the orthodox Christian tradition has an uncanny resemblance to the two words that might best describe Simon, a Samaritan magus, and have more in common with Simon than the Jesus of the New Testament.

This Jewish accusation against Jesus also corresponds to a passage in the Gospel of John: "Then answered the Jews, and said unto (Jesus), are we not right to say that thou art a Samaritan and hast a devil?" (8:48). Calling Jesus a Samaritan is highly unusual. Aside from the Woman at the Well story in the Gospel of John (a story perhaps designed to underline that Jesus was *not* known in Samaria), there are virtually no links between Jesus and Samaria in the New Testament, though there are innumerable references to his being in the two adjacent provinces, Judea and Galilee. Simon, on the other hand, was a highly prominent spiritual adept who was revered throughout Samaria during his lifetime.

In Acts, Simon Magus suffered name changes as part of the campaign to confuse his identity, calling him Elymas, Atomis, and Bar-Jesus. But there are also a number of Simons who lie, strangely, in very close proximity to Jesus in the New Testament. These include Simon, who was called in various biblical passages the Canaanite, Apostle, Pharisee, Zealot, Iscariot, and Nazarean. Who are these Simons, and why are they all quite similar to each other? Indeed, scholars have postulated that Simon the brother of Jesus, the apostle Simon the Zealot, and Simon of Jerusalem (who took over for James's ministry prior to the Jewish wars and led a large group of Jews to Pella to escape the destruction of Jerusalem) were all the same person.[2] This Simon seems to show up in post-crucifixion Jerusalem as a key player in the historical drama surrounding Peter, Paul, and James, though this man has been virtually wiped clean from biblical history. One wonders if there is any correlation between this Simon and Simon "the first Gnostic," head of the first Gnostic sect called the Simonians. Eisenman (1997) has offered extensive insights into how the New Testament has worked to hide and distort inconvenient history through the use of techniques such as name switching and name overlays. Clearly the extensive efforts to demonize, obscure, contort, and completely bury any footprints of a Simonian Gnostic Jesus by the mainstream Roman Christianity are at least clues that deserve more attention.

The subject of the brothers of Jesus is not widely known and is largely downplayed in the Christian tradition. This likely involved the highlighting of Mother Mary's virgin status where no man was involved in a divine conception. These brothers are mentioned twice in the Gospels, in Mark 6:3 and Matthew 13:55 though their identities have been explained as being cousins or half-brothers born from a different mother. Aside from James, who Eisenman investigates extensively, these brothers include Judas (also called Thomas and Didymus, both words meaning twin) and Simon.[3] The historical obscurity that surrounds both Simon and Judas is extensive, along with how Judas and Thomas (who, in the Gnostic texts, is one person, Judas Thomas) have multiple and sometimes contradictory identities. Simon and Judas are often paired in the Gospels, at times being related to each other with the surname Iscariot and Zelotes. In what has long been a highly awkward reference, found in the *Book of Thomas the Contender* (BTC) and the *Acts of Thomas* (AT), Jesus refers to Judas Thomas as his twin, called the "twin of Christ." Elaine Pagels has downplayed this as being more metaphorical, with the idea of Christ being a twin aspect of each person. However, an actual familial twin correlation may have fueled a long but largely unrecognized campaign by the Church to bury any references to the possibility Jesus had a twin named Judas the Twin (Thomas, Didymus). It is notable that the Catholic Church connects the two disciples Simon and Judas with the same saints' feast day, October 28. One wonders: who were the twins of the legends, the Dioscuri[4], and why were they so heavily edited out of the early Christian history?[5] These questions potentially throw the whole story of Jesus's birth into question, as Aslan has also postulated.[6]

The Gospel of John has always stood out as being cut from a different cloth than the synoptic Gospels, a name that refers to the similarity between Matthew, Mark, and Luke. Elaine Pagels (2003) believes that John's Gospel was written to directly counter the *Gospel of Thomas*, where the subtle Gnostic themes were reframed toward orthodoxy. However, in my reading, the Gospel of John appears to be more specifically geared toward minimizing a Simonian Jesus to promote the version of this savior figure as defined by St. Peter.

For example, it is odd that the first thing Jesus says in the Gospel of John is, "You are Simon son of John. You will be called Cephas (Peter)" (1:42). Jesus here seems to arbitrarily change this disciple's name from Simon to Peter. Simon Peter, as he is called in various books in the New Testament, is destined to be the key figure around which the orthodox Christian tradition coalesced. He was the pivot away from a Simonian theology to an orthodox Christian system, as was extensively hammered out in the Pseudo-Clementine literature. Might tagging the name Simon to Peter have been a part of a strategy of name scrambling which sought to absorb a Simonian personhood into the anti-Simonian Peter? This Simonian hall of mirrors is so obscure that even Eisenman, I believe, has had difficulty making sense of it. Though, of course, this Gospel excerpt could be inconsequential, in the context of this investigation, I believe it deserves further inquiry.

My research has found that the story of the crucifixion has been a major pivot that allowed the Jesus of the Gospels to gain traction by distancing this "dangerous likeness" with Simon Magus, who clearly lived past the date of the crucifixion. Just as there is barely a mention of the crucifix motif in the earlier Sethian Gnostic texts, the crucifixion narrative woven through various Gnostic and heresiological texts points to a very different story of this event, as will be explored in the Appendix. But here lies the problem: the accepted crucifixion drama is as central to the New Testament story of Jesus as whaleness is to Moby Dick, and hence, it is virtually impossible to counter.

There is also far more that can be said about Jesus's inner circle. I am not referring here to the inconsistent list of names and identities of his disciples, but rather to key players in this 1st century Novel Revelation. John the Baptist, Mary Magdalene, Mother Mary, Judas Thomas, Philip, Barnabas and St. Paul all played complex, controversial, and profoundly significant roles in the introduction and dissemination of these high teachings. However, a more thorough investigation of the historical personhood of Jesus and his core associates will require additional investigations.

On Human Origins

In light of this expanded Gnostic version of the creation myth of Adam and Eve, many questions remain around the origins of we humans, *Homo sapiens*. Were we merely the product of a Darwinian natural selection or did lower gods have a hand in the creation, or at least shaping, of our human species? Were we actually seeded with the luminous Epinoia, the divine spark of Sophia as the Deep Christ indicated? Was there some intelligent design that played a hand in our origins and our evolution?

The Sumerian stories of Enki and Enlil might offer some insights into our biological beginnings, though a sole reliance on a Zacharia Sitchen interpretation of these ancient myths is highly problematic.[7] Questions about the relationship between the Nephilim, Annunaki, and Hindu or Greek creator deities might be considered in inquiries about "gods" having a hand in our creation. This whole subject, however, involves the difficult intersection of myth and history and is riddled with uncertainty.

A number of people are working to understand the big picture of how the archons, as Christ called them, have influenced human history.[8] Some "seers" have access to higher dimensional information and insight and can be very helpful in mapping the history of our origins. I recommend caution, however, when juggling the necessary balance between metaphysical insight and pragmatic historical research. There are risks of depending on "channeled" or psychically acquired material for historical insight. Though a meta-physical view of the big picture can be helpful, extra-intuitive information can be clouded and even compromised by interference from within the "astral" realm and limits what could be considered a fourth-dimensional orientation.[9] In addition, the rabbit hole of non-traditional ancient history is endless, and one can easily get lost there.

It is this challenge that has led me to be ever more pragmatic in the use of first- and second-generation Gnostic texts in my research. With any dramatic conclusions about human history or human potential that are suggested here, I strive to be responsibly grounded within long-standing esoteric traditions that bring what Jung championed as of-this-world "clear and decisive cognitions."[10]

Grappling with the Problem of the Archons

It is no easy task to crack open the implications of this most problematical subject of the archons. For one, if these archons are real, then where are they now, and what impact might they still be having on us? And two, how can we look into this issue of the archons and remain safe from their subtle and highly sophisticated ways of seduction and exploitation?

Having been asked that question recently by a close friend and associate, I wondered if this might have to do with proportion. The anchoring in one's vibrational frequency of love and heart-based wisdom, I believe, needs to be at least 90% to counterbalance a 10% attention on what could be called the dark agenda. If you find yourself getting pulled into the shadowy corners of these otherworldly overlords without being solidly held in the Light of Sophia, for example, then you risk being pulled deeper into their trap.

On the other hand, this archonic control system can't be ignored if we are to fully reclaim our inner Divine Spark. To remain oblivious to their influence, as has been happening for much of human history, is to stay vulnerable to their ways of keeping us from accessing our latent potential.

That said, let's open Pandora's archonic box a crack to catch a glimpse of what is there. Christ describes the impact of the archons, which appears to be playing out in today's world, as a matrix of population management. "...They threw mankind into great distraction and into a life of toil, so that their mankind might be occupied by worldly affairs, and might not have the opportunity of being devoted to the holy spirit" (HA). In our modern era, to keep us from being in relation with the indwelling Light of the Shekinah, advanced technologies and strategies may be being utilized as part of a broad system of mass herding. Artificial intelligence, various mind control technologies, and what is called "transhumanism" all pose alarming risks to the unfolding of our divine human form. Some, like William Henry,[11] are sounding the alarm on what appears to be coordinated efforts to implement a sort of technological mimic to our biology that may be designed to replace what Sophia had originally intended us to be. A transhumanist agenda posits whether an archonic influence is at play through efforts by technological and cultural elites to plug the human form into an artificial cybernetic system that makes our unique biology and divine potential increasingly obsolete. This may sound like science fiction and it took me some time to open my eyes to this. I have concluded that the risks are real and quite serious.

Just in the last decade, within certain spiritual and deep history subcultures, there has been a great increase in the public discourse about archons. Though this newfound familiarity with what Christ talked about 2000 years ago is significant, there is much work to be done to fully excavate how this level of systemic control has influenced humanity from antiquity to our modern era. As this information becomes more available, we might better see how pervasive this overarching program of manipulation has been and continues to be very real. Certain elements within systems of finance and economic hierarchy, education, religion, social "castes," and the unlimited power of corporations, are all contributing, whether knowingly or unknowingly, to the long game of keeping humanity dumbed down. What is more, there seems to be increasingly brazen efforts to steer individual and social self-determination toward internationally coordinated "draconian" measures of control.[12]

And yet, the insights and spiritual resources found within the Sophianic mysteries, I believe, are some of the most advanced in understanding and hence navigating these threats. Indeed, the whole story of Sophia, the Deep Christ, the inner spark, and the archons offers invaluable insights into how we can navigate this crux of a technological versus bio-spiritual evolution.

This all begs the question: how can we responsibly engage with this incredibly difficult material? To bring concrete focus on the who, what, and where of the archons, I believe, is to step into a labyrinthine rabbit hole that requires cautious deliberation. I recommend that this exploration be accompanied by psycho-spiritual maturity and well-grounded critical thinking skills to responsibly navigate some of the deepest and most complex shadow territories. Though allegations of rampant pedophilia and child trafficking have intermingled with some Republican Party, anti-immigrant, and white nationalist ideologies, for example, this need not negate the evidence that there is an immensely powerful echelon of elite society that engages in an ancient form of dark ritual, where unimaginable crimes against humanity are allegedly being committed.

As well, it requires high levels of discernment to not recklessly toss around the phenomenon of the archons as it might relate to our interpersonal relationships. To accuse another of being under archonic influence is highly irresponsible. Archonic interference in human affairs happens typically on a meta-level, within the broader spheres of consensus reality and social trends. In the field of depth psychology, this might be understood in terms of how a person is influenced by archetypal phenomena as a result of disruptions within the wholesomeness of their psyche. In this way, we are all subject to these influences and a weaponized use of the idea of archons against another person is something that can be negligent and irresponsible.

To step into this level of — what has been passed off as — mere "conspiracy theory" requires enormous sobriety and sophistication to guard against this information being recklessly exploited to pit one group against another, as is happening in the United States with what has been termed the "culture wars."[13] The risk is to see everything tied into a grand conspiracy, which then whitewashes the nuances of so many levels and complexities of what is happening. This great cultural divide might be an unavoidable casualty, however, of being in these transition times as we move further into efforts by our society to become unhooked from a greater program of control. Like in any system of oppression, there is no easy route to liberation.

Instead of getting lost in this inane maze of the archons, as I have written in Chapter 11, I suggest we approach them as pre-verbal trauma impressions. Or, in the Jungian sense, consider this a "psychoid" reality (Ulanov, 2017) that is so deep and out of reach within the underpinnings of our collective unconscious psyche that all we can do is intuit or speculate on its nature by examining the effects this phenomenon might be having on our lives and the whole of human culture. The fact that the demiurge has a lead role in the Sophianic Mystery Play and is referred to multiple times by the Deep Christ suggests that this might, at the very least, be something important to consider.

If these archons, or more generally, nefarious non-physical "angelic" beings, are real, then our task, I believe, is to gain greater levels of inner spiritual resilience to guard against them, rather than just sitting back, wishing and waiting for them to one day disappear. As the Sophia mythos points towards, we don't need to be scared of the topic of the archons because we have within us a spark of divine Light which, like Sophia, and with divine assistance, we can become immune from their influence. The problem of the archons is not easy and, in a sense, we have to get over the archon hump to mine the real treasures of these Sophianic mysteries.

Are We Mature Enough to Have Access to this Divine Spark?

Though the phenomenon of free or "zero-point" energy is still elusive,[14] I wonder if humanity is somehow holding itself back from accessing this energy technology because we are not mature enough to take responsibility for being able to tap into this unlimited energy and not misuse it for exploitation and abuse of power. Likewise, are we mature enough to acquire superpowers that might come with a full awakening of the Divine Spark Within? Maybe this potential remains out of reach until we come to a developmental level that is consciously mature enough to have access to this mystery, as the X7 group so eloquently demonstrated.

Applying These Mysteries in Real Time: from the Individual to the Commons

> "The whole point of Jesus's life was not that we should become exactly like him, but that we should become ourselves in the same way he became himself. Jesus was not the great exception but the great example" (quote attributed to Carl Jung).

The grand journey of Sophia might be what Joseph Campbell called a "monomyth." Campbell's model of the Hero's Journey fits well with the prince and the four stages of the Soul's Journey, as I've outlined in Chapter 7.[15] Campbell also said that humanity, at this precarious stage in our evolution, has an urgent need for a new myth that offers a more unified guiding principle for the whole of humanity. Perhaps this ancient but newly recovered mythos of Sophia can help serve in this way, offering a roadmap that is more universal than the mystically reduced doctrines of the Catholic Church. This "gnosis" lies deep in the Jewish,[16] Christian, and Islamic traditions.[17] It moves through streams of Gnostic, Kabbalist, Sufi, Arthurian, Cathar, the Chinese Religion of Light, Taoist, and Zoroastrian religious and spiritual systems. This is a wellspring of expanded consciousness that swells beneath the surface of worn-out and rigid religious belief structures.[18]

That said, there is a need to bring this complex theology into practical terms. A significant question is how can we work with this meta-creation story within our broader community such that it can offer guidance and inspiration beyond the individual, where society at large can also benefit. There is a great need not only for individual consciousness growth but for collective transformation. How do we work within our relationships and broader communities to integrate a paradigmatic shift?

For many years, I have hosted a small, local, spiritual "support" group. We have had numerous meetings with keynote teachings, personal sharing, and rich interpersonal connections. This was all oriented toward supporting the process of shifting a consciousness paradigm that I equate with the awakening of each person's inner spark within the context of our current human and planetary transition.

Contemporary spiritual consciousness is fertile ground upon which an upgrade of humanity's relationship to the earth can be facilitated. Groups, like families, are complex systems, and sometimes, especially the larger they get, they can fall prey to dysfunction — or worse, abuse. This is why smaller, decentralized gatherings, where people can build stronger interpersonal relationships, seem healthier and more organically resilient than larger ones.

Based on what I learned from this group, here are some ideas for how to foster a spiritual community that can work with esoteric information that doesn't become dogmatic or override the nuance of each person's unique spiritual process.

Suggested Guiding Principles for Small, Local Spiritual Circles

1. A central question for the group might be: how is the archetype of the Inner Divine Spark moving in your life, and how do you experience it in relation to divine (non-archonic) realms? The burden of awakening is not dependent on a centralized teaching but is rather placed on each of us to be responsible for working with the gift of our lives. How can we at least bring more meaning and love to ourselves and the world, or more, to become our divine essential selves when "imagined to perfection?"

2. Honoring each person's subjective experience, their "truth," is paramount as long as it does not infringe on another's rights. Group beliefs can sometimes dominate over the individual's subjective experience, and so a group process that honors the primacy of subjectivity helps guard against this. This is not about adhering to a religious creed; rather, it is about meeting in a way that is grounded in the individual experience, where no one spiritual system or teaching has priority over what is moving through the individual. As this foundation of subjective truth is held, how might the spiritual process find common ground that serves the group as a whole?

3. The great gift of loving attention and compassionate witnessing toward another is invaluable and a fundamental basis of sustaining positive and clear relationships between group members. Loving attention consists of being aware of another person's experience, with particular attunement to their emotions, and then responding to them in a way that signals that you get it and that they matter to you. This offers the core elements of "attachment," or human relational bonding, arguably one of the most essential nutrients in our lives (Johnson, 2019).

4. This is not just about "Light"; it is also about being in the dark and dropping into the deeper soil of this world. This is the soul process of descent, as illustrated by the "fall" of Sophia. Surrendering into our inner unknowing, our emotional suffering, our wounds, and traumas create fertile ground upon which a latent spark might become more apparent. I tend, therefore, to avoid the word "ascension," which can carry an upward-leaning bias.

5.   Within the limits of a third-dimensional orientation, in the here and now of our physical world, there can be great divisions and polarizations. Especially in the United States, a cultural divide has developed within media, political, social, and even spiritual arenas. Aside from healthy discernment and critical thinking processes, each person's direct connection with the "divine source" and our inner child spark, is a way in which the group can come back to the broader "fifth-dimensional" connectivity that is shared and not caught in polarization.

6.   As this is not about a centralized teaching, each person participates in their unique spiritual process, bringing forth what is uniquely within them, where they come to the group dressed in their finest emanations of thoughts, emotions, and awareness, so to speak. From this, how can participants be in their higher consciousness while also being in relationship to each other, where there is some cross-connecting, and where the group "field" is enhanced?

7.   A far-reaching meta-Sophianic or fifth-dimensional metaphysical model draws us forward (*telos*) as we work in this world but are not bound by it. As this idea of the spark and the divine body are held as possibilities, the ego is humbled, and we stay open to the God Self as He/She moves through us.

8.   With all of the above in mind, a key task is to facilitate a process by which a unified frequency of coherence is created between group members that can, so to speak, sound a Holy Tone. This both serves to draw higher Wisdom to the group and also broadcasts a Wisdom frequency beyond those gathered.

These are loose guidelines that might be helpful in finding ways for the concepts found in this book to be explored beyond the personal level, where a collective desire to graduate to a post-archonic new world can be fostered.

Sophia and the Early French Gothic Cathedrals

Despite tremendous efforts at suppression, the archetype of the sacred feminine has been kept alive through two millennia of Christian patriarchy. Prominent figures like Mother Mary, who remains greatly adored, especially within the Catholic Church, and Mary Magdalene, who has enjoyed a recent surge in popularity have been key to this survival. The figure of Sophia as the grand archetypal Soul of the World, however, is little known beyond her relatively brief appearance in the Gnostic traditions of the first few centuries CE. Despite her obscurity, I believe there have been attempts to try to bring renewed attention to her, with push-back against the long-standing campaign to erase her altogether from the world stage. One extraordinary example of this is in images found in the earliest of the 12th- and 13th-century French gothic cathedrals. Following is a very brief overview of my findings.

Chartres Cathedral, left west portal

When reviewing photos I took during a trip to France in 2009, I began to notice an uncanny resemblance between the left west portal archway (tympanum) at the main entrance to Chartres Cathedral and the description of Christ's ascension found in the *Pistis Sophia* described previously in Chapter 12 (on p. 74-75). Though interpretations by scholars have been inconclusive, each of the elements in this image corresponds to Christ's description of his ascension found in the *Pistis Sophia*, a thesis I have outlined in my article *Chartres and the Pistis Sophia* (Morse, 2010).

Here, Christ is seen rising up in what could be a beam of Light. "It came to pass then, when that light-power had come down over Jesus, that it gradually surrounded him entirely. Then Jesus ascended or soared into the height, shining most exceedingly in an immeasurable light" (PS:58).

Angels below him appear to be singing and in a state of chaotic flight. This unique image is described quite specifically in the *Pistis Sophia*. "And all (the archons') bonds were unloosed and their regions and their orders; and every one left his order, and they fell down all together, adored before me, or before my vesture, and all sang praises to the interiors, being in great fear and great agitation" (PS:12).

Ten figures, not easily explained as the twelve disciples, are shown holding scrolls and looking up toward one direction and then another. This may correspond to how, during his remarkable ascension described in the *Pistis Sophia*, Christ disrupted the "horoscope-casters" accuracy as messengers of divination from within the archon-influenced lower heavens. "But now I have made them spend six months turned to the left and six months turned to the right" (PS:21).

After stumbling on the Gnostic correlation to this strange ascension scene, I subsequently became aware of other images found in the early French gothic cathedrals that also seemed to have striking parallels to themes found in the *Pistis Sophia*.

Coronation of the Virgin, Notre Dame de Paris

I found that numerous images of the Coronation of the Virgin, arguably the earliest of what was to become a prominent theme in 13th–15th-century Italian Christian art, looked much like Christ's rescue of Sophia as described in the *Pistis Sophia* which I presented in Chapter 11 (on p. 69). "It came to pass then, when Pistis Sophia had finished saying these words in the chaos, that I made the light-power, which I had sent to save her, become a light-wreath on her head so that from now on the emanations of the Self-willed [demiurge] could not have dominion over her" (PS:59). This coronation tableau has no textual correlation in the four Gospels. It is also odd that this young Mary hardly looks like she could be Jesus's mother. Indeed, who is "Our Lady" referring to?

In addition, the images of Ecclesia and especially Synagoga, displayed so prominently at the entrance to Notre Dame and other early French gothic cathedrals, though interpreted to mean the failure of Judaism and triumph of Christianity, have strong parallels to the captured and rescued Sophia in the Gnostic tradition.

Synagoga, Notre Dame de Paris

Here, Synagoga is seen with a hissing snake wrapped around her head, blinding her. This has a strange resemblance to descriptions of Sophia's "fall," where her Light was stolen from her and she became a captive of the beastly archons as Jesus described in the *Pistis Sophia*. "And the lion-faced power and the serpent-form and the basilisk-form and the dragon-form and all the other very numerous emanations of Self-willed surrounded Pistis Sophia all together, desiring to take from her anew her powers in her, and they oppressed Pistis Sophia exceedingly and threatened her" (PS:66). The corresponding image of Ecclesia featured on the Right side looking out from the cathedral, may be depicting the rescued Sophia.

Sophia and the Knights Templar

How is it possible that these radical and even heretical images, displayed so prominently on these great temples of Roman Catholicism, could have been so cryptically included? To help point towards further research, I have proposed a bare-bones theory that, of course, needs far more analysis to be seriously considered. The original nine Templars who resided and possibly conducted excavations at the Temple Mount in the early 12th century may have brought back to France a recovered copy of the *Pistis Sophia* or a text similar to it.[19] Designers from the mason guilds affiliated with St. Bernard of Clairvaux may have then worked these images onto the walls of Notre Dame, Chartres, and others before the original inspiration for these themes was lost in later cathedrals. When visiting the Cologne cathedral, for example, none of these subtle yet distinct Sophian images were on display. Bernard of Clairvaux personally may not have been aware of or endorsed these cryptic inclusions, however, his religious devotion had much in common with these gnostic undercurrents. He had a strong adoration towards Mother Mary and to the themes found in the Song of Songs. He was also a key sponsor and patron of the Knights Templars and was instrumental in organizing the construction of the original gothic cathedrals in and around Paris.[20]

I am introducing this far too brief summary of Sophianic themes on these cathedrals as background to presenting an image found at the entrance to Notre Dame de Paris that I am particularly fond of. A pillar stands in the center of the middle doorway of the main entrance to Notre Dame. Higher up on the pillar is Jesus standing above what appears to be a gate of two snake heads. Lower down the pillar, at chest level, to greet the pilgrim at this Temple to Our Lady, is the following image.

Central Pillar, West Royal Entrance, Notre Dame de Paris

Holy Sophia

Though I have been contemplating this image for years, only now as I write this am I finding more clarity as to who she might represent. She has been called Mother Alchemy (Franz, 2000), sitting on her throne of wisdom, with the nine rungs of what is believed to be a Hermetic process, surrounded by a number of symbolic panels that relate to the alchemical arts (Fulcanelli, 1984). From the very center of the Great Porch of Notre Dame, she seems to be saying something, or maybe she is trying to tell a story as if to lure us into some inner teachings. Could this be a metaphorical image of Sophia, or at least an emblematic symbol of the Sophianic mysteries?[21]

Here, she appears in her position in the (Sethian) 9th heaven (AJ), having been rescued by Christ, though she is still below the watery boundary of the Pleroma, the heavenly realm. The nine-rung ladder, instead of referring to the nine alchemical steps of labor, may suggest an invitation for us to climb through the gates of archonic control systems to, like her, be free from their influence. This ladder might also be an expression of her desire to fulfill her original intention: to come to this world to seed this region with incarnated beings of Light to inhabit. This is both a descent and an ascent.

She is referring to the inner teachings, the closed book hidden somewhat behind the open book of more public teachings. Or, at least I used to think that the front book represented the exoteric teachings such as the Bible that are available to all. However, as I ponder it now, the front book looks like its lock strap on the left has been thrown open. What *are* these texts and what might they reveal?

Our Lady Wisdom is holding a pineal image on top of a staff (similar to the small staff Christ is holding in the Coronation image shown above), perhaps points to our latent (spark) potential that runs up the spine and flowers in the pineal gland. Her staff covers her ring finger, possibly indicating that this process involves a sacred marriage, *heiros gamos*, the fulfillment of the mysteries of the Bridal Chamber.

She is waiting for her children whom she had "sent forth" that they, we, might one day return. When the regathering of the sparks is complete, she can then step back into the Pleroma, where she can once again be reunited with her sacred consort, the Christ.

The task before us is to step onto that ladder of liberation, to find that pearl of divine essence that is somewhere, somehow, within us. This droplet of Light might ultimately be something profound that brings radically expanded resources of human potential. But it starts simply with something that is creatively moving through each of us. This can be any movement that is as small as taking a deeper breath in this moment or just being in a state of not doing. Maybe there is a song in you that wants to be sung, a dance, a dream, an expression of affection, a poem, a tear. Maybe there is a powerful new insight or a letting go of something old that no longer serves. Maybe it is an opening of the heart after years of being guarded.

This is the process of the Creativa that counters the drag of the Negativa, the crux of the initiatory journey. And yet, simply expressing one's soul is not necessarily the answer. The divine inner spark is more like an unfathomable potential that needs divine energy to be fully activated. As an important spiritual maxim states, we need to reach out to be met. We have to ask in order to receive help. Either through prayer, ritual, or some form of an imaginal process, a bridge can be created where we can connect with Divine Wisdom or, as the Deep Christ called it, the Great Power, that lies largely outside our conscious awareness.

To *not* do this, to remain inactive and mundane, comes with great risk, as St. Thomas's Bring Forth saying warns. Reach out for help and also find that perfect tone, precise image, or dry tinder upon which that inner spark can catch fire.

These mysteries ring from a distant past and point to what is ours to reclaim.

Appendix

The Fog of Crucifixion

"Blessed is he who has crucified the world, and who has not allowed the world to crucify him.' The living Jesus." - Book of the Great Logos According to the Mystery (IE)

"Jesus came to crucify the world." - The Gospel of Philip (GP)

"I did not die in reality but in appearance..." - Second Treatise of the Great Seth (ST)

"I seemed to suffer in Judea but I did not really suffer." - Simon Magus in the Great Revelation (GR)

This book has delved into three mysteries of Sophia, Christ, and the Divine Spark, that point to the possibilities for psycho-spiritual transformation. Following the clues of the word "Sophia," we have peered into the thesis that a Revelation of High Wisdom emerged in the 1st century from the person I am generally referring to as the Deep Christ. This man, I argue, was the primary source for both a complex creation story, rituals and resources for overcoming the setbacks in the Sophianic plan to seed this world with beings of higher consciousness.

In this investigation, the name Simon Magus emerged as a prominent character who appears to be a close mirror image of the Jesus depicted in the Gnostic texts. It is difficult to ignore how the two seem to fit together like a hand-in-glove.

This puzzle of matching identities takes us into such an egregious controversy within an already difficult Christ mystery, where strong emotions are bound to be activated. Perhaps it is possible to consider that Simon, a key figure in the origins of Gnosticism, might be the same person as the Gnostic Jesus. But that would leave us with a far more troublesome question about the relationship between Simon and the New Testament Jesus.

I have resisted stepping further into this controversy within the main body of this book because I haven't wanted the inevitable intrigue around the identities of Simon and Jesus to interfere with the more important themes presented thus far. The notion that Simon and Jesus might be the same person is so untenable that even to suggest it risks undermining a reader's trust in this book as a whole. However, that this correlation between Simon and the Gnostic Jesus has been introduced, further substantiation of this thesis is warranted.

It is within the fog of the crucifixion drama that this outlandish Simon-Jesus thesis comes into more focus.

Robert Eisenman and the Historical Christ

This idea that Jesus is a reduced version of an earlier historical character is suggested by one of the most prominent researchers in this field. As an archeologist, historian, and scholar of ancient Israel, Eisenman's groundbreaking research into 1st century Jewish and early Christian history pushes the edges of mainstream opinions in the field. He has maintained a strong adherence to objective academic scholarship compared to the oftentimes unseen bias that can come with religious historical research. In his two encyclopedic books on the subject (1997, 2014), he stands out as one of the most prominent investigators of early Christian disinformation, exposing the playbook used by the editors and architects of the New Testament in their process of spinning the stories according to their various agendas.[1]

Eisenman himself is strongly rooted in Jewish historical research through his studies at Oxford, his archeological research in Israel, and his pioneering work in interpreting the Dead Sea Scrolls. Though Eisenman prides himself in not carrying a biblical bias, I have found that he is less oriented toward a Gnostic interpretation and rather holds a more Jewish lens in his research. Eisenman is a great fan of St. James, and for good reason, for the gigantic role that he played in 1st century Jerusalem is largely underappreciated.

Eisenman goes so far as to suggest that James may have been the historical person who inspired what was later constructed as the New Testament figure known as Jesus. Though Eisenman doesn't explicitly say it, he seems to circle around this thesis throughout the book,[2] culminating in a most notable last sentence where he suggests that who and whatever James was, Jesus was also.[3]

Prior to my exposure to Eisenman, I was aware of how the historical Jesus story, as presented in the New Testament, may have been tinkered with over the centuries. When I ultimately purchased his seminal *James the Brother of Jesus* (1997), I decided to step into this thick tome with a broad question in mind: where and how, in 1st century religious history in Palestine, does Jesus show up within a more disciplined investigation not caught in the bubble of the biblical version of that history? Clearly, Jesus was a highly influential religious figure, and so, where are the historical cross-references to his 1st century appearance?

I also studied Eisenman's book through the lens of my familiarity with the Gnostic system, scanning for the themes and language that were distinctly Gnostic. As I read, the name Simon Magus kept jumping off the page in a way I couldn't ignore. Simon, along with James, were key 1st century players, both of whom were victims of a near-complete erasure from what eventually became the orthodox Christian version of this history.

Ironically, even after years of my explorations into the Gnostic texts, I had little familiarity with the figure Simon Magus and hadn't fully taken in the possibility that Simon was believed by some to be the "first Gnostic." After reading Eisenman and then with the help of G. R. S. Meade (1892) and Stephen Haar (2003), I found a treasure trove of historical research that incited me to delve much more into who this man was.

The Enigma of Simon and Jesus

The strange interplay of identities between Simon Magus and Jesus is a mind-bender that has escaped clear analysis for the past 2000 years. In one recent and valuable contribution to this puzzle, Picknett and Prince (2019), in their book *When God Had a Wife: The Fall and Rise of the Sacred Feminine in the Judeo-Christian Tradition*, include a chapter on Simon Magus. They speculate on what they call a "dangerous likeness" between him and Jesus. So closely related are these two in time, place, and impact, I began to see that the mystic adept known as Simon Magus might well be the prototype for what Eisenman and many others have described as this heavily tailored, biblical savior figure known as Jesus.

Consider that Jesus and Simon Magus 1) were very close contemporaries, both being powerful spiritual leaders in the early 1st century CE Palestine, 2) were both highly influenced by John the Baptist and had extensive contacts with St. Peter, 3) had large followings and were disruptive to the Jewish status quo, 4) were considered messianic saviors and were identified with the Greek term "Christ," 5) used magic or performed miracles, and 6) both faced crucifixions. A big difference between the two, however, is that while Jesus was sacrificed, Simon survived past the time of the crucifixion. This distinction, as will be explored below, reveals what could be a crack in the whole Jesus story itself.

As I looked more deeply into this, I began to suspect that Simon the Samaritan and Jesus might be just two names for the same person and that the New Testament Jesus was a later redaction of a more historically original Simon. This Simonian Gnostic Christ was so controversial and metaphysically advanced that his Revelation of Wisdom teachings had to be marginalized and his unique personhood buried under a relentless campaign of character assassination. Gradually over time, with each heresiological spin, this high spiritual adept was morphed into a toned down, less esoteric, and less cosmological Roman-approved messiah.

This link between Simon and Jesus became for me like a missing puzzle piece in the investigation of the Gnostic Christ mystery, bringing a more theologically coherent throughline to the trajectory of Christian history. Like a chiropractic adjustment at the very origins of Christianity, this Simonian-source alignment opened up a surge of connections and insights for me around Christ and his message. Knowing how offensive this is at face value, it has taken me a full decade of work to integrate this mind-numbing correlation sufficiently enough to be able to even suggest it in this book.

The Fog of Crucifixion

Just as the theatrical fog has shrouded the very character of Jesus in the Sophianic Creation Story, so have the mists of obscurity weighed heavily on the most seminal scene in the Jesus story: the crucifixion and its counterpart, the resurrection. The execution of Jesus has been fundamental to the Christian religion since this scene was locked into each of the four Gospels, in the latter decades of the 1st century. To question the historical accuracy of the crucifixion is to potentially upset the whole Christian apple cart which is why it is virtually impossible for any crucifixion counter-narrative to be taken seriously. Dismantling the Christian crucifixion story equates to how the big banks are too big to fail because this would result in the financial system, or, in this case, the whole Christian theological system, being thrown into turmoil.

The crucifixion has elicited boundless compassion and love for this man through the centuries. I do not wish to detract from this rich culture of devotion towards the heroically sacrificed Jesus and I fully support each person's beliefs about this. As an archetypal motif, the crucifixion works on many levels and is a valuable model for overcoming the ego-self, for example, to make way for the Great Self. Mary Magdalene, who many have turned to more recently as a woman of great wisdom and who was very close to Jesus, figures prominently in the crucifixion story. Her faithfulness and adoration expressed to the crucified and risen Jesus need not lose value in the face of conflicting historical versions of this event.

However, like much of what has been explored in this book so far, we are again faced with how to grapple with some unusual and at times conflicting narratives that abound in texts not included in the New Testament. Plenty of theories have sprung up over the years that try to account for the historical discrepancies surrounding the crucifixion. Some suggest that Jesus didn't die on the cross but rather survived the horrid execution attempt, being rescued and revived from near death by Joseph of Arimathea. Rumors that Jesus survived the crucifixion have circulated for 2000 years, though this idea has been wholeheartedly dismissed by Christian historians. As in the fog of war, when digging deeper into the whole crucifixion drama, it is filled with confusion, false leads, and shrouded historical accounts. Such is the haze that surrounds orthodox Christianity's victorious campaign to control the narrative.

Simon of Cyrene

The story of Jesus's dramatic death march through Jerusalem to

Golgotha, with cross in tow, lines the interior walls of Catholic, Anglican, and Protestant churches throughout the world in what is called the Stations of the Cross. In the fifth station, as described in the synoptic Gospels,[4] a man named Simon of Cyrene took the cross from the stumbling Jesus. "Then they led [Jesus] out to crucify Him. Now Simon of Cyrene, the father of Alexander and Rufus, was passing by on his way in from the country when the soldiers forced him to carry the cross of Jesus." This has always been an odd detail in the story, and, strangely, there is no specific reference to Simon giving the cross back to Jesus. This is no accident, I believe, for, as it turns out, this scene appears to be a pared-back version of a crucifixion account that was likely earlier, more elaborate, and even more confusing.

The Substitution Theory

You might want to buckle your seatbelt through this one because it is a rough ride.

In following the clues of the keyword "Sophia" into the mystery story of the Deep Christ, there appears to be a coherent and consistent crucifixion storyline found in a variety of ancient texts, where the identities of Jesus and Simon seem to be thrown into a mind-bending hall of mirrors. The basic template of this pre-orthodox crucifixion story is very odd, almost repulsive.

The plotline is simply this: Jesus had been scheduled for crucifixion, but something happened where another was executed in his place. This substitution theory suggests that some sort of magic was used so that this sacrificed man was made to look like Jesus, where Jesus appeared to be killed but was not. After the crucifixion, there was then much confusion and conflicting accounts about whether this Jesus had died or not. Astonishingly, in some of the early versions, instead of Simon of Cyrene just carrying Jesus's cross, Simon is the one who was killed while Jesus survived unharmed. Of the nine texts listed below, two refer to the name Simon as the substitute, one refers to confusion of identities around the crucifixion of Simon Magus, three refer to a substitute who is not named, and another three texts report that both Jesus and Simon Magus were thought to have died but didn't, with no mention of another being killed in his place.

Following is a review of these accounts.

Apocalypse of Peter

Peter was the disciple who famously fulfilled Jesus's prediction that "before the rooster crows, you will deny me three times." The Gnostic *Apocalypse of Peter* (APe) version of this scene offers a strange twist or at least a stark contrast to Peter's denial. In this Gnostic text, Peter is speaking to Jesus after the crucifixion: "And I [Peter] said 'What do I see, O Lord? That it is you yourself whom they take, and that you are grasping me? Or who is this one, glad and laughing on the tree? And is it another one whose feet and hands they are striking?' The Savior said to me, 'He whom you saw on the tree, glad and laughing, this is the living Jesus. But this one into whose hands and feet they drive the nails is his fleshly part, which is the substitute being put to shame, the one who came into being in his likeness. But look at him and me'" (APe).

Here, the "living Jesus" explains to Peter that he climbed up a tree and looked onto the crucifixion of another, a substitute who looked like Jesus, who was killed on the cross. This raises the possibility of a backstory to the New Testament's version of Peter's denial.

First Apocalypse of James

The *First Apocalypse of James* offers a glimpse of what appears to have been confusion at the time of the crucifixion. James thought that Jesus had died on the cross, but Jesus assures him that he did not "suffer."

"The master appeared to [James]. He stopped praying, embraced him, and kissed him, saying, 'Rabbi, I've found you. I heard of the sufferings you endured, and I was greatly troubled. You know my compassion. Because of this, I wished, as I reflected upon it, that I would never see these people again. They must be judged for what they have done, for what they have done is not right.' The master said, 'James, do not be concerned for me or these people. I am the one who was within me. Never did I suffer at all, and I was not distressed. These people did not harm me. Rather, all this was inflicted upon a figure of the rulers, and it was fitting that this figure should be [destroyed] by them'" (FstAJ).

Here, the Gnostic Jesus is telling James that the one who was killed had some connection to the Roman authorities and his death was something that they brought on themselves. James, who was known as the brother of Jesus, shows great compassion and concern, as was true to his character.

Acts of John

This 2nd-century document says, "Thou hearest that I suffered, yet did I not suffer" (ActJ), a statement also found in the *Second Treatise of the Great Seth* as well as in Simon's *Great Revelation. Acts of John* is complex, not clearly Gnostic, and is a text that is generally less reliable as a source. However, it may present a certain explanation of the confusion around the death of Jesus which was circulating at that time.

"Nothing, therefore, of the things which they will say of me have I suffered: ... Thou hearest that I suffered, yet did I not suffer; that I suffered, yet did I not suffer; that I was pierced, yet I was not smitten; hanged, and I was not hanged; that blood flowed from me, and it flowed not; and, in a word, what they say of me, that befell me not..." (ActJ).

Here is a clear denial from the Gnostic-leaning Jesus that he did not "suffer" the punishments of crucifixion, in contrast to the news that must have been spreading through the communities at that time that this man suffered piercing, bleeding, and crucifixion.

Irenaeus, *Against Heresies*

In his 2nd century *Against Heresies*, Irenaeus describes the beliefs of various Gnostic groups, whereupon he works to discredit them. Here is one paragraph from Book I – 24:4, where he refers to an astounding interpretation from the 2nd century Alexandrian Gnostic teacher Basilides, saying that Simon of Cyrene died and Jesus survived.

"Wherefore he [Jesus] did not himself suffer death, but Simon, a certain man of Cyrene, being compelled, bore the cross in [Jesus's] stead; so that this [Simon] being transfigured by [Jesus], that Simon might be thought to be Jesus, was crucified, through ignorance and error, while Jesus himself received the form of Simon, and, standing by, laughed at them."[6]

Writing about a century after this event, Basilides might represent a second-generation version of the crucifixion, which now includes the figure of Simon of Cyrene. Simon was made to look like Jesus, and Jesus was made to look like Simon. Therefore, they crucified the Jesus-looking Simon, and the Simon-looking Jesus got away scot-free. Here, we are in the thick of the fog of this crucifixion scene.

The following are two more accounts of Jesus being spared from crucifixion in Acts and the Koran.

St. Paul on the crucifixion

St. Paul made vague references to the crucifixion, mostly as a metaphor where he urged his followers to "crucify the flesh" and, by doing so, die to a life of sin (Rom 6:6; Gal 2:20 and 5:24). Paul wrote so little about the historical Christ that it makes one wonder why. Did he just not know about his life even though he was close associates with James, Peter, and, as Eisenman suspects, Simon and Thomas too? Clues suggest that Paul was less ignorant than he let on, and he, or the editors of his writings, were trying to skirt the awkward details of Jesus's life.

In Acts, Paul is depicted as defending himself against accusations by the Jewish community in Jerusalem to the Roman governor, Festus. This account mentions one notable accusation made against Paul. His accusers, the chief priests and the elders of the Jews, "had some points of dispute with (Paul) about their own religion [Judaism] and about a dead man named Jesus who Paul claimed was alive" (25:19). Did Paul, like the Gnostic Peter and James as quoted above, also know that Jesus had survived the crucifixion despite many who believed he had been crucified? Remember, Paul claimed to have had some direct line into the mystery teachings of Christ, which were later woven into his Hellenized version of Christianity (Pagels, 1975). At the very least, this odd passage deserves further inquiry.

The Koran

The Koran contributed to this whole confused crucifixion storyline, though it was likely influenced by earlier scriptural accounts. "And their saying, 'Indeed, we have slew the Messiah, Issa, the son of Maryam, the messenger of Allah.' And they did not slay him, nor did they crucify him; but it only appeared to them. And indeed, those who differ over it are in doubt. They have no knowledge of it except conjecture. And they did not slay him, for certain."[10] In other words, it looked like they crucified this man Issa and many are confused about this. One thing is for "certain" however, "they did not slay him."

Second Treatise of the Great Seth

The *Second Treatise of the Great Seth* gives the most extensive account of the substitution theory: "And I was in the mouths of lions. And as for the plan that they devised about me to release their error and their senselessness [i.e. to kill him], I did not succumb to them as they had planned. And I was not afflicted at all. Those who were there punished me, yet I did not die in reality but in appearance, in order that I not be put to shame by them because these are my kinsfolk. I removed the shame from me, and I did not become fainthearted in the face of what happened to me at their hands. I was about to succumb to fear, and I suffered merely according to their sight and thought so that no word might ever be found to speak about them. For my death, which they think happened, happened to them in their error and blindness, since they nailed their man unto their death. Their thoughts did not see me, for they were deaf and blind. But in doing these things, they condemn themselves. Yes, they saw me; they punished me. It was another, their father, who drank the gall and the vinegar; it was not I. They struck me with the reed; it was another, Simon,[7] who bore the cross on his shoulder. It was another upon whom they placed the crown of thorns. But I was rejoicing in the height over all the wealth of the rulers and the offspring of their error, of their empty glory. And I was laughing at their ignorance" (ST).

What is striking about this is that Jesus claims he was the one who was whipped with the reed, but that after that, another took the cross and was crucified. We can begin to paint a picture here that Jesus was scheduled to be crucified but that something happened, possibly employing magic, where another stepped in, looking like Jesus, who was then crucified. It is also notable that this account suggests that the ones trying to kill Jesus put in a substitute to spare them all from shame because they were related. "… I did not die in reality but in appearance, in order that I not be put to shame by them because these are my kinsfolk." That this Jesus (and Simon Magus, as Josephus documented) might have had some Roman connections is a question to consider.

This is all extraordinary, and I believe this rare book found in the Nag Hammadi Library comes very close to the epicenter of the mystery of the Deep Christ. Further research is encouraged to investigate whether, given how similar they are in story, tone, and theology, the *Second Treatise of the Great Seth* may be the second *Great Revelation* (GR) of this Simonian Christ.

Simon Magus: "I did not really suffer"

The edited and Christian orthodox-approved New Testament clearly states that Jesus's life ended at about 33 years of age, while Simon Magus lived well past this age, with alleged appearances before Nero (post 54 CE). It is barely known, however, that Simon Magus indicated that he went through his own crucifixion drama. In his *Great Revelation*, he wrote that people believed he had been crucified but was not: "And I seemed to suffer in Judea but I did not really suffer" (GR).

Simon's use of the word "suffer" is similar to how it is used in the *First Apocalypse of James*, the *Acts of John*, and the *Second Treatise* (all quoted above), where this word "suffer" specifically refers to the various inflictions of pain associated with a deadly crucifixion. Also, the crucifixion of Christ is famously known as the Passion, from the Latin word *pati*, meaning "to suffer."

Here, Simon has written one brief sentence suggesting there was confusion around whether he was crucified or not ("I *seemed* to suffer"). Given how little remains of Simon's writings, this speaks volumes. Keep in mind that this is Simon Magus writing about a crucifixion confusion that is eerily similar to other accounts involving Jesus's death, where Jesus also says, much like Simon Magus, "I did not suffer" (ActJ).

There is also a curious detail about a likely historical figure known as Dositheus the Samaritan who is referred to in a number of the heresiological accounts. Dositheus, being one of John the Baptist's prominent students, took over John's ministry after John was murdered. Despite Simon Magus being considered John's most accomplished students, Dositheus "falsely gave out that Simon was dead." This rumor vanished when Simon returned from Egypt and shortly thereafter usurped Dositheus's position and became head of this assembly.[5] Could this detail involve Simon's claim that he "seemed" to be killed but was not?

Simon Magus and Faustus

As discussed in Chapter 15, the Pseudo-Clementine literature made a brazen effort to take what was likely earlier historical accounts from the 1st century and weave them into fanciful stories that had spin, polish, name changes, and identity distortions, all to steer the emerging New Testament narrative in favor of orthodoxy. Eisenman writes extensively about this and suggests that parts of Acts can be included in this "romance literature."

The reader might be familiar with the odd and tragic magician named Dr. Faust, made famous by Marlowe and Goethe. However, what is less known is that a Faustus character appeared much earlier in the 2nd-century Pseudo-Clementine *Recognitions*.[8] This story has an uncanny resemblance to the crucifixion stories of Jesus and Simon, with the same themes of confused identities, where one was killed and another was spared. This story features Faustus and Simon Magus, with St. Peter playing a key role. Instead of Faustus being killed, his identity was switched with Simon Magus, and, therefore, Simon died while Faustus was saved by the hand of Peter, the favored disciple of the Christian orthodox architects.

The story is complicated, but here are the key elements: 1) There are twin boys named Faustus and Faustinus (also named Nicetas and Aquila) who, since their boyhoods, were educated by Simon Magus. 2) The twin's father, Faustus, is related to Emperor Augustus. The mother takes the twins and flees Rome, but they are shipwrecked. Cornelius the Centurion tries to drive Simon away with threats. However, Simon changes the face of Faustus into Simon's own likeness by smearing it with magic juice in hopes that Faustus will be put to death instead of Simon himself. 4) Faustus then goes to Antioch in the guise of Simon, where he fully denounces Simon's attacks against Peter. 5) Faustus is almost killed but is saved by Peter and restored to his original identity.

In this identity hall of mirrors, it is not Simon of Cyrene but Simon Magus who is killed, sparing another who looks like Simon. This version is so close to the others as presented above that it is clear that they are related. Faustus seems to stand in the place of the orthodox Jesus, who is exalted, while Simon is damned.

Likewise, the wholesale condemnation of Simon Magus and praise of Peter is put on full display here, a theme also found in Acts.[9] This is one of a number of differing accounts of Simon Magus's death that are found in the heresiological and romance literature, so desperate were they, it seems, to just make him go away.

A Theory of Explanation

If Jesus survived past the time of the crucifixion, then this would be devastating to the colossal Christian religion that built itself around a theology of Jesus's sacrifice. The substitution explanation of what happened at the crucifixion is so outrageous that it is hard to imagine it as a fabrication, as indicated by the relatively consistent storyline in the above references. It certainly raises questions about who actually died and what could easily be seen as an egregious moral insult, if not a crime, that another was killed instead of Jesus.

If Jesus did live past his 33rd year, then this would shed a whole new light on the Gnostic scriptures, most of which barely mentions the crucifixion. He is often referred to as "Living Jesus," where just his voice is heard. Might this have been a Docetist explanation for how he delivered his mystery teachings after the time of his supposed death? That the Roman Church sought to bury these Gnostic teachings, it makes sense that they would heavily promote the crucifixion narrative and negate any post-crucifixion teaching as being purely heretical.

How do we fathom the "Living Jesus," who looks eerily similar to some damning accounts of Simon Magus as described in this post-crucifixion period? How do we explain this highly unusual story that both Jesus and Simon Magus claimed to have survived the crucifixion?

This then begs the question: were Simon Magus and Jesus the same person? This Appendix is only able to offer one angle of evidence that sheds more light on this possibility, though it is unable to take on the enormous challenge of "proving" this thesis, as far more research and investigations are required.

That said, if we are to entertain the possibility of a single Simon-Jesus identity, let us try to make sense of the various accounts that Simon-Jesus was not crucified. Through some use of magic (something Simon was most noted for), another, let's call him X, was made to look like Simon-Jesus, which resulted in X being crucified. In later edited versions, instead of Simon-Jesus being in contrast to this other person X, rather, Simon-Jesus is separated into Simon of Cyrene and Jesus, where Simon is either the one who was crucified or, as found in the New Testament, was the one who simply helped Jesus carry the cross. This character Simon of Cyrene may have been introduced in later editions of this tale as a means of detaching the Christ Simon of Cyprus identity away from an orthodox version of Jesus.

This conflation of the names Cyprus and Cyrene is similar to how Acts inserted these two names, together side by side, in a way that does not make sense in the sentence and suggests an intention to create confusion between them. "Now they which were scattered abroad upon the persecution that arose about Stephen [more likely James] travelled as far as Phenice, and Cyprus, and Antioch, preaching the word to none but unto the Jews only. And some of them were men of Cyprus and Cyrene, which, when they were to come to Antioch, spake unto the Grecians, preaching the Lord Jesus" (11:19-20). In the second sentence, Cyprus is redundant from the first and may have been included as a way to blend and confuse the names Cyprus and Cyrene. These two sentences are clearly confused, with Antioch, for example, being named as both the origination and destination of the travelers. As Eisenman (1997) explores extensively, this is a classic example of the technique of name scrambling in the New Testament that serves to deflect and obscure the reader away from a more accurate but less welcomed history.

Again, instead of there being two people, Simon and Jesus, the thesis is that there was one called by both names. Furthermore, Jesus-Simon did not die, but another died in his place, and there was much confusion around this in its aftermath. As opposed to Simon Magus of Cyprus, Simon of Cyrene was a character that the later orthodox designers of the scriptures likely invented to throw a curveball into the identity of this Jesus-Simon, where questions of who died and who survived were shrouded in fog to confuse the more original story. In the final version that was locked into the Gospels, there is no confusion that Jesus was crucified and Simon of Cyrene helped carry Jesus's cross on his grueling walk to Golgotha.[11]

An Earlier Version of the Cross

Though images of the cross currently adorn Christian churches worldwide, common use of the crucifix in churches took centuries before it came into prominence. There is evidence of an earlier esoteric cross symbol used as an expression of the Deep Christ teachings that may have eventually become replaced by the crucifix. In the *Second Treatise*, Jesus writes, "It was my cross that the world did not accept." One wonders if this might relate to Simon's lost book, *The Four Quarters of the World*,[12] where he may have presented a more elaborate, even cosmological, cross symbol that was rejected and eventually replaced with an image of the crucifixion of Jesus.

From my review of this Deep Christ literature, there was an earlier cross symbol that presented a complex map of the entire Sophianic cosmology that, I believe, was later overlaid with a two-dimensional cross of crucifixion. In the *Acts of John*, Christ shows John a "Cross of Light" and says, "And as it is Wisdom in 'harmony,' there are those on the Right and those on the Left- powers, authorities, principalities, and daemons, ... and the Lower Root from which hath come forth the things in genesis. This, then, is the cross which by the Word hath been the means of 'cross-beaming' all things – at the same time separating off the things that proceed from genesis and those below it... this is not the cross of wood which thou shalt see when thou descendest hence; nor am I he that is upon the cross..."[13]

In other words, instead of this being a symbol of Jesus's sacrifice (which he says specifically didn't happen to him), it is a sort of cosmological map showing the path of Christ's descent from the upper Region of the Right down through the lower Region of the Left, which seems to include the history as recounted in the Book of Genesis. This is a rare glimpse at what might have been the meaning of a more original cross of Jesus.

There is also a most significant clue, I believe, to what may well have been a cross that originated from the earliest teachings of the Deep Christ. This is known as the St. Thomas Cross.

The St. Thomas Cross

The *Acts of Thomas*, at least in part, is believed to have emerged from the writings of St. Thomas possibly as early as 40 CE. This version of AT, however, is clearly a later edited version that includes the scrambling of names and identities of three key figures as is typical in the New Testament: "James the son of Alphaeus and Simon the Canaanite and Judas the brother of James" (AT).

There is a curious story in this unusual text of how Jesus tricks Judas Thomas "which is also the twin" into being sent off to India. This story may not be too far from the truth, for there is historical evidence outside of the

Acts of Thomas that points to Thomas going to India for missionary work and founding a sect of Indian Christians called The Nasrani or St. Thomas Christians. Nasrani is a Syriac term that stems from the word Nazarene, associated with the early Christians.[14] The Syriac written language is derived from the Palestine region's Aramaic and is the written language in which many of the Gnostic scriptures were translated from their Greek originals. This unique language emerged in the region of Edessa in the 1st century CE, where, evidence suggests, Thomas famously resided.

Within this tradition that still exists today, records indicate that Thomas first came to Northern India ~40 CE into the court of King Gondophares. (Ironically, if Jesus did send Thomas to India at this time, as the *Acts of John* recalls, this would have happened after the time of the crucifixion). In 52 CE, the St. Thomas Christian community records him arriving in the Kerala region in Southern India. There, he spent twenty years establishing seven churches that included the Syriac language as part of the church ritual,[15] until he was killed, allegedly, by a Hindu priest.

When the Portuguese Vasco de Gama and his fellow explorers arrived in Kerala in 1498, they found a network of Thomas Christian churches, all having one item on their alters, known as the Cross of St. Thomas. The oldest of these crosses they uncovered was believed to be the stone Thomas himself carved and was clutching when he was killed.[16]

St. Thomas Cross, carved in granite.
This modern replica may be close to the original one carved by St. Thomas.

A contemporary wood version of the St. Thomas Cross

This cross is strikingly different from the crucifixion cross of Jesus. If this image had been seeded into southern India in the mid 1st century, it may well have escaped the later orthodox-leaning version of the crucifix and represents an earlier cross motif associated with the Deep Christ.

It is also interesting to note that St. Thomas is featured in the anti-Simonian John's Gospel as being the one who doubted that Christ hung on the cross. This is an egregious distortion and, I believe, a glaring cover-up of what was likely a far more profound and elaborate story of Thomas's role in the dissemination of what appears to be a cross that depicts the whole drama of Christ Sophia. Given that the early French gothic cathedrals did not include images of the crucifixion, the phenomenon of the Thomas cross could provide insights into why the Knights Templars, according to reports from their interrogations, rejected the Catholic crucifix.

These Thomas crosses are popular not only in the Nasrani churches but in churches around the world, though often not recognized nor understood. The Episcopal Church in Northern California, for example, where the priest preached about the heresy of Gnosticism after my conversation with him, features an artistic variation of a silver metal Thomas Cross positioned on the wall behind the main altar.

Interpreting this image of a Thomas Cross, from the top center, there is an emanation that lands on two pillars, with exploded clouds of energy. This could be representing the 12 aeons of the Pleroma that then intermingle from Light to materiality as it enters into the "midst" of the transitional 13th aeon. This is all above the crossbar, in the Region of the Right. Then, this Light energy enters into the materiality in what is called the Region of the Left, as signified by the stone pillars.

From above, a bird descends into a ball on the top of the cross. This invokes the key theme of the Great Emanation as found in the first sentence of the *Pistis Sophia*, "…in the second space of the First Mystery which is before all mysteries, -- the Father in the form of a dove" (PS:1). This bird is likely equated with the dove, a symbol of the Holy Spirit, the feminine aspect of the divine emanation, the higher Sophia. The ball could equate to the program of the Sophianic seeding of the Divine Spark as it was brought down from the Pleroma and into the Regions of the Left.

At the ends of the crossbars are a larger and then a smaller ball. This, I believe, equates to the idea of the fruit on the tree and even inside the fruit, the seed, or the Divine Spark. This recalls the Simonian notion of the Tree and the Fruit in the *Great Revelation*. Let's revisit this passage.

"But as for the fruit of the tree, if its form is perfect and it assumes the true shape, it is gathered into the storehouse, not thrown into the fire. For the fruit is produced in order to be stored away, but the bark of the tree, having served its purpose is destined for the fire, as it was produced for no purpose in its own right but only to protect the fruit" (GR).

This tree and fruit, I believe, are metaphors for our physical and spiritual bodies accordingly. The ephemeral physical body gives rise to the spiritual body. This whole cross image even goes further by identifying the seed within the fruit, that spark of the latent fire from the heavens which was planted into the human form here in these lower regions of creation that can give birth to our body of light.

Base of the St. Thomas Cross

The lowest section at the base of the Thomas cross is highly significant. If this cosmic map of the Great Emanation equates to the Kabbalah's Tree of Life, then this bottom section would be in the position of the Malkuth, the Kabbalah's 10th sephiroth, earthly home to the shekinah. The classic interpretation of this part of the cross is that it equates to the lotus flower, a prominent Hindu religious symbol common to this region in southern India. However, if viewed according to a Thomas-Deep Christ model, this may well represent an explosion of divine Light from within the small indwelling seed/spark.

The "Living Jesus," not the one hanging from the cross, said, "Blessed is he who has crucified the world, and who has not allowed the world to crucify him" (IE). Forego the glut of temptations of physical pleasure that numb our ability to access the ultimate pleasure, the awakening of our essential Divine Spark Within.

This Thomas cross seems to illustrate that the Holy Light within us is made of the same stuff as the fire of Ein Soph Or, the Great Power, that radiates from the Source and is carried down into materiality by the Sophianic Holy Spirit. Incredibly, this may be the earliest illustration of what both Thomas and the Deep Christ meant by the phrase, "Bring forth what is within you."

ENDNOTES

Introduction

1. Incidentally, Sophia was not so marginalized by the Eastern Church, and author Sergei Bulgakov (1879–1944) was one of her great proponents.

2. I presented *The Myth of Sophia: Recalling an Ancient Gnostic Creation Story* (Morse, 1998) for my Master's degree project at Matthew Fox's former University of Creation Spirituality in Oakland. See https://www.matthewfox.org/university-of-creation-spirituality.

3. Joseph Campbell used the term "monomyth," taken from James Joyce, to describe the Hero's Journey as a broad archetypal template that can take numerous forms in myth, folklore, and religious motifs. Similarly, the creation story of Sophia can be viewed as an overarching meta-creation story.

4. See Henderson, 2005, for a valuable analysis of the archetype of initiation.

5. Such as the influence of Ibn Arabi. See Corbin, 1998.

6. See Klimkeit, 1993.

7. Regarding the Nestorian Monument in China, see https://archive.org/details/nestorianmove00saekuoft.

Chapter 2: Historical Context of the First Century Novel Revelation of Wisdom

1. Eisenman (1997) writes extensively about references, including from Josephus, to a Jewish religious leader who strongly resembles James being pushed down the steps of the temple and who was eventually killed, which Eisenman believes was an event that triggered the Jewish Wars from 66–70 CE.

2. Aslan, 2011, p. xxx.

3. Eisenman, 1997, p. xxxii.

4. Robinson, Editor, 1978. "In none of these Sethian instances can one derive the texts or their mythology primarily from Christian tradition…" p. 8.

Chapter 3: An Introduction to Gnosticism

1. From a former website (https://www.westarinstitute.org/resources/forum/reflections-on-the-category-Gnosticism/). "The April 2016 issue of Westar's academic journal, *Foundations and Facets Forum*, has just been posted online. The articles in this issue, from Westar's Fall 2014 meeting, acknowledge that the category of 'Gnosticism' is not an ideal tool for making sense of the first- and second-century movements that led to the emergence of Christianity."

2. Haar, 2003, p. 73. For an updated review of this definition, see Dillon, Matthew J. (2016), *"Gnosticism Theorized: Major Trends and Approaches to the Study of Gnosticism"* https://hcommons.org/deposits/objects/hc:34032/datastreams/CONTENT/content.

3. Layton, 1987, p. 14.

4. Heresy, from the Greek *haíresis*, means roughly a sort of philosophical pursuit of diverse opinion. The word heresy associated with heterodoxic or open-ended thinking became demonized by the more rigid Christian doctrine. Irenaeus helped codify the word "heresy" as being a derogatory word that meant a violation of the more accepted orthodoxy.

5. See http://gnosis.org/library/bookss.htm.

Chapter 4: Introduction to the Creation Story of Sophia

1. Mead, 1900, p. 594. See http://gnosis.org/library/grs-
    mead/fragments_faith_forgotten/fff72.htm. Also, Isaiah 66:8.
    "…as soon as Zion travailed, she brought forth her children."

2. See https://www.wisdominallthings.com/wisdom/old-testament-
    scriptures-wisdom/.

3. Layton, 1987, p. 12.

Chapter 5: Introduction to the Deep Christ

1. Pagels, 1975, p. 5.

2. Ibid, p. 10.

3. See https://www.westarinstitute.org/.

4. Matthew 28:19 is the only reference to the full "Father, Son and
    the Holy Spirit" in the four Gospels.

5. Petrine doctrine and the Primacy of Peter refer to Peter as the
    founding pope of Roman Christianity. The historical accuracy of
    this has been disputed by Eisenman and Tabor.

6. This is a quote taken from the Ritual of the Bridal Chamber (Miller,
    2004). Rosamonde Miller, an ordained Priestess of the Gnostica
    Ecclesia in Mountain View, CA, held sacred Gnostic services for
    many years. Her devotion to this work was inexhaustible, as she
    and her husband, David Miller, created a few different sanctuaries
    in the South Bay area as the need for newly leased spaces arose.
    The story is that, after her tortured political imprisonment and
    subsequent release from a Cuban prison (Segal, 1995, p. 199–203),
    Rosamonde was initiated into the Holy Order of Mariam of
    Magdala, which claims its origins to the 1st century, and Mary
    Magdalene as its founder. This lineage was private until it was
    decided that it was time to become public, and Rosamonde was the
    one to do this. She was also ordained by the acclaimed Gnostic
    priest and author Stephan Hoeller.

7. There is a consensus amongst scholars, including Eisenman and
    Aslan, who believe that the Slaughter of the Innocents is a fable as

there is no corroborating historical record of such an event. See https://en.wikipedia.org/wiki/Massacre_of_the_Innocents#CITE REFMaier1998.

8. Eisenman, Robert. Historical Jesus Lectures, presented at Cal State Long Beach. https://www.youtube.com/watch?v=V8tBkuLftDA.

9. See Conner, 2011, p. 90.

10. Layton, 1987, p.12. "Gnostic myth is the literary creation of theological poets - an elaborate theological symbolic poem, and not the spontaneous product of a tribe or culture. Philosophical myth of this kind was generally fashionable in the second century A.D., following a revival of interest in Plato's mythic tale of creation, the Timaeus, in the previous two centuries."

Chapter 7: The Four Stages of the Soul's Journey

1. Referring to Matthew Fox's book *Original Blessing*, his website (https://www.matthewfox.org/donation-store/original-blessing-a-primer-in-creation-spirituality) says this: "The sacredness of creation and of our role in it is a starting point—what the mystical tradition calls the Via Positiva, the path of joy and delight, awe and gratitude. The Via Negativa is the past of darkness and silence and also of suffering and of letting go and letting be. The Via Creativa is the path of creativity. And the Via Transformativa is the path of justice and compassion. All four paths constitute an adult spiritual journey. Each feeds the others."

2. Layton, 1987, p. 12, presents a four-part structuring of this myth of origins. Act I. The Great Emanation from source. Act II. Creation of the material world. Act III. The creation of Adam, Eve, and their children. Act IV. The subsequent history of the human race. What he calls a "subplot" to this grand myth of origins is the whole theme of the Divine Spark. Act I. The expansion of the "divine power" that fills the universe. Act II. The theft of this power by the archons. Act III. Via a trick, the planting of this seed into humans. And Act IV. The process of a great return of the sparks back to Source.

Chapter 8: The Great Emanation

1. Scholem, 1974, p. 100.
2. Ibid, p. 95.
3. Scholem, 1991, p. 159.
4. Scholem, 1941, p. 264.
5. Ibid, p. 261.
6. Corbin, 1978, p. 114.
7. Scholem, 1974, p. 96.

Chapter 9: The "Fall" of Sophia

1. In the *Pistis Sophia*, Jesus describes the source as the First Mystery as the 24th "aeon" in the complex "dimensional reality" of the Pleroma, the heavenly realm. From that source, the aeons emanate out in pairs, going down in numbers starting at 24, with the 13th aeon being the last in the Pleroma. This has also been identified as a transitional aeon and, according to the Pistis Sophia, is where Sophia came from. The 12th aeon and below (in other texts, the 7th heaven) lie outside the Pleroma and is where these lower beings called archons reside. It is in these lower regions where Sophia becomes trapped.

2. Evans (2015) argues that the editors or compilers of this rendition of the *Pistis Sophia* were referring to the "thirteenth aeon" as a region outside and not inside the Pleroma by a "Jeuian" Gnostic sect that he believes was intent on demeaning the Sethian Sophianic mythos.

3. This very specific and unusual motif of an archetypal feminine figure who abandons her post, which then results in anger from her brothers, appears specifically in the Old Testament Song of Songs (also called the Song of Solomon). "The sons of my own mother they grew angry with me; they appointed me the keeper of the vineyards [although] my vineyard, one that was mine, I did not keep" (1:6). I speculate that, amongst many other parallels, this suggests that the Song of Songs may be a poem that emerges out of

the same later 1st century proto-Gnostic roots as the Sethian Gnostics, including how this same highly unique motif is found in the Pistis Sophia. Two other key points contribute to this theory: 1) that the great philosopher of Old Testament religious allegory, Philo, who died in 50 CE, made no mention of the Song of Songs, the greatest poetic expression of allegory in the Old Testament, and 2), I have found no specific reference to this text prior to Rabbi Akiba's praise for it in 90 CE. This also points to the possibility that the Song of Songs arose out of a 1st century new Revelation of Wisdom literature, possibly involving St. Thomas, and may have been part of an effort to make this novel Gnostic system more compatible with Judaism. See https://sophiaproject.net/post/song-of-songs/.

4. Also, this parallels the Song of Songs (5:7): "The watchmen that were going about in the city found me. They struck me, they wounded me. The watchmen of the walls lifted my wide wrap off me."

Chapter 10: Reflections on Sophia and the Archons

1. Jung, 1976, p. 33. Letter written to Erich Neumann on 1/5/1952.

2. Lash, 2006, p. 158.

3. "Studying Intrusions from the Subtle Realm: How Can We Deepen Our Knowledge" by Dr. John E. Mack, in Steinfeld, 2021, p. 136 – 157.

4. https://www.theguardian.com/world/2022/feb/05/ufos-america-aliens-government-report. Also, https://www.c-span.org/video/?520133-1/hearing-government-investigation-ufos.

5. For a study on pre-verbal trauma and memory, https://www.researchgate.net/publication/15719501_Trauma_in_ the_Preverbal_Period_Symptoms_Memories_and_Developmental _Impact/link/5c983dab299bf1116945695b/download.

6. Kalshed, 2013, p. 58, discusses the transitional space between a child's outer experience and their inner world of imagination. Early trauma can result in a break between these worlds, though through

trauma healing work this can be linked once again by the recovery of the innocent (child) self that, as he describes, acts like a spark across the synapse of these two worlds. Also, Kalshed's insights into the "dark side" of devils and fallen angels as a psychological function can provide a context to the phenomenon of the archons in a way that offers an alternative to the problem of proof of their existence.

7. "Then a voice called out to them..." corresponds to a "Docetist" view of the post-crucifixion appearances of Jesus, where some believe that Jesus was non-physical and only appeared to his disciples in a spirit-body.

8. Regarding this idea of "faith," Jung clarified that to him, religion did not mean a simple creed. A religious belief or philosophy is originally based on both a numinous experience and also on faith (*pistis*) and trust that this experience has undoubtedly impacted the consciousness. Jung is saying that religion refers to a particular viewpoint that has been changed by an experience of the *numinosum*. Edinger (1999), p. 25–26.

Chapter 11: The Rescue of Sophia

1. This is listed as the 68th Psalm in the *Pistis Sophia* but is known in the Bible as the 69th Psalm.

2. Song of Songs, 5:7. The implications that the *Psalms* of David may have been drawn from the laments of Sophia are quite compelling. Was David tapping into these ancient songs of Sophia, or is this dialogue designed to help root this obscure text in a Jewish scriptural tradition to help give it more context in the face of increased marginalization? I am only able to speculate and am unable to offer clear insight into this question.

3. Song of Songs, 2:12.

Chapter 12: Emergence

1. To better understand the *Pistis Sophia* (which was not a part of the Nag Hammadi Library), we have to see it in the context of the

spectrum from the earliest Gnostic texts to the scriptures becoming more Christianized over time. The *Pistis Sophia* is the longest of all Gnostic texts, which includes extensive depictions of the story of Sophia. This text is arguably a later (2nd or 3rd generation) version, likely written in the mid-4th century, and includes telltale Christianized features. The extensive dialogues with the disciples, in an almost prescriptive manner, are one of the features of this trend. Also, linking the songs of Sophia with Old Testament Psalms may have been a device sought by the authors to bring greater "scriptural justification" of the Gnostic system to the Jewish communities (Ethan, 2015, p. 233).

2.   Also see the Robe of Glory theme in the *Mandean Book of John* (Mead, 1924). This also equates with Paul's reference to "putting on the whole armor of God" (Ephesians 6:10–18).

3.   One possible explanation is that the *Pistis Sophia* could have been written as an elaboration on the chronologically earlier Luke Gospel. However, if we look at the strategies employed by the editors of the New Testament as outlined exhaustively by Eisenman (1997), there is the possibility that Luke is a later, more reduced version of an earlier, more complex ascension narrative that found its way into this copy of the *Pistis Sophia*.

4.   Turner, 2001, p. 80–84.

5.   For the curious reader, there is a cryptic phrase that is described as having been written on Christ's robe by the "most High," and in the *Pistis Sophia* (PS:10), Christ gives a lengthy translation of this message.

6.   On the concept of a walk-in, see https://en.wikipedia.org/wiki/Walk-in.

7.   This debate in Christianity was settled in part by the Athanasian Creed that concluded that Jesus was both divine and human, called the hypostatic union.

Chapter 13: Lost Teachings of the Gnostic Christ

1.   Pagels, 1975, p. 3.

2. Robinson, 1978, p. 8.

3. Also, Luke's attempt in Acts to place Christ within a Jewish Pharisaic lineage may well have been a part of the effort to circumvent the role that Gnosticism played in the early formation of Christianity.

4. Robinson, 1978, p. 377.

5. Christ's higher self is equated with what is termed the Logos, the Word, and Christ. Pagels refers to him as the One Man, the "Anthropos." He is also identified with an aspect of that original trinity at times identified as the Logos, also called the Word, but which is associated with this archetypal divine figure of "man," called Anthropos in Greek, and Adam Kadmon (Primal Adam) in the esoteric Jewish texts of Kabbalah. The Greek word *Christos* would be the title associated with this aspect of his higher self. Another identification for the Word is "Standing" and "being upright within himself because he exists in everyone" (GTr). This Word is also associated with the "epinoia" or "ennoia," which equates with the Divine Inner Spark of Sophia and also of Christ.

6. Schmidt, 1978, p. 116.

Chapter 14: The Descent – from the Gnostic Christ to the New Testament Jesus

1. Mitchell and Young, 2008, p. xiii.

2. Ibid, p. xiii.

3. Filoramo, 1990, p. 5.

4. Haar, 2003, p. 78.

5. Couliano (1992, p. 31) explains this turning point in Gnostic history. Here is the Episcopal Nicene Creed from the Book of Common Prayer: "We believe in one God, the Father, the Almighty, maker of heaven and earth, of all that is seen and unseen. We believe in one Lord, Jesus Christ, the only Son of God, eternally begotten of the Father, God from God, Light from Light, true God from true God, begotten, not made, of one Being with the Father. Through him, all things were made. For us and for our

salvation he came down from heaven: by the power of the Holy Spirit, he became incarnate from the Virgin Mary and was made man. For our sake he was crucified under Pontius Pilate; he suffered death and was buried. On the third day, he rose again in accordance with the Scriptures; he ascended into heaven and is seated at the right hand of the Father. He will come again in glory to judge the living and the dead, and his kingdom will have no end. We believe in the Holy Spirit, the Lord, the giver of life, who proceeds from the Father and the Son. With the Father and the Son, he is worshiped and glorified. He has spoken through the Prophets. We believe in one holy catholic and apostolic Church. We acknowledge one baptism for the forgiveness of sins. We look for the resurrection of the dead, and the life of the world to come. Amen."

6.   In an original version of the Nicene Creed, a tag line was added: "We don't accept this line 'There was a time when he was not.'" Here, they are likely denouncing the Gnostic concept of the "Ineffable," "Unknowable" God.

7.   Josephus was an educated Jew from Jerusalem who fought in the Jewish uprising but was captured by the Roman army. He then turned on his cause and, likely as a means of gaining favor, managed to get word to the Roman military commander Vespasian that Vespasian himself would be the one to fulfill the Jewish prophecy of the long-awaited Messiah (Meshiach). To Josephus's good fortune, this "prophecy" was fulfilled, at least to some degree, when, in the wake of Nero's suicide, the revered Vespasian became Emperor of the Roman Empire. Josephus was adopted into this Flavian family, where he spent decades meticulously documenting the history of that era, including a whole book on the Jewish wars. Though there is a need to recognize his obvious bias in favor of the Romans, he was still incredibly detailed in his descriptions and historical accuracy, having the unique viewpoint of being both a prominent Jew and Roman citizen.

8.   Josephus, Book VIII, Chap 3, paragraph 3. "Now there was about this time Jesus, a wise man, if it is lawful to call him a man; for he was a doer of wonderful works, a teacher of such men as received

the truth with pleasure. He drew over to him both many of the Jews and many of the Gentiles. He was [the] Christ. And when Pilate, at the suggestion of the principal men amongst us, had condemned him to the cross, those that loved him at the first did not forsake him; for he appeared to them alive again the third day, as the divine prophets had foretold these and ten thousand other wonderful things concerning him. And the tribe of Christians, so named from him, are not extinct at this day." If we take this paragraph at face value, it appears to align with the familiar (orthodox) story of Christ. If we look at this paragraph in the context of not only Josephus's writing in general but the paragraphs immediately preceding and following it, it stands out like a sore thumb.

9. Josephus: *Antiquities of the Jews*. Book 20, Chapter 9, paragraph 1.

10. Sanhedrin 43a. See https://en.wikipedia.org/wiki/Yeshu#Yeshu_the_sorcerer.

11. See https://en.wikipedia.org/wiki/Historical_Jesus.

Chapter 15: Simon Magus

1. See http://gnosis.org/library/grs-mead/grsm_simon_magus.htm

2. Here is the full paragraph from Acts 8: 9-24. "But there was a certain man, called Simon, which before time in the same city used sorcery, and bewitched the people of Samaria giving out that himself was some great one: to whom they all gave heed, from the least to the greatest, saying, 'This man is the great power [Greek. *Dynamis Megale*] of God.' And to him, they had regard, because that of a long time he had bewitched them with sorceries. But when they believed Philip preaching the things concerning the kingdom of God, and the name of Jesus Christ, they were baptized, both men and women. Then Simon himself believed also: and when he was baptized, he continued with Philip, and wondered, beholding the miracles and signs which were done. Now when the apostles which were at Jerusalem heard that Samaria had received the word of God, they sent unto them Peter and John: who, when they came down, prayed for them, that they might receive the Holy Ghost:

(for as yet he was fallen upon none of them: only they were baptized in the name of the Lord Jesus). Then laid their hands on them, and they received the Holy Ghost. And when Simon saw that through laying on of the apostles' hands the Holy Ghost was given, he offered them money, saying, 'Give me also this power, that on whomsoever I lay hands, he may receive the Holy Ghost.' But Peter said unto him, 'Thy money perish with thee because thou hast thought that the gift of God may be purchased with money. Thou hast neither part nor lot in this matter: for thy heart is not right in the sight of God. Repent therefore of this thy wickedness, and pray God, if perhaps the thought [Greek. *Epinoia*] of thine heart may be forgiven thee, for I perceive that thou art in the gall of bitterness, and in the bond of iniquity.' Then answered Simon, and said, 'Pray ye to the Lord for me, that none of these things which ye have spoken come upon me.'" Simon's attempts to purchase the gifts of the Holy Spirit are known to this day as the sin of "simony."

3. See https://en.wikipedia.org/wiki/Clementine_literature.

4. Eisenman, 1997, p. 77.

5. Haar, 2011, p. 31–71.

6. Ibid, p. 71.

7. Irenaeus, *Against Heresies* (Book I, Chapter 23). For an online copy, see https://www.newadvent.org/fathers/0103123.htm.

8. See http://www.earlychristianwritings.com/hippolytus.html.

9. https://www.earlychristianwritings.com/text/hippolytus6.html. For more insight on the viability of the *Great Revelation* being authored by Simon Magus as it relates to Irenaeus, see DeConick, 2016, p. 102. Also, regarding the Greek name, *Apophasis Megale*, the word *apophasis* refers to a Greek rhetorical device of negation where a speaker will say they will not bring up a subject but by saying it they are in fact bringing it up. "I refuse to discuss rumors that my opponent is a drunkard" is an example of this. As it can be ascertained from the Pseudo-Clementine and this Great Revelation literature, Simon appears to have had a strong Greek education and that he may have purposely used the word *apophasis*, not to denote

"Revelation" (or in some translations "Declaration"), but rather, that he is pointing towards a Godhead which is ineffable and hidden from our direct knowing. Hence the title may more accurately be interpreted as, "A Great Revelation of something which can't be revealed."

10. Epiphanius quoted in Haar, 2011, p. 127.

11. Mead, 1892. http://gnosis.org/library/grs-mead/grsm_simon_magus.htm

12. Ibid.

13. Ibid.

14. I wonder if the odd Christian theme of "Christ's ransom" — i.e., Christ's sacrifice as an atonement to the devil for Adam and Eve's sin — is a distortion of this more original Simonian reference to "ransom."

15. This theme appears in the Gospel of John (John 15) which may suggest how later proto-orthodox versions emphasized the Savior Jesus as being the key figure in this metaphor. "I am the vine; you are the branches. If you remain in me and I in you, you will bear much fruit; apart from me, you can do nothing. If you do not remain in me, you are like a branch that is thrown away and withers; such branches are picked up, thrown into the fire, and burned." Here, Jesus is the vine, his disciples are the branches, and the fruit comes as they maintain devotion to him. The proto-orthodox writings in this Gospel may have been written as a way to distance Simon's esoteric teachings of human transformation toward a theology of dependency. Again, the emphasis is less on the fruit and more on the problem that we, the branches, are being separated from Christ the Savior. Or maybe this was a deliberate placeholder of the more advanced teaching so that someday, we could break the code and reclaim its deeper meaning.

16. *Homilies*, Chap 23. https://en.wikisource.org/wiki/Ante-Nicene_Fathers/Volume_VIII/Pseudo-Clementine_Literature/The_Clementine_Homilies/Homily_II/Chapter_23.

17. Eisenman, 1997, p. 62.

18. *Homilies*, Chap 24. https://en.wikisource.org/wiki/Ante-Nicene_Fathers/Volume_VIII/Pseudo-Clementine_Literature/The_Clementine_Homilies/Homily_II/Chapter_24 (Note: descriptions of the killing of Dositheus are likely part of *Homilies'* "romance" elaborations).

19. Mead, 1892. It is interesting to note that in the *Pistis Sophia*, Jesus is also depicted as referring to the "four corners of the world." "Jesus said unto his disciples: 'Draw near unto me.' And they drew near unto him. He turned himself towards the four corners of the world, said the great name over their heads, blessed them and breathed into their eyes" (PS:141). Also see https://en.wikipedia.org/wiki/Gospel_of_the_Four_Heavenly_Realms.

20. Ibid, p. 36.

21. The "red thread" motif found in contemporary religious and spiritual circles that honor Mary Magdalene may harken back to a spiritual lineage, sisterhood, or even bloodline associated with Jesus. However, I have not found first- or second-generation textual references to this red thread theme and Mary Magdalene.

22. Haar, 2011, p. 120.

23. Eisenman, 1997, p. 533–534.

24. Simon Magus allegedly wrote in the *Great Revelation*, "This is why, in truth, the poet Stesichorus was deprived of his sight when he treated her rudely in his verses. This is the reason, too, when he afterward recanted and wrote new verses, extolling her virtues, he received his sight again" (GR). Also see https://en.wikipedia.org/wiki/Stesichorus.

25. Haar, 1892.

26. For a full text of the *Kerygmata Petrou*, see http://www.earlychristianwritings.com/text/kerygmatapetrou.html

27. Quoted in Picknett and Prince, 2019, p. 226. For a synopsis of the Pseudo-Clementine *Recognitions* see https://www.newadvent.org/cathen/04039b.htm.

28. See https://www.newadvent.org/fathers/0815.htm.

Chapter 16: Simon and the Gnostic Jesus

1. Haar, 2011, p. 120–121.

2. Ibid, p. 92.

3. The symbol of water, I believe, refers to the boundary between the heavenly pleroma and the outer world of creation.

4. Haar, 2011, p. 124–125.

Chapter 17: Sparks of the Latent Fire

1. See http://gnosis.org/naghamm/nhlintro.html.

2. Meade, 2018, p. 124, and Kalsched, 2013, p. 164. Kalsched, 2013, p. 17 also equates this "splinter of divine radiance we call soul" with the motif of the pearl in the *Acts of Thomas*, "Hymn of the Pearl."

3. Like the word Ein Soph, the Kabbalah once again provides a term, Shekinah, that helps clarify what the Gnostics worked to describe, and I use this word personally to invoke this indwelling Sophianic spark of the divine within me.

4. Wilhelm, 1963, p. 21.

5. This psycho-spiritual orientation is inspired by Coherence Therapy. See Ecker, Ticic, and Hulley (2012) and www.coherencetherapy.org.

Chapter 18: Adam and the Sophianic Eve

1. The *Hypostasis of the Archons* (HA) is possibly a 3rd-century Gnostic text that may have been developed from the same source text as *On the Origin of the World* (OW), where both interpretations were taken from what were likely earlier, more original texts.

2. This quote from Paul (from possibly as early as the 2nd century) validates this as being a text from St. Paul that has had little editing or "redaction" over the centuries. "For we are not contending against flesh and blood, but against the principalities, against the

powers, against the world rulers of this present darkness, against the spiritual hosts of wickedness in the heavenly places" (St. Paul. Ephesians 6:12).

3.   Christ speaks in the *Trimorphic Protennoia*, a text that has many cross-references to the writings and teachings of Simon Magus. "And the Archigenetor of ignorance reigned over Chaos and the underworld, and produced a man in my likeness. But he neither knew that that one would become for him a sentence of dissolution, nor does he recognize the power in him (Adam)" (TP).

4.   Turner 2001, p. 74.

5.   One theme that appears in the Gnostic texts that is confusing, if not troubling, is the idea of the "Race" and the Seed of Seth. I subscribe to the theory that Adamic Man, *Homo sapiens*, is of a genetic group that carries this Divine Spark or some aspect of latent divine potential. To assert any one particular "race" as being the carrier of the Seed of Seth is to open the door to the obvious inanity of any group's claim to racial superiority. Gnosticism has endured a long history of being pushed underground, where it then became the breeding ground for many secret and dark groups that sought to exploit sacred wisdom to assert their own superiority, the Nazis being one example of this. That said, this idea of the "seed" of Seth is spoken of in the *Apocryphon of John* (AJ) as being in contrast to an elite genetic group that had some relationship to the archons, which I explore further in Chapter 20.

6.   Josephus recounts in *Antiquities* a story where Seth, Son of Adam, leaves two stone tablets (or two pillars) made of stone and clay high in the mountains that would survive either flood or fire. These were inscribed with advanced science, including astrological information for his future offspring. This Three Steles motif is also noted in the *Gospel of the Egyptians* (GE) and the *Revelation of Adam* (RA). Also see https://www.marquette.edu/maqom/giants.html.

7.   The story of Norea also appears in the Nag Hammadi collection as a Sethian praise to the divine, an "ode" or hymn called the *Thought of Norea* (TN). Norea represents the voice that commands support from the higher angelic (non-archonic) realms. "It is Norea who cries out to them" (TN).

8. Tabor, 2012, p. 11 explains that Paul's model of resurrection was less a physical rising from the dead but rather a transformation of the body into what he calls a "life-giving spirit" (1 Corinthians 15:45) and a process of becoming cloaked with a new spiritual body (2 Corinthians 5:1-5). Hence for Paul, Jesus represented a new Adam, a wholly novel species of human spirit beings he called Children of God.

9. Such a change involved 'putting off' the body like clothing, but not being left 'naked,' but 'putting on' a new spiritual body with the old one left behind. So transformed, Jesus was, according to Paul, the first 'Adam' of a new genus of Spirit-beings in the universe called 'Children of God,' of which many others were to follow."

Chapter 19: Retaining the Childlike Spark Within

1. As a psychotherapist, I contracted as a Military Family Life Consultant and was stationed at numerous military bases around the US and Europe. One of my roles was to provide emotional and behavioral support to children and their parents and the child care worker staff in the Child Development Centers.

2. From a pamphlet published by "Youth Liberation" in Ann Arbor, MI, in the 1970s. https://en.wikipedia.org/wiki/Youth_Liberation_of_Ann_Arbor.

3. Neil, 1960, p. 67.

4. Of course, there are innumerable layers to all this, involving the dynamics of my family system and how both my psychology and temperament also factored into what was an overall caring and well-supported upbringing. The role of socialization is multifaceted and, ideally, essential in helping young people enter the world so that his or her spark can be engaged with others as a valuable offering.

5. For information about Neil Douglas-Klotz, see https://neildouglasklotz.academia.edu/.

6. For an overview of Neoteny, see https://en.wikipedia.org/wiki/Neoteny.

7. I looked at age difference using the basic template of Hegelian dialectic theory and applied it to a general theory of change, where there is a "thesis" or a given condition that is then countered with an "anti-thesis." The thesis then works in response to this anti-thesis and vice versa, whereupon a third, "synthesis" can result in a new outcome from the old duality. Jung's concept of the Transcendent Function (Miller, 2004) can also be used as a model for understanding this. The main point is that, like in Freire's *Pedagogy of the Oppressed (1993),* it is the consciousness of the one who is oppressed that becomes the force whereupon an abuse of power can be challenged, shifted, and transformed. It was a half-priced book, *The Oppression of Youth,* I found at a local bookstore that provided the ground upon which my spirited child-self found some footing to stand up and push against the ominous forces of adult acculturation. "The oppression of youth is one form of the oppression dialectic; its aim is to maintain power, to perpetuated the social system, and, most important, to defend against the fear and anxiety associated with the possibility of radical or extreme changes." (Clark, 1975, p. 156) This book spoke poetry for me, naming the unseen forces of control that guard the status quo against each new generation's potential to initiate change.

8. Ironically, it was the same church in Santa Rosa where my Gnostic intrigues were curtly shot down from the pulpit that, years earlier, the resident Episcopal priest with a strong Jungian orientation played the pristine-quality pipe organ as part of a musical accompaniment to one of my bardic presentations on Sophia.

9. According to Jung, "the alchemical operations were real, only this reality was not physical but psychological. Alchemy represents the projection of a drama both cosmic and spiritual in laboratory terms. The opus magnum had two aims: the rescue of the human soul, and the salvation of the cosmos." From 1952 interview at Eranos, quoted in https://carljungdepthpsychologysite.blog/2020/10/24/the-alchemical-operations-were-real/#.YvFXD-zMJfU.

Chapter 20: Overcoming the Counterfeit Spirit

1. Sigmund Freud, in a letter to Jung, dated August 20, 1911.
    Printed in McGuire, William, ed. 1974. p. 438.

2. Carl Jung, in a letter to Freud, dated August 29, 1911. Printed
    in McGuire, William, ed., 1974. p. 439. Jung wrote the Greek
    Sophia, σοφ´ια (Greek: sigma - s, omikron - o, lower case phi -
    ph, iota - i, alpha - a) and ended the sentence with "...an
    Alexandrian term particularly suited to the reincarnation of
    ancient wisdom in the shape of A" (Greek uppercase alpha).
    For Jung, the Gnostic Sophia was a theme, though rarely
    mentioned, that seemed to weave through the underground
    strata of his work. Also, the figure Simon Magus features
    prominently in his inner explorations, showing up as an
    imaginal wise old man (senex) he called Philemon.

3. From the preface to "Gnostic Cathechism" by Stephan
    Hoeller. http://gnosis.org/ecclesia/catechism.htm#Preface.

4. From Meade's "Living Myth" Podcast, Episode 260: Myth
    Makes Meaning, 12/22/2021.

5. "Standing" is a prominent theme in the Simonian system,
    relating to Simon's claim to being the Standing One, the Christ.

6. Mead, 1900, p. 589, postulates that the *Pistis Sophia* may have
    been taken from a more original but lost book called
    Questions of Mary. Also found at
    http://gnosis.org/library/pistis-sophia/ps003.htm.

7. "Do you think I came to bring peace on earth? No, I tell you,
    but division. From now on there will be five in one family
    divided against each other, three against two and two against
    three" (Luke 12:51–52).

8. This identification with the physical body as being one part of
    the enslaved self, I believe, is referring to the lure of, at times,
    addictive carnal pleasures that can distract us from our exalted
    potential. Though the theme of the body being corrupt is
    certainly present in the Gnostic tradition, this, however, can be
    viewed in contrast to the central importance of the very
    physical vehicle, the "bodily dwelling," which was key to the

process of becoming embodied as Children of Light.

9. Mary further clarifies Christ's analogy of the house equating to our own being. She again quotes from Christ's parable teachings: "The foes of the man are the dwellers in his house" (Matthew 10:36). In the Pistis Sophia, Mary describes how "the dwellers in the house of the soul are the counterfeiting spirit and the destiny, which are hostile to the soul the whole time, making it commit all sin and all iniquities" (PS:11320).

10. Kaia Ra, 2016, p. xiv–xvii.

11. Christ also told his disciples during the discussion on the counterfeit spirit that he will present vast details about all of this at some future time he calls "at the expansion of the all, and after that I will tell you why all this has occurred" (PS:132). This is a highly cryptic reference that suggests that, if this information was not already given to his disciples during this time of the mystery teachings, at some future date, after some cosmic "expansion" event, the full story will then be able to be told.

Chapter 21: The Bridal Chamber

1. The precession of the equinoxes is the circular movement of the earth's axis that wobbles one complete cycle over the course of approximately 26,000 years, with 2,160 years marked as a distinct astrological age.

2. Scholem, 1941, p. 274–280.

3. The HeartMath Institute: https://www.heartmath.org/.

4. Institute of HeartMath. 2003, p. 1.

5. Ibid, p. 3.

6. Ibid, p. 7.

7. Anonymous, 2010, p. 4.

8. Scholem, 1991, p. 140–196.

9. Ibid, p. 5–6.

10. Anonymous, 2010, p. 42.

11. It is possible that the sheer quantity of time this group spent deep in the salt mine, however, might have given them the advantage of severe sensory deprivation, a condition that can make the development of higher perception abilities come more easily.

12. Ibid, p. 20. Also, I refer the reader to Kalshed (2013) for insights into what might be seen at face value as spiritual "visions" which, though not dismissing them as mere hallucinations, can nevertheless be seen in the context of how, in the face of trauma, these spiritual experiences can be understood as arising out of the deep Self's process of self-preservation.

13. This may be a later version of "The Mystery of the Forgiveness of Sins" as described by Christ in *The Great Logos According to the Mystery*. "For it is necessary that every man who will believe in the Kingdom of the Light should perform the mystery of the forgiveness of sins only once. For to every man who will perform the mystery of the forgiveness of sins, all the sins which he has committed knowingly or unknowingly, from his childhood until today, and which he committed since the foundation of the world until today, will all be erased, and he will be made to be a pure light and taken to the Light of these Lights… And when those who have received these mysteries and the mystery of the forgiveness of sins come forth from the body, all the aeons (archons) draw back (one) after another, and they flee to the west to the [region of the] left…" (IE p. 104).

14. An exquisite and ancient version of a Bridal Chamber ritual was performed for decades in Northern California by the esteemed Gnostic Priestess Rosamonde Miller in her "Gnostic Mystery of the Eucharist" (Miller, 2004). See https://www.gnosticsanctuary.org/eucharist.html

15. The English and then the Aramaic translations.

    Our Father: *Abwoon:* O Birther! Father-Mother,

Who art in heaven: *D'washmaya:* you create all that moves in light.

Hallowed be thy name.

Nethqadash: Your name, your sound

Shmakh: can move us if we tune our hearts as instruments for its tone.

16. See my longer translation and accompanying notes in Song 20 at https://www.sophiaproject.net/post/song-20.

17. The voice of Sophia from the *Book of Theophanies* by Ibn 'Arabi. Quoted in Corbin, 1997, p. 174.

18. Anonymous, 2010, p. 40–41.

19. Ibid, p. 13.

20. See my translation and notes in Song15 at https://www.sophiaproject.net/post/song-15.

21. See Mary the Prophetess https://en.wikipedia.org/wiki/Mary_the_Jewess.

22. A rough metaphysical model of dimensions. Third dimension: physicality as defined within space/time. Fourth Dimension: subtle, non-physical, astral level, psyche, emotions, dream space, synchronicity. Fifth dimension: unity consciousness, outside of duality, Christed consciousness and is best exemplified by the achievements of the X7 group.

23. There are other examples of this process of the awakening of the divine Light Body, such as the phenomenon of the Rainbow Body found in the Tibetan Buddhist tradition of Dzogchen, the Chinese alchemical process described in *The Secret of the Golden Flower* (Wilhelm, 1962) and the Quechua (Incan) shamanic work with the emergence of a new human species they call "homo luminous." In various Gnostic texts, it is called "The Robe of Glory" and equates with St. Paul's "the whole armor of God" (Ephesians 6:11). Also, Mead's book (1919), *The Doctrine of the Subtle Body in Western Tradition,* offers an investigation into this phenomenon as found within a variety of esoteric traditions. I know a man who described to

me how he witnessed his spiritual teacher shift into his body of light, an eyewitness account that is highly extraordinary. The X7 testimony, however, is being used here as the primary example because it holds such a clear correspondence to the "Gnostic concept of Sophia."

24. McGilchrist, 2018. The studies into the nature of the left and right hemispheres by McGilchrist constitute a monumental contribution to our understanding of the nature of human consciousness. Whereas the left brain dissects, analyzes, maps, and creates impersonal disconnection, the right brain offers a more advanced baseline function where we both perceive and become a part of the gestalt of connection, relationship, and meaning-making that ultimately grounds us in a position of love, the most fundamental and essential fabric of reality.

25. Rudolf. 1983, p. 245.

26. Corbin, 2014, p. 111.

27. Ibid, p. 163. Henry Corbin, Islamic, Sufi, and Persian Mysticism scholar extraordinaire, wrote in a posthumously published collection called *Jung, Buddhism, and the Incarnation of Sophia; Unpublished Writings from the Philosopher of the Soul* (2019) of the enormous value of Jung's *Answer to Job* (2010), which Corbin calls Jung's "Sophianic" book. Corbin wrote, "The reign of the Holy Spirit as feminine hypostasis [underlying reality] ...and identifying itself with Sophia, is thus the vision of 'the dawning of a new aeon.' And this is the answer to Job." A year after Jung published his book, he wrote to Corbin, saying that Corbin "understood completely" what was occurring in this book.

28. http://gnosis.org/ecclesia/homily_Descent.htm.

29. Sapientia is Latin for "wisdom."

Epilogue: Thesis Implications and Areas of Further Research

1. Mead, 1903, p. 288.

2. For reference, see

https://en.wikipedia.org/wiki/Simeon_of_Jerusalem.

3. This may not be significant, but in both Gospel references, the names Simon and Judas are reversed. The fourth brother is called Joses. The identity of this highly elusive brother, I suspect, might equate with a key 1st century figure, Barnabas of Cyprus, the famed associate of St. Paul, whose birth name was Joses or Joseph.

4. Harris, J. Rendel, *The Dioscuri in The Christian Legends,* 1903. https://archive.org/stream/cu31924099385084/cu319240993 85084_djvu.txt.

5. It is curious that in October, 2006, Pope Benedict presented an address to the Vatican's General Audience titled "Our Identity Is Not to Be Toyed With." His talk focused on the two least-known disciples, Simon the Canaanite and Judas Thaddeus, "son of James." In this address, the Pope appeared to be upholding orthodoxy with a warning to Christians about the dangers of "unacceptable teachings" (such as, I suspect, the contemporary publications of 1st century Christian and Jewish scholar, Robert Eisenman). The Pope reported that his main concern was to alert Christians against those who entertain heretical teachings which can lead to divisions within the Church. See https://www.catholic.org/featured/headline.php?ID=3717

6. Aslan, 2013, p. 33.

7. Zacharia Sitchen has published numerous books that work with the Sumerian tablets to develop theories that are extraordinary, even extreme. Though his work has been a major influence in studies of ETs and ancient history, I believe one cannot rely on his research for definitive findings of the Sumerians.

8. A list of contributors: Paul Levy, Sol Lukman, Lisa Renee, William Henry, Meg Benedicte, Corey Goode, David Wilcock along with Pete Peterson, Sean Stone, David Icke, Laura Eisenhower, Vidya Frazier, Darren Starwynn, and Debra Giusti's Ascension Panels at conscious festival gatherings. I

utilize rigorous discernment processes as I investigate information from these sources.

9. My loose definition of the fourth dimension, apart from just "time," is an astral-psychoid frequency range of consciousness, where synchronicity and dreams are found, for example, and where Space-Time (third dimensional) framework is loosened.

10. Jung wrote about this in a most insightful way. He had psychic encounters with a Gnostic figure Basilides, from 2nd-century Alexandria, who was featured in his *Seven Sermons of the Dead* (1916). Jung later wrote in his autobiography (1989) that he often felt like the deceased were in the room with him, waiting to hear his insights into their own destiny. He came to understand that the dead were dependent in some fashion on the living, those in the world, for answers to their questions. The broader consciousness assumed to be available to the deceased, they seemed to indicate, relied on a "soul bound in a body." The mind of the living, he suggested, held an advantage over that of the dead "in the capacity for attaining clear and decisive cognitions" (p. 308).

11. William Henry is sounding a serious alarm that biological technologies are increasingly becoming incorporated into our human experience and are a threat to our natural bio-spiritual potential. See https://www.williamhenry.net/whblog/.

12. The World Economic Forum and its ideological leader, Klaus Schwab, is an example of this, where, though on the surface appears to do good to attend to real-world challenges, the Great Reset platform may exploit the power of Artificial Intelligence in social and biological engineering that, unchecked, ultimately serves the technocratic elite.

13. The work of Charles Eisenstein is helpful in navigating this difficult terrain. See https://charleseisenstein.org/essays/the-conspiracy-myth/. "It is a myth with an illustrious pedigree, going back at least to the time of the first century Gnostics. Gnostics believe that an evil demiurge created the material world out of a preexisting divine essence. Creating the world in the image of his own distortion, he imagines himself to be its

true god and ruler. One needn't believe in this literally, nor believe literally in a world-controlling evil cabal, to derive insight from this myth — insight into the arrogance of the powerful, for example, or into the nature of the distortion that colors the world of our experience." Also helpful is Eisenstein's conversation with Paul Kingsnorth at https://www.youtube.com/watch?v=okO4H_Y6704.

14. https://en.wikipedia.org/wiki/Zero-point_energy.

15. For reference to Campbell's model of the hero's journey, see https://en.wikipedia.org/wiki/Hero%27s_journey.

16. See Gershom Scholem's writing on Jewish mysticism.

17. See Henry Corbin's writings on Persian and Islamic Sufi mysticism.

18. Indigenous spiritual systems likely lie deeper still and hence deserve honor and respect as a unique source in contrast to these esoteric traditions.

19. See my article, https://www.sophiaproject.net/post/the-templars-and-the-sacred-feminine.

20. If indeed there is a correlation here, it would be astounding that these cryptic Gnostic images etched into Catholic cathedrals remained invisible to Rome while the Church, in the same (13th) century that Notre Dame was built, embarked on a genocidal crusade against the Gnostic-leaning Cathars of southern France.

21. In 1625 a large fountain was built on the West area in front of Notre Dame to provide water for villagers. According to Fulcanelli (1984, p. 63) in its center featured a large statue of a man holding a book in one hand and a snake in the other. The inscription read, "You who are thirsty, come hither: if by chance the fountain fails, the goddess, by degrees, prepared the everlasting waters." This cryptic image, like Mother Alchemy, sprang up in the early centuries of this temple's life. In 1748 this was taken down to expand the West side's open plaza called Parvis Notre Dame. In contrast, on the East side of Notre Dame, was erected in 1910 the Fountain of the

Archbishop, featuring a statue of the Virgin and child, accompanied by three archangels defeating the allegorical figure of heresy (see https://curate.nd.edu/show/1r66j101b7r).

And yet the everlasting waters remain.

Appendix: The Fog of Crucifixion

1. In his book, *James the Brother of Jesus,* Eisenman (1997) makes an exhaustive investigation into how early Christian writers used "misinformation" with a pattern of deceit to steer the emerging theology in their favor. Words he uses to describe this are: "malicious substitutions," "distorted," "covered up," "reversed or inverted," "historical obliteration and transformation," and "neutralizing and deflecting."

2. Eisenman, 1997, p. xxvii. "That is not to say that the Jesus of history did not exist, only that the evidence is skewed and that the problem is more complex than many think."

3. Ibid, p. 963.

4. Mark 15:21-22, Matthew 27:32, Luke 23:26.

5. In Pseudo-Clement's Homilies II, Chapter 24. https://en.wikisource.org/wiki/Ante-Nicene_Fathers/Volume_VIII/Pseudo-Clementine_Literature/The_Clementine_Homilies/Homily_II/Chapter_24

6. Irenaeus, *Against Heresies,* Book I, Chapter 24, Section 40. See http://gnosis.org/library/advh1.htm. Also, the 4th century Epiphanius may have taken this interpretation from Irenaeus: "This second monologue mounts another dramatic piece for us in his account of the cross of Christ; for he claims that not Jesus, but Simon of Cyrene, has suffered. For when the Lord was marched out of Jerusalem, as the Gospel passage says, one Simon of Cyrene was compelled to bear the cross. From this, he finds his trickeries opportunity for composing his dramatic piece and says: Jesus changed Simon into his own form while he was bearing the cross, and changed himself into Simon, and delivered Simon to crucifixion in his place. During Simon's

crucifixion, Jesus stood opposite him unseen, laughing at the persons who were crucifying Simon. But he himself flew off to the heavenly realms after delivering Simon to crucifixion and returned to heaven without suffering. It was Simon himself who was crucified, not Jesus. Jesus, Basilides says, passed through all the powers on his flight to heaven, till he was restored to his own Father" (Williams, 2009, p. 78).

7. It is possible that the name "Simon" was added to an earlier version, just as "she who was a whore" was likely added after the name Sophia in this ST text, but we can only speculate.

8. For full document, http://www.documentacatholicaomnia.eu/03d/0050-0150,_Pseudo_Clemens,_Recognitions_[Schaff],_EN.pdf. Chapters LIII (p. 354) to LXII (p. 364).

9. This raises the question of whether the later Faust stories of Goethe and Marlow were drawn from earlier romance literature fictions designed to demonize Simon Magus and exalt St. Peter, such as in the legend of St. Cyprian and his beloved Justin. If this is the case, then the story of St. Cyprian the magician, along with the Faust tale, might offer more clues to the life of Simon Magus, such as his possible ties to the Roman aristocracy and his connection to the island of Cyprus. See Palmer and More, 2013, p. 42–52 (The Sources of the Faust Tradition). For a further analysis of Marlowe, Faust, and Simon Magus, see https://www.jstor.org/stable/458629.

10. The Holiest Koran 4:157. See https://corpus.quran.com/translation.jsp?chapter=4&verse=157.

11. It is curious that the orthodox Christian promotion of the crucifixion and blaming the Jews for his death seems to reinforce a doctrine of Jesus being sacrificed for the sins of the people, thus fostering a dependence on the church, where, with the help of tithing, people can be exonerated for their sins that Jesus so heroically suffered for. It is also important to note that profound devastation has resulted from the New Testament's version of the crucifixion of Christ, where blame

on the Jews has been a convenient excuse for rampant and devastating antisemitism over all subsequent centuries. Luke (Acts) takes great liberty in blaming the Jews for Jesus's death while minimizing the role of the Roman rulers. Here, this narrative from the late 1st century and later writings served to downplay any negative view of Roman rule, acting as apologists to the Roman-sponsored Christian orthodoxy. The Gospel's version that the Judean governor Pontius Pilate was innocent and the Jews were to blame for this crucifixion speaks volumes in light of the historical fact that Pilate was so bloodthirsty and cruel that he was recalled back to Rome by the emperor Tiberius to be interrogated for his crimes (Eisenman, 1997, p. 106.)

12. Mead, 1892.

13. Mead, 2006, p. 257–258.

14. This term Nazoreans is riddled with confusion between the Jewish zealot movement of James and the emerging non-Jewish early Christian movement associated with Jesus and Paul.

15. See https://www.nasrani.net/revival-syriac-language-worship-grass-root-level-new-model-liturgical-reformation-syro-malabar-church/. The Thomas Cross carved in granite featured at the top of this article might be a close replica of the original cross created by St. Thomas, though this is only my speculation. Depicted are the twelve aeons emanating down into the thirteen, that transitional region depicted at length in the *Pistis Sophia*, which then descends into the eight aeonic regions of the material world.

16. For information about the Bleeding Stone of St. Thomas, see http://www.talentshare.org/~mm9n/articles/sliva/8.htm.

Glossary of Terms

13th Aeon: A transitional aeon between the Pleroma and the lower worlds of creation. The location from which Sophia resided and descended, according to the *Pistis Sophia*.

Aeon: Frameworks of dimensionality that emanate from Ein Soph-Ineffable. Hosted by male and female deities (sometimes also called Aeons), who take responsibility for the maintenance of that structure. A broader context to time/space reality.

Anthropos: Archetypal Man, blueprint of the divine human form, equated with the Kabbalah concept of Adam Kadmon, Primal Adam. "Image" of God. Associated with the "Son" aspect of the threefold original trinity emanation.

Archon: Physical and/or higher dimensional nefarious beings who have, from the inception of *Homo sapiens*, exploited and manipulated humanity and positioned themselves as the quintessential overlords of this world.

Barbelo: A term used in *Apocryphon of John* which identifies the male and female (higher Sophia) aspects of the original Great Emanation.

Deep Christ: A general term for the person known as Jesus Christ but who requires a broader identification beyond how he is depicted in the New Testament to include how he is portrayed historically and theologically in the Gnostic texts and, in particular, the Simonian system.

Docetism: The theory that Christ was not a physical being but rather came to his disciples from a disembodied spirit form. This philosophy seems to have sprung from confusion surrounding the crucifixion drama.

Ein Soph: (Kabbalah) Sole source, The Ineffable, monad, singularity.

Ein Soph Or: (Kabbalah) Radiance of the Ineffable. Equated with The Great Power.

Ennoia: Female Thought Holy Spirit radiation or emanation from the singularity at the onset of creation. Simon's Helen was said to be an incarnation of Ennoia.

Epinoia: From the Greek Thought, indwelling female principle in the Gnostic system, similar to the Luriac Kabbalah's *shekinah*.

Gnosis: Deep wisdom, expanded (higher dimensional) consciousness, transformational insight.

Great Emanation: The original radiance that exploded from the Ineffable-Ein Soph that has a threefold nature.

Great Power: The Fire as associated with either the male aspect of the original emanation or the three-fold nature of the original emanation, equated with the First Mystery in the *Pistis Sophia*.

Kabbalah: A stream of Jewish mystical literature, beginning in the 1st century CE and flourishing in the Middle Ages, that delves into the mysteries of Ein Soph (Source, Ineffable) and its relationship to this mortal world.

Pleroma: Meaning "Fullness." Specifically referring to the heavenly divine region outside the control of the archons. Also called the Treasury of Light and Light Land in the *Pistis Sophia*.

Pronnoia: Female Thought Holy Spirit radiation or emanation from the singularity at the onset of creation.

Shekinah (in the Luriac Kabbalah): Indwelling presence of divinity that is feminine in nature.

Sophia: In her higher nature, she is an original feminine emanation, identified as Thought/Holy Spirit. In her "lower" nature, she is known as "daughter of light" (AT), propagator and regent of the material world, and consort to, or feminine aspect of, Christ.

Tzimtzum: Contraction. The Divine Mind within Ein Soph retreated into itself prior to the Great Emanation.

Yaldabaoth/Demiurge: Lead archon who plays a key role in the entrapment of Sophia.

Index

List of Abbreviations and Text Web Addresses

Abbreviations reference quotes taken from texts published on the listed websites. For easy access, see https://www.sophiaproject.net/post/list-of-abbreviations-and-text-web-addresses

ActJ: Acts of John

http://gnosis.org/library/actjohn.htm

AJ: Apocryphon of John, translated by Frederik Wisse
http://gnosis.org/naghamm/apocjn.html

AJ-D: Apocryphon of John translated by Stevan Davies
http://gnosis.org/naghamm/apocjn-davies.html

Allo: Allogenes
http://gnosis.org/naghamm/allogene.html

AP: Act of Peter
http://www.earlychristianwritings.com/text/actspeter.html

APa: Apocalypse of Paul
http://gnosis.org/naghamm/ascp.html

APe: Apocalypse of Peter
http://gnosis.org/naghamm/apopet.html

AT: Acts of Thomas
http://gnosis.org/library/hymnpearl.htm

BTC: Book of Thomas the Contender
http://gnosis.org/naghamm/bookt.html

CGP: Concept of the Great Power
http://gnosis.org/naghamm/cgp.html

ES: Exegesis of the Soul
http://gnosis.org/naghamm/exe.html

Eug: Eugnostos the Blessed
http://gnosis.org/naghamm/eugn.html

FstAJ: First Apocalypse of James
http://gnosis.org/naghamm/1ja.html

GE: Gospel of the Egyptians
http://gnosis.org/naghamm/goseqypt.html

GM: Gospel of Mary
http://gnosis.org/library/marygosp.htm

GP: Gospel of Philip
http://gnosis.org/naghamm/gop.html

GR: Great Revelation
https://www.sophiaproject.net/post/the-great-revelation-by-simon-magus

GT: Gospel of Thomas
http://gnosis.org/naghamm/gosthom.html

GTr: Gospel of Truth
http://gnosis.org/naghamm/got.html

HA: Hypostasis of the Archons
http://gnosis.org/naghamm/Hypostas-Barnstone.html

IE: First Book of IEOU
https://fdocuments.us/document/1-book-of-ieou-books-of-jeu-and-the-untitled-text-in-the-bruce-codex-schmidt-macdermot-part-ipdf.html

LPP: Letter of Peter to Philip
http://gnosis.org/naghamm/letpet.html

NHL: Nag Hammadi Library
http://gnosis.org/naghamm/nhl.html

OS: Odes of Solomon
http://gnosis.org/library/odes.htm

OW: On the Origin of the World
http://gnosis.org/naghamm/origin.html

PS: Pistis Sophia
http://gnosis.org/library/pistis-sophia/

RA: Revelation of Adam
http://gnosis.org/naghamm/adam.html

SJC: Sophia of Jesus Christ
http://gnosis.org/naghamm/sjc.html

ST: Second Treatise of the Great Seth (Bullard and Gibbons)
http://gnosis.org/naghamm/2seth.html

TN: Thought of Norea
http://gnosis.org/naghamm/nore.html

TP: Trimorphic Protennoia, First Thought in Three Forms (Turner)
http://gnosis.org/naghamm/trimorph.html

TPM: Thunder, Perfect Mind
http://gnosis.org/naghamm/thunder.html

TSS: Three Steles of Seth
http://gnosis.org/naghamm/steles.html

TT: Tripartite Tractate
http://gnosis.org/naghamm/tripart.htm

Bibliography

Anonymous. *The Mysterious Story of X7: Exploring the Spiritual Nature of Matter.* Findhorn, Scotland. Findhorn Press, 2010.

Aslan, Reza. *Zealot: The Life and Times of Jesus of Nazareth.* New York: Random House, 2013.

Atwill, Joseph. *Caesar's Messiah: The Roman Conspiracy to Invent Jesus.* Charleston, South Carolina. CreateSpace, 2011.

Baigent, Michael., and Richard Leigh. *The Dead Sea Scrolls Deception.* New York: Simon and Schuster, 1993.

Clark, Ted. *The Oppression of Youth.* New York: Harper and Row, 1975.

Conner, Miguel. *Voices of Gnosticism.* Dublin, Ireland: Bardic Press, 2011.

Corbin, Henry. *The Man of Light: In Iranian Sufism.* New Lebanon, New York: Omega Publications, 1994.

Corbin, Henry. *Alone With the Alone: Creative Imagination of the Sufism of Ibn 'Arabi.* Princeton University Press, 1998.

Corbin, Henry. *Jung, Buddhism and the Incarnation of Sophia.* Rochester, Vermont: Inner Traditions, 2014.

Couliano, Ioan, P. *The Tree of Gnosis. Gnostic Mythology from Early Christianity to Modern Nihilism*. San Francisco, California: Harper, 1992.

DeConick, April, D. *The Gnostic New Age: How A Countercultural Spirituality Revolutionized Religion from Antiquity to Today*. New York: Columbia University Press, 2016.

Douglas-Klotz, Neil. *Prayers of the Cosmos: Meditations on the Aramaic Words of Jesus*. HarperSanFrancisco, 1990.

Ecker, Bruce., Robin, Ticic., and Laurel Hulley. *Unlocking the Emotional Brain. Eliminating Symptoms at Their Roots Using Memory Reconsolidation*. New York: Routledge, 2012.

Edinger, Edward F. *Psyche in Antiquity: Book Two, Gnosticism and Early Christianity*. Toronto, Canada: Inner City Books, 1999.

Eisenman, James. *James the Brother of Jesus. The Key to Unlocking the Secrets of Early Christianity and the Dead Sea Scrolls*. New York: Penguin Books, 1997.

Eisenman, James. *The New Testament Code: Gospels, Apostles and the Dead Sea Scrolls*. Old Saybrook, Connecticut: Konecky and Konecky, 2014.

Evans, Erin. *The Books of Jeu and the Pistis Sophia as Handbooks to Eternity: Exploring the Gnostic Mysteries of the Ineffable*. Leiden, The Netherlands: E. J. Brill, 2015.

Filoramo, Giovanni. *A History of Gnosticism*. Cambridge, UK: Basil Blackwell, 1990.

Franz, Marie-Louise von, *Alchemy*. Toronto, Canada: Inner City Books, 1980.

Franz, Marie-Louise von. (edited with commentary). *Aurora Consurgens, A Document Attributed to Thomas Aquinas on the Problem of Opposites in Alchemy*. Toronto, Canada: Inner City Books, 2000.

Freire, Paulo. *Pedagogy of the Oppressed.* New York: Continuum Publishing, 1993.

Freke, Timothy., and Peter Gandy. *The Jesus Mysteries: Was the "Original Jesus" a Pagan God?* New York: Three Rivers Press, 1999.

Fox, Matthew. *Original Blessing.* Rochester, Vermont: Bear and Company, 1983.

Fulcanelli. (translated from French by Mary Sworder). *Fulcanelli: Master Alchemist, Le Mystere de Cathedrales, Esoteric Interpretation of the Hermetic Symbols of the Great Work.* Las Vegas, Nevada: Brotherhood of Life, 1984.

Haar, Stephen. *Simon Magus: The First Gnostic?* New York: Walter de Gruyter Press, 2003.

Henderson, Joseph. *Thresholds of Initiation.* Asheville, North Carolina: Chiron Publications, 2005.

Higdon, Nicholas, and Huff, Mickey. *Let's Agree to Disagree: A Critical Thinking Guide to Communication, Conflict Management and Critical Media Literacy.* New York: Routledge, 2022.

Holy Bible. New International Version, Zondervan Publishing House, 2011.

Hurtak, J.J., and Desiree Hurtak. *The Pistis Sophia: A Coptic Gnostic text with commentary.* Los Gatos, California: The Academy for Future Science, 1999.

Institute of HeartMath. *The Energetic Heart: GCI (Global Coherence Initiative) Edition.* Boulder Creek, California: Institute of HeartMath, 2003. https://www.heartmath.org/gci/.

Interstellar. Directed by Christopher Nolan. Paramount Pictures, 2014.

Irenaeus of Lyon. Against Heresies: On the Detection and Overthrow of Knowledge, Falsely So Called. ~ 130-202 CE. http://gnosis.org/library/advh1.htm.

Johnson, Sue. *Attachment Theory in Practice. Emotionally Focused Therapy (EFT) with Individuals, Couples and Families.* New York: Guilford Press, 2019.

Jonas, Hans. *The Gnostic Religion.* Boston, Massachusetts: Beacon Press, 1963.

Josephus, Flavius. *Antiquities of the Jews.* Translated by William Whiston, 2017. https://www.gutenberg.org/files/2848/2848-h/2848-h.htm.

Jung, Carl G. *Flying Saucers.* https://press.princeton.edu/books/paperback/9780691018225/flying-saucers.

Jung. Carl G. *Seven Sermons of the Dead.* 1916. http://gnosis.org/library/7Sermons.htm.

Jung, Carl G. *Letters Vol. II 1951-1961.* Princeton U. Press, 1976.

Jung, Carl G. *Memories, Dreams and Reflections.* New York: Vintage, 1989.

Jung, Carl G. *Answer to Job. From Volume 11 of the Collected Works.* Princeton University Press, 2010.

Kaia Ra. *The Sophia Code, A Living Transmission From The Sophia Dragon Tribe.* Mt. Shasta, California: Kaia Ra and Ra-El Publishing, 2016.

Klimkeit, Hans-Joachim. *Gnosis on the Silk Road: Gnostic Texts from Central Asia.* HarperSanFrancisco, 1993.

Lash, John L. *Not In His Image.* White River Junction, Vermont: Chelsea Green Publications, 2006.

Layton, Bentley. *The Gnostic Scriptures.* New York: Doubleday, 1987.

McGilchrist, Ian. *The Master and His Emissary: The Divided Brain and the Making of the Western World.* Yale Press, 2018.

McGuire, William, ed., *The Freud/Jung Letters.* Princeton University Press, 1974.

Mead, G. R. S. *Fragments of a Faith Forgotten.* 1900. http://gnosis.org/library/grs-mead/fragments_faith_forgotten/index.htm.

Mead, G. R. S. *Did Jesus Live 100 B.C.?* London, UK: Theosophical Publishing Society, 1903. http://gnosis.org/library/grs-mead/jesus_live_100/index.htm.

Mead, G. R. S. *The Doctrine of the Subtle Body in Western Tradition: An Outline of What the Philosophers Taught and Christians Taught on the Subject.* London, UK: J. M Watkins, 1919.

Mead, G. R. S. *Simon Magus: An Essay on the Founder of Simonianism Based on the Ancient Sources With a Re-Evaluation of His Philosophy and Teachings.* London:The Theosophical Society, 1892. http://gnosis.org/library/grs-mead/grsm_simon_magus.htm

Mead, G. R. S. *Echoes from the Gnosis.* Wheaton, Illinois: Quest Books, 2006.

Mead, G. R. S. *Gnostic John the Baptizer. Selections from the Mandaean John Book.* London, UK: Theophania Publishing, 2012.

Meade, Michael. *Awakening the Soul: A Deep Response to a Troubled World.* Vashon, Washington: Green Fire Press, 2018.

Miller, Jeffrey C. *The Transcendent Function: Jung's Model of Psychological Growth through Dialogue with the Unconscious.* Albany, New York: State University of New York Press, 2004.

Miller, Rosamonde. *Ritual of the Bridal Chamber, The Gnostic Mystery of the Eucharist.* Redwood City, California: Gnostic Sanctuary, 2004.

Mitchell, Margaret., and Francis M. Young. *The Cambridge History of Christianity; From Origins to Constantine.* Cambridge, UK: Cambridge University Press, 2008.

Montague, Ashley. *Growing Young.* Granby, Massachusetts: Bergen and Garvey, 1981.

Morse, Dan. (unpublished). *The Myth of Sophia, Recalling an Ancient Gnostic Creation Story.* Master's Thesis to fulfill graduation requirement at the University of Creation Spirituality, 1998.

Morse, Dan. *Chartres and the Pistis Sophia: On the thesis that images on the Left West Royal Portal of Chartres Cathedral are direct references to scenes described in the ancient Gnostic text, The Pistis Sophia.* 2010. https://www.sophiaproject.net/post/chartres-and-the-pistis-sophia.

Munther, John. *The Samaritan Jesus.* http://themirroredbridalchamber.com/images/pdfs/The_Samaritan_Jesus. pdf and http://www.themirroredbridalchamber.com/

Neil. A. S. *Summerhill: A Radical Approach to Childrearing.* London, UK: Hart Publishing, 1960.

Pagels, Elaine. *The Gnostic Gospels.* New York: Vintage, 1979.

Pagels, Elaine. *The Gnostic Paul, Gnostic Exegesis of the Pauline Letters.* Harrisburg, Pennsylvania: Trinity Press, 1975.

Pagels, Elaine. *Beyond Belief: The Secret Gospel of Thomas.* New York: Random House, 2003.

Pagels, Elaine. *Revelations, Visions, Prophecy and Politics in the Book of Revelations.* New York: Penguin, 2013.

Patten, Terry. *A New Republic of the Heart: An Ethos for Revolutionaries.* Berkeley: North Atlantic Books, 2018.

Picknett, Lynn., and Clive Prince. *When God Had a Wife: The Fall and Rise of the Sacred Feminine in the Judeo-Christian Tradition.* Rochester, Vermont: Bear and Company, 2019.

Price, Robert. *The Christ Myth: Theory and Its Problems.* Cranford, New Jersey: Athiest Press, 2011.

Rasimus, Tuomas. *The Three Descents of Barbelo and Sethian Initiation in the Trimorphic Protennoia.* © 2014–2016 https://www.academia.edu/23699007/The_Three_Descents_of_Barbelo_and_Sethian_Initiation_in_the_Trimorphic_Protennoia.

Robinson, James M. General Editor. *The Nag Hammadi Library: Revised edition.* San Francisco, California: Harper and Row, 1978.

Rudolph, Kurt. *The Nature and History of Gnosticism.* New York: Harper and Row, 1983.

Scholem, Gershom. *Major Trends in Jewish Mysticism.* New York: Schocken Books, 1941.

Scholem, Gershom. *Zohar: The Book of Splendors.* New York: Schocken Books, 1949.

Scholem, Gershom. *Kabbalah.* Jerusalem, Israel: Keter Publishing, 1974.

Scholem, Gershom. *Origins of the Kabbalah.* Princeton, New Jersey: Jewish Publication Society, 1987.

Scholem, Gershom. *On The Mystical Shape of The Godhead. Basic Concepts in The Kabbalah.* New York: Schocken Books, 1991.

Schmidt, Carl. ed. *The Books of Jeu and The Untitled Codex.* Leiden, The Netherlands: E. J. Brill, 1978.

Segal, Robert A. ed. *The Allure of Gnosticism.* Peru, Illinois: Open Court Publishing Company, 1995.

Smith, Houston. *Jesus the Magician.* San Francisco, California: Hampton Roads, 2014.

Steinfeld, Alan. *Making Contact. Preparing for the New Realities of Extraterrestrial Existence.* New York: St. Martin's Essentials, 2021.

Tabor, James D. *Paul and Jesus: How the Apostle Transformed Christianity.* New York: Simon and Schuster, 2012.

The Silver Chalice. Directed by Victor Saville. Warner Bros, 1954. Based on the book, *The Silver Chalice, A Novel.* by Thomas Chastain, Random House LLC, 2011.

The Matrix. Directed by Lana Wachowski and Lilly Wachowski. Warner Brothers, 1999.

Turner, John D. *Sethian Gnosticism and the Platonic Tradition.* Québec, Canada: Les Presses De L'universite Laval, 2001.

Tyson, Joseph B. *Marcion and Luke-Acts, A defining struggle.* Columbia, South Carolina: University of South Carolina Press, 2006.

Ulanov, Ann B. *The Psychoid, Soul and Psyche; Piercing Time Space Barriers.* Einsiedeln, Switzerland: Daimon Verlag, 2017.

Wilhelm, Richard. *The Secret of The Golden Flower.* New York: Harcourt, Brace and World, Inc., 1962.

Williams, Frank. *Panarion of Epiphanius of Salamis: Against Basilides Book 1 (Sects 1–46).* Boston, Massachusetts: E. J. Brill, 2009.

Acknowledgments

To my most trusted editors and sounding boards: Marjorie Bair, Hari Meyers, and Marien Grace. Your attention and care escape words of appreciation.

To Darren Starwynn, Lorna Sass, and Luminessa Enjara: for your wise reflections and support.

To fellow travelers on the Path of Gnosis: Kayleen Asbo, Elizabeth Kelly, Christy Michaels, Diana Marie Kelly, and Melissa Sophia Joy.

To our local 5d Community: Cherished.

To the YaYas and the Laguna Men: Gratitude Abounds.

To artist Daniel Holeman: For help in imagining.

To mentors: Bruce Ecker and Michael Meade. Invaluable.

In loving memory of Rosamonde Miller: Guide, Beacon, Carrier of the Light.

To Robert Eisenman: For the guts to dig deeper.

To Wisdom Keepers: G. R. S. Mead, Carl Schmidt. Elaine Pagels, Stephen Hoeller.

To Lance Owens and the team at Gnosis.org: Stewards of great treasures.

To my beloved family.

About the Author

Dan Morse is a Licensed Marriage and Family Therapist (Daniel Craig-Morse, MFT) with over 20 years of practicing depth-oriented psycho-spiritual therapy in Northern California. He has been researching Gnosticism and the esoteric traditions for nearly three decades and has presented lectures on the Mysteries of Sophia in a variety of spiritual, religious, and psychological forums. His grassroots spiritual support gatherings have helped anchor "new paradigm" "5d" consciousness within his local community where key cosmological frameworks, as outlined in this book, for example, are being explored and integrated. Dan's multi-instrumental and looping soundscapes have been used in bardic presentations of the Myth of Sophia since first presented for a Master's degree at the University of Creation Spirituality in 1997. www.sophiaproject.net.